AD PRIMERS

Spatial Intelligence

Erie Charalampous

Spatial Intelligence

New Futures for Architecture

LEON van SCHAIK

John Wiley & Sons, Ltd

Published in Great Britain in 2008 by John Wiley & Sons Ltd

Copyright 2008   John Wiley & Sons Ltd, The Atrium, Southern Gate, Chichester,
West Sussex PO19 8SQ, England
Telephone +44 (0)1243 779777

Email (for orders and customer service enquiries): cs-books@wiley.co.uk

Visit our Home Page on www.wiley.com

All Rights Reserved. No part of this publication may be reproduced, stored in a retrieval system or transmitted in any form or by any means, electronic, mechanical, photocopying, recording, scanning or otherwise, except under the terms of the Copyright, Designs and Patents Act 1988 or under the terms of a licence issued by the Copyright Licensing Agency Ltd, 90 Tottenham Court Road, London W1T 4LP, UK, without the permission in writing of the Publisher. Requests to the Publisher should be addressed to the Permissions Department, John Wiley & Sons Ltd, The Atrium, Southern Gate, Chichester, West Sussex PO19 8SQ, England, or emailed to permreq@wiley.co.uk, or faxed to +44 (0)1243 770620.

Designations used by companies to distinguish their products are often claimed as trademarks. All brand names and product names used in this book are trade names, service marks, trademarks or registered trademarks of their respective owners. The Publisher is not associated with any product or vendor mentioned in this book.

This publication is designed to provide accurate and authoritative information in regard to the subject matter covered. It is sold on the understanding that the Publisher is not engaged in rendering professional services. If professional advice or other expert assistance is required, the services of a competent professional should be sought.

Other Wiley Editorial Offices

John Wiley & Sons Inc., 111 River Street, Hoboken, NJ 07030, USA

Jossey-Bass, 989 Market Street, San Francisco, CA 94103-1741, USA

Wiley-VCH Verlag GmbH, Boschstr. 12, D-69469 Weinheim, Germany

John Wiley & Sons Australia Ltd, 42 McDougall Street, Milton, Queensland 4064, Australia

John Wiley & Sons (Asia) Pte Ltd, 2 Clementi Loop #02-01, Jin Xing Distripark, Singapore 129809

John Wiley & Sons Canada Ltd, 5353 Dundas Street West, Suite 600, Etobicoke, Ontario M9B 6H8, Canada

Wiley also publishes its books in a variety of electronic formats. Some content that appears in print may not be available in electronic books.

Executive Commissioning Editor: Helen Castle

Project Editor: Miriam Swift

Publishing Assistant: Calver Lezama

ISBN   978-0-470-72322-7 (hb)
        978-0-470-72323-4 (pb)

Design and cover design by Karen Willcox for aleatoria.com

Printed and bound by Conti Tipocolor, Italy

Dedication

To Peter Lyssiotis, for imaging what words can only suggest

Acknowledgements

Thanks to Helen Castle, Executive Commissioning Editor for her clear and incisive advice; to David Grahame Shane whose close reading of early chapters was encouraging; to Melisa McDonald, my Executive Assistant, whose pursuit of missing links has been invaluable; to Abigail Grater for the copyediting; to Project Editor Miriam Swift and Publishing Assistant Calver Lezama; and to Karen Willcox for the design of the book.

Contents

Introduction	008
Chapter One: The mechanics of spatial intelligence	022
Chapter Two: How spatial intelligence builds our mental space	036
Chapter Three: The disruption of the unity of time, place and architecture, and some precursors of reunification	057
Chapter Four: Intuitives: confronting spatial intelligence – tracing the use of spatial intelligence	082
Chapter Five: Pioneers of mental space – tracing the use of spatial intelligence	140
Chapter Six: New futures for architects: new roles for practitioners	164
Chapter Seven: New professionalism – new practice manifesto	182
Index	201

Introduction

Spatial intelligence, one of the seven acknowledged human capabilities, is the result of millions of years of evolution, but is an underrated human capability, mainly because people use it unconsciously all the time as they navigate their way through their daily lives. Linguistic, mathematical, kinetic, natural and musical intelligence are more consciously applied in daily living, as are inter- and intra-personal intelligence.[1] Architecture is bereft of a theoretical underpinning in spatial intelligence. As a discipline it is pursued through precedent and challenged with experience, but the role of every individual's history in space, the unfolding and developing of their spatial intelligence is not accounted for. This creates a discontinuity between architectural endeavour and everyday life. This book argues for a continuum between our spatial intelligence, usually surfaced only in eidetic recall, and architecture.

What if architecture were the product of our spatial intelligence? Neither 'carved nor moulded',[2] not cut out of solid matter, not assembled from twigs

Peter Lyssiotis, *Though we are unaware of this, we are the prisoners of our mental space*, photomontage for Spatial Intelligence, 1998 – completed as part of an Australia Council New Media Arts Fellowship at RMIT, Melbourne, Australia.

and branches, not draped from poles, but instead forged from our ideas about space, our histories in space, our communal mental space all built upon that combination of inherited capabilities that have evolved into us over millennia, and the unfolding of those capabilities in specific environments? That complex of abilities – of which we are so little aware as adults – that enable us to negotiate our ways through our worlds, little and large. Would our built world be very different to the ones that prevail today? Would we be content to inhabit the horizontal slabs of space pressed between the minimum ceiling heights specified by building codes that are layered through our cities ubiquitously from Cape to Cairo?

And if we answer that it would be different, even if only slightly, what form would that difference take? This is a question that could not be posed until now – even though it has been foreshadowed by Henri Lefebvre (1901–1991), a pioneering observer who spent his life acutely, minutely and obsessively considering how new technologies were altering the spatial perception of those around him. Penetratingly he remarked on the flattening out of our spatial awareness by the combined effects of travelling at speed and of seeing the world, not with our heads free in the air, but with them poised in a capsule of space, shielded by screens from the effects of moving. He thought this flattening of our awareness in time and spatial duration was compounded by the way in which we have become accustomed to receive information from screens – whether through movies, TV or terminals and monitors. Perhaps he felt that when we read books – in pre-industrial tempos – we still activated our spatial imaginations in pre-industrial ways.

We are so little aware of what has changed that it takes a book like *Pandaemonium*[3] to remind us about how drastically (and similarly) our aural world has changed. Once, when going about our daily business, we might have seen a colleague chopping wood across a paddock. We would have seen the stroke of his axe, and some seconds later we would have heard the thwack of it biting into the timber. That delay – with all the clues about space and time that it gave – has gone from our lives. We are never alone in the world now, without deliberate effort. We carry manufactured sound with us everywhere. Through this ubiquity and propinquity, sound has for us – in our daily lives – pretty much lost its physical dimensions. We can also say that just as sound has lost its spatiality, space has lost its 'aurality'. Many of us, but not all, snatch the connection between them back into our lives only when we go to a concert hall, or go on holiday.

Perhaps in earlier times, when we relied on the ability to 'read' our environments – in order to stalk prey, find food (tubers, roots and fruits), secure shelter in rock overhangs or tree cradles, trace the best possible path through forest or savannah, between swamp and ridge of hill, pick the best gradually rising contour across an uncharted foothill flank – we were constantly in touch with our spatial intelligence. We accorded the status of magician to those who could survey a way through the dense mantle of growth that obscured the surface of the earth and who could drive a straight line[4] across valleys from one point to another hidden beyond many dales. We gave the same status to those who tracked the heavens and the seasons. Around the world we erected 'observatories' – structures that embedded in their form observations of the movement of the sun, the planets and the stars. Just looking at these structures told you about what they 'observed'. And slowly we handed over to those who surveyed and observed, and to their descendants, the business of being conscious about all of this so that we could relegate our spatial awareness to the humdrum – the unselfconscious background to what seems to us the more pressing matters of everyday competition and survival. Paradoxically in doing this we have slowly lost touch with the processes that ensure our survival. We have come to take it for granted that water comes from pipes, milk from bottles, food from supermarkets. Now we have to struggle to think our way back up the supply chains to rediscover the origins of our water and food – and we do this more and more, even if it seems too few of us, too late.

But we have not even begun to think our way back into an understanding of what the space we inhabit does to us, how demeaning and oppressive our spatial environment – except in those few set-pieces in the best monuments and squares of our cities – has become. After a depressing day in the office, we tend to lay the blame on our social situation (which may be at fault), but we seldom – except in crisis – reflect on the psyche-crushing effect of sitting under acres of acoustic tile ceiling punctuated with luminaires, sensors, sprinkler heads and emergency exit signs. And if we do not work in an office but rather in a factory, in a warehouse or on a farm, there it is, with rare exception, another space-debilitating norm – the ubiquitous portal frame, obliterating through its repetitive sameness all spatial particularity, and doing this most surely where the frame strikes an obstacle and deforms to accommodate a site boundary as if a knife has been taken to a loaf of bread – so that what is evident is the failure of the site to conform to the pattern, not the intelligence with which the conflict has been resolved.

As with water and our surrounding ecologies, we have become so complacent about our ability to house our activity that we have lost our awareness of what space does to us, and we are having to fight our way back to an understanding of how, for example, beautiful space in a hospital reduces anxiety and promotes healing. The collection of the data that proves this is one of the initiatives of the UK's Commission for Architecture and the Built Environment (CABE).[5] To some extent we can blame our profession for what has happened. Every true profession nurtures an area of human knowledge and takes care (to the best of its ability) of that knowledge for society. Think of Medicine and Law. When architecture was professionalised in the 1840s it sought out as its 'body of knowledge' the notion of being Master Builders. I suspect that this area of human endeavour was selected

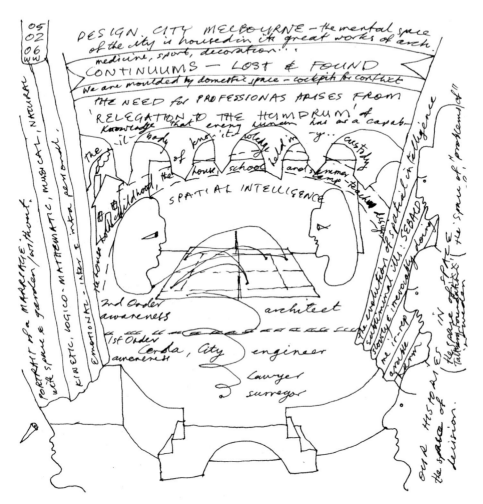

by those who formed the new profession of Architecture (new because until then it had been an 'art' open to practice by any enthusiast), because they envied the celebrity of Engineers in the emerging industrial economy. These makers of engines, bridges, tunnels and ships were often photographed with one foot raised onto part of their latest invention, as if they were the 'hunters' of the new age. So to compete with this practical glamour our architectural forebears went to the heart of the making of architecture – its technologies of carving, moulding, draping or assembling – when they staked their claim to be caretakers of a body of knowledge for society. The architectural capacity to think and design in three and four dimensions,

Leon van Schaik, *Ideogram on Spatial Intelligence*, presented at Melbourne Conversations, BMW Edge, Federation Square, Melbourne, 2006.
My ideogram is based on a shoebox theatre. We are the audience, and the profiles on the lower left and along the right-hand side represent some of that audience. People are there to remind us that everyone has a personal history in space, built up around our spatial intelligence. Some profiles contain key points about spatial intelligence. The curtains to the left list other human intelligences and note that our intelligence is emotionally framed, and inflected by our relationships. The right-hand curtains note the evolution of our spatial intelligence over millennia, and cite WG Sebald as a writer who describes life through space. The proscenium arch notes 'Design City Melbourne: the mental space of the city is housed in its great works of architecture ...'. Drops note the search for continuums in human experience of space: domestic to professional, and the phenomenon of 'relegation to the humdrum' that erodes our spatial awareness in everyday life. On the stage a banner quotes Gaston Bachelard's *Poetics of Space*: 'the house holds childhood motionless in its arms'. Below this on the stage two personae watch a spatial tennis game ... while in front of them a spiral of spatial engagement twirls, the first-order awareness of the surveyor followed by the lawyer, then the engineer, and now the second-order awareness of the architect. Each side of the stair are mnemonics for spatial analyses of spaces domestic and workaday.

our highly developed spatial intelligence, was overlooked, and for the profession space became, by default, something that resulted from what was construction. Some of this resultant space was utterly marvellous: the floating glass of the Crystal Palace, the breathtaking engine shed at St Pancras .... But it was engineered space, and where the architects ended up was in dressing the engineering with narratives like the Scottish Baronial fantasy on the front of the shed at St Pancras, or designing the pylons that disguise the fact that the soaring arch of the Sydney Harbour Bridge (amongst many) rests on a small, confidence-eroding, expansion joint.

This is not to sneer at the storytelling function of architecture. The expression of civic narratives is an important and legitimate function of architecture, and some practitioners (Venturi, Scott Brown of Philadelphia, Edmond & Corrigan of Melbourne and FAT of London) put it at the forefront of their approach to design. Another way in which architects have dealt with engineer-envy is in presenting themselves as masters of the organisation of human activity in plan. Systems approaches developed by engineers at NASA are used to document the needs of the users of giant complexes like hospitals, and efficiencies of relationship may well be achieved, but that is not what we experience as we wind our ways through the seemingly unordered mazes of horizontal and vertical circulation that characterise these blastocysts, looking for our sick or dying loved ones. Unconsciously we hate the architecture of these places, despise the architects when we pause to be aware of the baleful influence on our current situations of their failure to deploy their spatial intelligence. The engineer-*manqué* ploy has not worked for Architecture and society is by and large confused by our claims. Do builders and engineers not share the same knowledge base? So what is so special about architects? Are they not just adding to the expense of projects?

What if our forebears had professionalised architecture around spatial intelligence rather than the technologies of shelter? Might society find it easier to recognise what is unique about what our kind of thinking can offer? Might we now have architectural approaches that focus on the provision of space that nurtures and supports us? We can all point to architecture in every age that does this. Connoisseurs like architectural historian Nikolaus Pevsner (1902–83) (when he was pursuing the line of English architectural beauty and not promoting the factory aesthetic of modernist ideology), poet John Betjeman (1906–84) who eulogised the grounded and authentic beauty of unspoiled parish churches and villages in unspoiled countryside, anthologists of great English architecture John Julius Norwich (1929–) and Simon Jenkins

(1943–) and so on, all revel in such special architecture. They collect it, describe it and discuss it, so building it into the popular culture of their community. As in Art, the canons of Architecture are by and large those buildings that are so loved that they survive the depredations of development cycles from one generation to the next. Examining them, we conduct an archaeology of the spatial intelligence of previous generations – a pursuit that can take us all the way back to the earliest manifestations of our spatial intelligence at work: the seeking out of caves like those at Lascaux by the Neanderthals, for instance. Tourists flock to places with these qualities in a perhaps desperate search for something that is missing from their daily lives. Knowing what we do about the sustainability of these mass migrations in the pursuit of beauty architectural and 'natural' – with their now crowded-out destinations in the 'hushed' cathedral, the 'exclusive' palace, the 'contemplative' gallery or on the 'pristine, untouched' beach, the 'untrodden' mountain pass or the 'unsullied' meadow – we must learn again how to satisfy this need where people live and work. To design interior and urban spaces that satisfy this need, we have to look back to the spatial intelligence that is the source of everyone's longing for spatial wonderment, lack of the exercise of which sets us off on our travels. If we understood this better, perhaps we would recast the basis of architectural knowledge so that the profession would become acutely aware of the architectural capability to think spatially and to create space that awakens the spatial intelligence of clients and users.

There are other reasons for seeking out such awakenings. Chief amongst these, I think, are the dangers inherent in being unaware of the role of spatial intelligence in our lives – both how we inherit it as a capability and how it unfolds in specific places, forming individual and communal histories in space that are particular to the experience of being in those places. Colonisation is a practice that is filled with the unconscious export of spatial (and not only spatial) histories and their attendant customs. Unthinking replication of spatial histories formed in Europe has wrought havoc on the ecosystems of Australia, before global warming exacerbated the conditions. Students of the Australian climate point out that this is the only continent where through history the climate from one year to another has been more different than from one season to another. Settlers in South Australia spread north in a wet period, imagining a climate that could sustain European-style agriculture, and did well for some years, but then had to retreat south as 'bad' years followed one another in long succession. One way of understanding this (in retrospect) peculiar belief that all was as it had been in Europe is to note how unexamined that European spatial history was as an internalised system of expectations about the nature of the world. A more spatial-intelligence-aware society might have asked: 'What spatial constructs does this new place allow?' They might have wondered what wisdom played through the forty thousand years of stewardship of this landscape exercised by the Aboriginal population, and why – although introduced to agricultural practices from the north over the centuries – they did not practise agriculture. There are haunting similarities to the story of the settlement of Greenland by the Danes over a thousand years ago, and the slow decline of their pastoral economy over the following four hundred years, ending with their population dwindling to nothing while their Inuit neighbours adapted to the resurgent ice age. Today pastoral practice is possible again … will the lesson of awareness be heeded this time? These are broad-brush examples. Any exile from one country to another will be able to give an account of how differently space is constructed in the new country. You only have to cross the border between the Netherlands and Germany to see what is at stake. There is no dramatic change of geographical features, and yet as you cross everything changes. Road verges are differently sized and mowed, trees are planted to different patterns. Roof tiles change, modes of construction alter. <u>All because of an invisible line on a map, a line that divides differing spatial histories.</u>

Many who are aware of the power of reawakened awareness of the sensibilities that create such differences and the wonder with which we regard these when we are tourists believe that what we have to do is to go back to the past glories of what we admire in that state of wonder, unsullied by queues, and replicate them. We cannot however recreate the mindsets that created those glories, nor the socioeconomic conditions that framed them.

We soon find that going back in order to recreate past glories is almost an impossible thing to do. The spatial awareness that we have is something that has evolved, and it continues to evolve. In a very real way, we cannot go back. With effort we can imagine a valley that is spatially delineated by the sound of a woodsman's axe, but the way back to that state of being is thwarted for us by our technological successes and the huge numbers of us that are now alive in the world. Replicas can entertain – as Disney's Worlds and Lands or Clough Williams-Ellis's picturesque collage of domes, cupolas and facades in the seaside village fantasy of Portmeirion in Wales (1925 onwards) do – but these are isolated tourist destinations, tiny fragments of mimicry that do not, even in the new urbanism settlement commissioned by Disney in Florida, wield much influence on the lives we lead today. Cities like

Warsaw and Dresden have been reconstructed to conform to images of what they had evolved into before they were destroyed – but these constructs do not extend well into new domains. A few wealthy people have been served by the talents of someone like Raymond Erith (1904–73),[6] who worked in a neoclassical idiom but inventively and with a genial humour rather than academically, producing some entertaining follies such as the Croquet Shed at the Pediment (1964–5) and the Folly in Hertfordshire (1961) as well as more ponderous edifices such as his competition design for St Paul's Cathedral Choir School, London (1962).

Henri Lefebvre, the lonely observer with whom I opened this discussion, now chimes in to remind us of the space-flattening screens that are so much part of our lives. We need historians, novelists or filmmakers to bring the spaces of the past to life in the light of the mental space of those who commissioned, designed and made them. They are all as much political constructs as they are architectural wonders. Contemporary architectural scholar Li Shiqiao describes how two neoclassical buildings – Christopher Wren's Trinity College Library, Cambridge (1675–95) and Henry Aldrich's Peckwater Quadrangle, Christ Church, Oxford (1707–14) – look to us today as if they are in the same genre, but divided contemporaries into two warring camps.[7] Supporters of Wren's design which presented a facade that did not reflect the section behind it, considered themselves functional realists and were allied to the Tory faction in Parliament, whereas supporters of Aldrich's more purist design were idealists in the Platonic sense, and were allied to the reformist Whig faction in Parliament. Re-creation of past vernaculars plucks aspects of their imagery from the past and applies these with just as much ultimate authenticity as that achieved by the forgers of paintings. Succeeding generations cannot believe that anyone was fooled. It is instructive to look at any city and see how succeeding waves of spatial order have been applied. Studious tourists uncover such tides of ambition wherever they go.

Let us now examine a city that receives much architectural pilgrimage. Wandering through Helsinki[8] one observes the way in which the conquering Swedes in the 1640s applied their 'Athens of the North' sensibility to the city's dock edges, how this was in the 1800s grown back inland in a series of avenues and squares and then how a succeeding generation in the 1900s cooked up a 'national' style that drew on the heady mix of decorative arts that also curiously influenced the 'national' style of that other architecturally compelling province – Barcelona. Here a distinct quarter of the city rings the neoclassical core running up towards the new

Wandering through Helsinki, one observes the way in which the conquering Swedes in the 1640s applied their 'Athens of the North' sensibility to the Finnish city's dock edges.

infrastructure of the 19th century. In Helsinki the local working through of the ideas about industrialisation then being addressed across Europe emerges as a masterpiece of spatial design in the form of the Main Railway Station (1906–16), the work of Eliel Saarinen (1873–1950). So it is that the awakened observer can discern how the founding architecture is taken up by the succeeding generation of architects, and is applied to the topography to create some powerful set pieces in the manner of – but different to – Stockholm. Then a succeeding generation, more independent and also more widely connected to the European intelligentsia, evolves an architecture that expresses a local take on the ideas then current in the arts and sciences of the continent. Luckily, a masterpiece emerges from this. In this city generation after generation of architects have used their locally developed spatial intelligence consciously to modulate and adapt what could so easily have remained – as is the case in less culturally driven societies – generically applied 'international' styles. That the architect Alvar Aalto (1898–1976) emerges from this milieu is less startling when the city's architecture is considered as the product of an actively cultivated 'mental space'.

I have taken this seeming detour to bring our attention to Aalto, whose works are readily shown to be the result of putting a locally developed spatial intelligence to work. In part this is because he avoided the mainline ideology of modernism. Perhaps it is a sign of his awareness of his creative marginality or, perhaps better, his spatial specificity, that he holidayed often in Barcelona, that other city with a long history of being aware of and cultivating – also for political reasons – its own 'mental space'. Where, in the Anglo-Saxon imperium with its fantasies (past and present) of globalisation in its own image, would Antonio Gaudí (1852–1926) have found a client? So many of Aalto's buildings seem to be sensing out a boundary between internal and

Alvar Aalto, House of Culture, Helsinki, Finland, 1955–8. Aalto is working in a third term, neither carving or moulding, nor assembling or draping, but sensing a boundary between inside and outside.

external spatial forces or needs. This is particularly the case with the fine House of Culture in Helsinki (1955–8). It is not that he ever 'shrink-wraps' the skin of his buildings to a definition of the programme to be housed within it – that profoundly anti-three-dimensional thinking process that functionalism adopted. Rather, it is as if he were working in a third term, neither carving or moulding, nor assembling or draping, but sensing a boundary between inside and outside that makes both spatial realms beautiful to inhabit.

And it is precisely this 'sensing' that the current generation of architects have ubiquitously the tools to do. If, that is, they could situate themselves within the technology with a full awareness of what human spatial intelligence is and what it does for architects when they are aware of it, and cultivate it as a culture, a mental space, individually and together. And this is also a moment when, if the knowledge base is redefined and re-engaged, architects, using spatial intelligence, can enter into virtual environments and help people recapture the socio-spatial nuancing that they have lost as so many of our face-to-face exchanges have become internalised in a new shrinking of spatiality that would, I am sure, have shocked our lonely observer were he still alive today.

Here is an example. In 1992 'World Wide Web' and 'Internet' technology became multifunctional; and, as this matured (from 1997 in particular), some of the most intense trading floors in the world began to lose their need for face-to-face contact.[9] As Caitlin Zaloom describes, the Chicago Board of Trade futures trading hall – a vast, four-storey-high, granite-lined room housing tiered pits on the steps of which traders were arrayed day after day selling and buying – began to be invaded by people using laptop computers. And then, slowly, the spatially organised system – in which the most established traders occupied the highest tiers, while beginners worked their way up from the floor as they established contacts and built up trust in their trading behaviour – began to erode away. Dealers used to enter the floor announcing opportunities and catching the eyes of those who would deliver of their deals. There was an elaborate sign language for selling and buying, a process of recording trades on scrips, runners who took scrips from the floors to clerks who reconciled the deals in off-the-floor offices. Reputations were made and lost in these spaces. People would gauge their time to retire from them by their zest or lack of zest for the everyday fray, the full day spent standing, eyeing competitors. Perhaps there was relief that the spatiality of the process was superseded by the new technologies. And yet, as Zaloom found, there has evolved in the de-spatialised information environment of online trading, a primitive simulacrum of that face-to-face environment. People find ways of identifying their bidding by using a regular suffix amount – 142,000 rather than 100,000, for example. And the research shows that online gossip is rife as people try to establish who is doing what. Asymptote's design for a real-time virtual simulacrum of the New York Stock Exchange (2000) is an example of how architecture could intervene. This pioneering work reconstructs the stock exchange in virtual space. All of its functionality is embedded in the model. Trading can be observed online: a trading position that is running hot can be zoomed in on. Action replays can be mounted so that trades can be analysed. And the entire operation is as readily negotiated as its real-space original. The model engages the spatial intelligence of those using it where almost all other models prior to this had been two-dimensional, desktop, page-on-page click-through systems.

This project seems so much to presage the future that we must wonder why it has not yet led to other commissions for architects. Perhaps it is because it mimicked the existing space, and did not venture into new spatial formulations that might offer an advantage over the replication of what exists. Certainly some researchers think so, and for seven years now Tom Kovac has been pursuing architecturally informed information environments that offer complex manifestations of social encounters in the pursuit of specific educational outcomes. This work challenges and awakens the connoisseurship that spatial intelligence allows. It may lead to new roles for an architecture that holds 'spatial intelligence' as its knowledge base.

Be that as it may, the old roles of architecture become very vital as the pressure on resources mounts. The old technocratic approach enshrined in the way the profession was established leads to the ever thinner spread of spatial quality that is the norm for offices, warehouses and factories all around the world. It also switches symbol for actuality in our housing, so that our ever expanding suburbs are filled with facades that refer to architectures of quality but do not provide that quality – only a picture that stands for what we may have experienced on our holidays, or seen in a picture book, or read about in a novel. If we as architects can invoke our spatial intelligence in the service of our clients and the potential users of the spaces we devise, we can perhaps return a fullness to spatiality that will engage people and slow their seemingly unstoppable pursuit of the things that promise paradise but destroy it by giving us access to it – cars, flights and so on. We use these in a fruitless pursuit that has come to replace the pleasures of being in a place and enjoying its slow progression through the day and the night and the years. So comprehensively that on the lagoon of Burullus an owner of one of hundreds of broad-beamed sailing ships with a design perfected over centuries for sailing in water no more than two metres deep, and that comb across that vast expanse of water in near silence capturing every breeze, can fail to appreciate what he has in his arms, and lament the lack of the 'entertainments' of the city, and long to leave. And is driven to that by an ever tightening economic noose, as demand for fish outstrips supply. There is a restlessness in us that drives us to seek the new, and I am aware that I am in danger of entertaining the naiveté of Marie Antoinette here, suggesting that we can play at being peasants while around us people are being deprived of their livelihoods by our very success as a species. But like the founders of slow food, I do suspect that slow architecture can help us to adapt to a more pleasurable, healthier and sustainable way of living – and do that both in the physical realm and in virtual environments.

In pursuit of the question of what an architecture based on spatial intelligence might be, the following chapters look into what we know about this human capability, and how it is supported by other intelligences such as kinetic, natural, linguistic, logical, mathematical, musical and personal.

There will be an emphasis on the need for individual awareness of histories in space and the relationship of such individual histories to the evolving mental space of communities, especially as we grapple with adaptive change to an increasingly dynamic climate. In this pursuit various approaches to the capturing of the 'mental space' of individuals or communities are discussed.

In further chapters we will encounter conflicting accounts of how this intelligence has evolved, and discover the impact of these accounts, and consider how a new account could be constructed and what it might offer.

In the final chapters we will explore future roles for architecture conceived of as being the utilisation of spatial intelligence. We will consider how designing with spatial intelligence could enable and awaken the spatial intelligence in all of us, creating a new practice rooted in an inclusive cultural tri-polarity in the architecture of the future; contemplate what intellectual change in the practice of architecture might then come about; and imagine how we could build new forums for public behaviours that capture the spatial knowledge of participants in design, creating designs that elicit eidetic recall, and realising such designs in linked real and virtual environments.

In conclusion, we assess the extent to which activating spatial intelligence as the knowledge base for architecture might assist in taking on the challenge of what the 2006 London Architecture Biennale described as a 'call to arms': 'The task for current architecture is to propose architectures that navigate and negotiate between these polarities – surveillance, eco-damage, 24-hour working, ubiquitous curvilinearity at the expense of social, ethical or radical ideas – and vicariously create future cities that are liberating, equitable, sustainable and spatially exciting … .'

References

1 Howard Gardner, *Intelligence Reframed: Multiple Intelligences for the 21st Century*, Basic Books (New York), 1999.
2 Leon van Schaik, 'Neither carved nor moulded: an architecture of the third term', in Leon van Schaik (ed), *Tom Kovac: Architectural Monographs No 50*, Academy Editions (London), 1998, pp 24–8.
3 Humphrey Jennings, Mary-Lou Jennings, Charles Madge, *Pandaemonium: 1660–1886: The Coming of the Machine as Seen by Contemporary Observers*, Papermac (London), 1995.
4 Alfred Watkins, *The Old Straight Track*, Abacus (London), 1974.
5 CABE presentation at RIBA Research symposium, September 2007, www.architecture.com
6 Lucy Archer, *Raymond Erith Architect*, The Cygnet Press (Burford, Oxfordshire), 1985.
7 Li Shiqiao, *Power and Virtue: Architecture and Intellectual Change in England 1660–1730*, Routledge (London), 2007: Trinity College Library (1675–95) by Christopher Wren, p 42; Peckwater Quadrangle, Christ Church, Oxford (1707–14) by Henry Aldrich, p 120.
8 Jonathan Moorhouse, *Helsinki: Birth of the Classic Capital, 1550–1850*, SKS Finnish Literature Society (Helsinki), 2003.
9 Caitlin Zaloom, *Out of the Pits: Traders and Technology from Chicago to London*, University of Chicago Press (Chicago, Illinois and London), 2007 (reviewed by Donald MacKenzie, Fellow of the Institute of Advanced Study, University of Durham, *London Review of Books*, Vol 29, No 21, 1 November 2007, p 22).

1

The mechanics of spatial intelligence

Of course, it's rather grave for all of us because, whether you believe in heredity or environment, either way we are boiled, shut up here with this old sub-human of a father!

Jassy on Uncle Matthew, from Nancy Mitford's *Love in a Cold Climate*[1]

What if Henri Lefebvre, my lonely observer,[2] were alive today, pondering in his isolated Belgian village on what science has since discovered about our capabilities and how they work? Much has been discovered that makes the existence of spatial intelligence an ever stronger presence in the ways that we work in the world. But we (my observer and all the scientists at work in the field of cognition) would have to acknowledge that we face a central mystery: while we know more and more about how we are put together, and of the material that constitutes us, and how it organises itself and faces the challenges of being in the world, a working hypothesis on how the bundle of matter that we are achieves consciousness eludes us. How does the assemblage of particles of which we consist, organised within the observable laws of physics, self-organising and replicating through the coding of DNA, achieve self-awareness and consciousness of its being in the world? And how extensive is the phenomenon itself? Is all life conscious? Are plants conscious to some extent? Does the universe 'learn'?[3]

Peter Lyssiotis, *We comprehend and negotiate space using our spatial intelligence ...*, photomontage for *Spatial Intelligence*, 1998 – completed as part of an Australia Council New Media Arts Fellowship at RMIT, Melbourne, Australia.

We simply do not know. Worse still, we cannot work out how to begin to know – even though we have more and more facts about how we (our neurones, that is) perceive and experience the world.[4]

The problem of consciousness and intelligence

Thoughtful commentators ruefully acknowledge that this is a problem that has to be set aside, for the moment. There have been moments when artificial intelligence has been thought to give the key to this question. People have argued that if we can create a machine that is intelligent, we may have uncovered the nature of consciousness. There is a famous 'test' for artificial intelligence: the Turing test. Mathematical philosopher Alan Turing (1912–54),[5] credited with cracking the Germans' Enigma Code and turning the tide of the Second World War at sea, was also a lonely observer! His test is disarmingly simple. We will know we have created intelligence when we recognise it in a machine, just as we recognise it in other beings. Such recognition has not yet occurred. Some mathematicians believe that computers are inherently incapable of fully recognisable intelligence. One of these, Roger Penrose (1931–), in proving this (at least to his satisfaction) gives a wonderful account of how our perceptions of human intelligence are shifting as discovery proceeds.

We now know, he argues, that every cell in the body has enormous calculating capability – as much as we once attributed to the brain itself. Cells consist of bundles of micro tubules lined with pouches arrayed around a central tube – each looking, I imagine, rather like a Giacometti sculpture – and these are suspended in water that has its molecules aligned rather in the way that heavy water has aligned molecules. Each sac on each tubule may contain or not contain a particle – and this gives the cell a binary memory capability. When we talk of human (or animal – though perhaps not of plants because they do not have a nervous system) intelligence, we now have to consider that intelligence is a distributed system: not something held like a command centre in the brain and distributed, but something that is present throughout the organism, and linked together through the nervous system but also possibly through quantum effects made possible by the alignment of the molecules in the water in each cell. (So plants might have a 'quantum'-enabled diffuse intelligence after all?)[6]

Intuitively we have known this – partly through observing what happens to us after traumatic accidents. We now think that the 'lost limb' syndrome in which an amputee feels pain or other sensations in a removed limb, and is still sometimes confronted with the spatial presence of the lost limb, may be explained by continuing memories in the body adjacent to the lost limb, and to the spatial self-perception of the whole being – not just the perception held in the brain.[7] A PhD candidate at RMIT[8] has discovered a range of experiments in which blind people gain a form of navigational spatial awareness when a video camera is mounted on their heads, and the image is projected onto the skin of their abdomens. Being 'differently abled', as are some people who are described as 'autistic', has been shown to intensify a person's awareness of their own spatial intelligence such that they can draw what they have seen with total recall, while in one case at least awareness of the ways in which others respond to space – even if unconsciously – has become the basis for a career in the humane design of cattle handling facilities.[9] Entertainingly, architect Peter Wilson (1950–) describes in conversation (perhaps apocryphally) how an autopsy on the great German architect Karl Friedrich Schinkel (1781–1841) – a renowned master of spatial design – revealed that he had suffered from a brain wasting disease, and was practising out of the stem of the brain – supposedly its oldest part – suggesting that architectural intelligence is a primitive, or indeed primal, business!

Kinaesthetic intelligence: its spatiality

In other realms, we may be able to understand the extremes of spatial intelligence at work in some kinetic environments. How the rugby player Jonny Wilkinson, 'squeezing out the crowd' by bringing his hands together, sensing the breeze and imagining his position oblique or acute on the rectangle of play, can then marshal all of his 'consciousness' to kick that ungainly ovoid ball accurately between two distant posts. Or how English footballer David Beckham, whose 'ability to compute and execute the exact angles and forces required to score a goal from a free kick', is a 'genius' in his spatial intelligence.[10] Or how a golf professional like Tiger Woods can summon up the concentration – not just by visualising it in his mind, but by suppressing the conscious command of the mind and working through the whole of his bodily distributed intelligence – to create a spatial awareness in a complex geography of vales, ponds, bunkers and roughs, and a varying microclimate, that allows him to hit a hole in one far more often than the laws of probability would allow. These are miracles of awareness. They are not confined to sport, though

Jonny Wilkinson 'squeezing out the crowd' by bringing his hands together, sensing the breeze and imagining his position oblique or acute on the rectangle of play.

more observable in sport than in other fields of endeavour, perhaps because sport necessarily brings the whole of the body into play.

Aboriginal art in Australia is perhaps an example of distributed intelligence at work.[11] There is an often-remarked-upon 'uncanny' resemblance between some 'dot' paintings and the landscape inhabited by their creators, but it is a resemblance that they can never physically have observed. It is as if they had hovered over the landscape in a helicopter, or worked from aerial photography. Distributed intelligence offers an (unproven) explanation: a person who knows a landscape through walking over it barefoot, knows where the watercourses are, where the plants offering edible tubers are, where the animals will shelter, who has learned its dimensions through the kinetic intelligence of hunting – stalking, running, spearing – such a person 'knows' the landscape in a way that engages the whole of their distributed intelligence; and in painting, with its repetitions and its quiet 'squeezing out' of distractions, all of this knowledge resolves itself into a simulacrum of that landscape seen from the air.

Spatial intelligence uncovered

This speculation brings what we are discovering about our intelligence into the realm of design and spatial intelligence. Architects know that the complex problems they work with cannot be solved parameter by parameter. I think that even people who claim that they solve problems like this are aware – if they care to admit it – that it does not work that way. They just do not find what actually happens 'respectable', or logical, or sensible. What really happens – as we know from account after account, beginning with Archimedes in his bath at his Eureka moment – is that when we embark on a quest, we become well primed about our prospective journey, and we seek out everything we can know about its likely course. But the way is made clear not by a logical step-by-step system – though such a process may be a necessary part of beginning the quest – but by some unexpected concatenation that suddenly brings everything together. Often we 'sleep on it', and wake with our solution. Archimedes was relaxing in a bath, and the moment of awareness was so apposite that we have probably learned the wrong lesson from his experience. Well, now even the most unpoetic of us can relax. There is an explanation, and it comes from twenty years of sleep research combining neurological mapping of what is happening in the brain, and observing the kinds of sleep that we are having – deep sleep, or

REM (rapid eye movement) sleep. What is being discovered is that at night we use a form of 'weak force' intelligence to process the events of the day.[12] Experiments have shown that in sleep we can make connections between things that the awake mind resists. It is this 'weak' connection capacity that allows us to forge resolutions to complex problems requiring some form of reconciliation between numerous conflicting requirements.

Space and emotional intelligence: our capabilities and the role of sleep

The ever expanding mapping of the way in which the brain reacts to stimuli and to emotions is rapidly extending our hypotheses about how our intelligences work, paving the way to the formulation of what some now call 'emotional intelligence'. Sleep research and this mapping have led researchers to speculate that during dreaming we are assessing all of our experiences of the day in their fullest form. Awake we are barely aware of our spatial and kinetic intelligences – unless we play in the top echelons of sports, or achieve the obsessive contemplation of an artist or a spatially tuned-in architect. Some of us will have been consciously using our musical intelligence, our natural intelligence; we will all unconsciously have been using the miracle of our linguistic intelligence. And in varying degrees we will, in our inter- and intra-personal relationships, have been using or abusing our 'emotional' intelligence.[13]

What underlies all these intelligences is that they are all innate human capabilities. They have evolved – so our best hypotheses and observations indicate – over millions of years. We argue about how they have evolved – whether by a form of social Darwinism in which the needs of survival draw us to select for certain capacities, or whether they are fortuitous accidents randomly generated and then adopted because they confer advantage in the pursuit of survival (or, if you are a teleologist, in the pursuit of an ever growing awareness or consciousness). Recent research in palaeontology suggests the existence of some 'clock' that drives the growing capacity of the human cranium, shifting the relationship between the spine and the skull in stepped evolutions that bring ever greater pressure to bear on the lower jaw. The evidence is there, but what do we make of it?

At the moment the most fascinating sustainable hypothesis for designers lies in the relationship between neurological mapping and sleep research.

What this suggests is that all these capabilities that we inherit unfold in the world that we are born into, and adapt to our specific surroundings, both social and environmental. We commonsensically understand this about our linguistic intelligence, for example. Born in France, we speak French, inflected by the dialect of our specific locale or class. Born in China, we speak the form of Chinese common to our region. Argument rages about just what the building blocks of that intelligence are – is it deep grammar, or are there smaller particles of in-built sense associated with certain sounds? Evidence is adduced, challenged, and the research continues. What is now observable about the relationship between the 'theories' with which we arrive in the world, and our experience of the world, is that during REM sleep the brain is using parts of itself devoted to different forms of intelligence to assess whether what has happened in the day has impacted on the understandings provided by the capabilities that we have inherited.

So 'dreaming' is a kind of mapping. And we know that during sleep calcium is fired into synapses of the brain to form new pathways which hard-wire changes into our mental networks that we believe are the product of our learning from the events of the day, in our specific environment.[14] Much that we think is rejected as not worthy of assimilation; and perhaps that is what a nightmare is – a rejection of possible changes to our awareness. These are hypotheses, but they are the best-informed hypotheses that we have to date.[15] And they have the merit of making sense of things that we have intuitively – even commonsensically – known. We must bear in mind, however, that as yet there has not been much mapping of the distributed intelligence that Penrose describes.

Distributed intelligence proposition supports the concept of mental space

That we may conceive of our intelligence as even more widely distributed becomes evident when we try to understand how we build realities through our engagement with the world. Discussion of the role of location – inside us? outside us? – in the way we build 'realities' confronts us with the fact that, while formed through the engagement of our brains with what our senses tell our insides, these appear to us to exist 'outside'.[16] This exteriority may be brought about by kinetic extension (using that distribution of intelligence throughout our being) into the spatially extended 'phenomenal' world that we seem to inhabit – as our lonely observer noted – by moving through it. By adding that to what we know about sporting prowess, we can understand what an architect means when he says of a line that he has drawn: 'There are fifteen years of hard-won experience in that line. There is stuff that my hand knows that I don't know that I know. I have to respect that line.'[17] Knowing how to access this 'interior' or internalised knowledge, forged by the unfolding of our inherited capabilities in the world, is acknowledged to be the key to effective creativity. Recognising these emerging facts, Ignasi de Solà-Morales proposed that we think of architecture that acknowledges these 'soft' pathways through our intelligence as 'weak architecture'.[18] Later we will consider how this might be defined, and whether consciously created exemplars are emerging through contemporary design practice.

We are also presented with new ways of thinking about how we as individuals and as members of groups of individuals occupy and navigate space, and how, being conscious about what is happening in every one of us all through our lives, we never stop 'learning', never stop building new synapses – though the rate of construction varies through our development. And there is more at work in our spatial intelligence than we have allowed during the relatively short period of professionalised architectural practice.

Neurone mapping in primates and in humans proceeds apace. Recent study of neurones activated by our actions has led researchers to postulate that the purpose of our memory – that networked terrain constantly remapped in our sleep – is to act as a 'projectory,' or a predictor of upcoming events in all their dimensions: emotional, intellectual, physical and spatial.[19] These researchers believe that they have an answer for the strange but familiar experience of *déjà vu* – one that we all have from time to time, when we feel that we have lived through an experience before. We have, argue these researchers, envisaged everything before we experience it, using our memories of similar past events.

Other researchers are tracking what are called 'mirror neurones' because they seem to induce mimicry (we all must have wondered why it is that if one of us yawns, all of us begin to yawn?).[20] These neurones seem to assist us in learning from others, helping us to – unconsciously – map and imitate those around us. This throws some light onto how language is transmitted from adults to their young. It also perhaps begins to account for the ways in which our awarenesses are shared with the groups with which we have attained them. Interestingly in humans these neurones do not always fire – suggesting that they do in macaque monkeys, in whom they were first identified – but are suppressed by the act of conscious observation. This further suggests that we build up memory/projectory through a combination of unselfconscious imitation and conscious learning.

This is hardly a new concept, but as the mechanisms are beginning to emerge, we find that our intuitions about some forms of learning are substantiated. In sport, the art of 'visualisation' has long been a recognised way of teaching the body to perform actions that are difficult to mimic through observation. Here perhaps suppressing that act of observing forces athletes to use their imagination to picture a motion holistically. Vangelis, the composer who scored *Blade Runner* and *Chariots of Fire*, writes that composing is a matter of 'consciously not thinking'. He talks of detachment and trying to be totally 'available'.[21] Again we can find anecdotal examples closer to architecture. The Swiss-Italian architect and educator Aurelio Galfetti (1936–) – founder of the School of Architecture at Mendrisio, where he boasted that the average age of the foundation staff was seventy – once stated in a seminar at RMIT that all he thought you could hope to do for aspiring students of architecture was 'to put them in the position of being an architect'. Learning through doing, or through visualising and then doing, does seem to lie at the core of many of our more complex activities. This is learning of a very powerful and too often tacit kind, and if we induct students into a certain vision of architecture unconsciously, as we do with the one proposed around the practicalities of construction and technology for example, we are – as Beatrix Potter had her Gardener entrap her rabbit hero – picking up pots that we intend to 'pop upon the top of Peter'.

In the 1960s Iona and Peter Opie conducted their famous research into the games that children play, tracing many street games and their accompanying rhymes back in a continuous tradition to ancient Greece.

Much that is group consciousness is learned through empathy – mostly unconscious observation and mimicry. In the 1960s Iona and Peter Opie conducted their famous research into the games that children play, revealing that each succeeding generation since ancient times has inherited its games and ditties – at least in part – from previous generations (see Chapter Four).[22] It is that very osmotic process, combined with the prodigious amount of mapping between our inherited capabilities and theories and the contingent realities of our lives, that makes accessing our spatial knowledge so difficult once we feel that we have mastered it. This is precisely why we have evolved 'professions', groups who are charged with taking care of a body of knowledge on our behalf, nurturing it, extending it and ensuring that its horizons are joined to the horizons of the knowledge that is emerging in other fields.

Ways of being in the world supported by new research

This leads to contemplation of systematic ways of being in the world that are assisted by research, through which we are increasingly aware of how we 'work', if only at some levels. However, we have to be aware that what we consciously observe is very much the product of what we set out to observe. In the mid-20th century, progressive development through learning was the accepted paradigm. Swiss philosopher, natural historian and development psychologist Jean Piaget (1896–1980) identified a progression of awareness through close observation of the behaviour of infants. For example, he posited a phase during which infants fear that when a person or a thing leaves a room they no longer exist, followed by a phase when continuity of existence is assumed (birth to two years). Succeeding stages of increasingly sophisticated awareness are then posited and observed, with motor skills following (two to seven years), thinking logically about concrete events (seven to eleven), and abstract reasoning (eleven+). It was as if our many capabilities were 'booted' one after the other in a logical sequence. The step-by-step development Piaget charted has been disputed by those who argue that our awarenesses are developing in parallel – it is just that observers find what they set out to observe. There have been huge changes in our view of babies over the past thirty years. As Alison Gopnik, Professor of Cognitive Psychology at the University of California at Berkeley, wrote in 2003: 'We now know that babies know more about the world than we would ever have thought possible. They have ideas about other human beings, about objects and the world – right from the time they are born. And these are fairly complex ideas, not just reflexes or responses to sensations.'[23] She continues: 'Newborn babies have an initial theory about the world and the inferential learning capacities to revise, change and rework those initial theories on the evidence they experience from the very beginning of their lives.' Other research shows that this process continues throughout life.

Psychologists studying adults also posited hierarchies of awareness, running in a spiral of increasingly sophisticated modes of understanding of the complexity of our world,[24] from 'first order' awareness – in which the mode of awareness entertained is conceived of as the only possible mode, to second order – in which the simultaneous uses of different modes are first accepted, then transcended. These stages were argued to map onto many of the staged systems of enlightenment developed by humans in recorded history. These ascending diagrams tend to appeal to those who feel that they themselves have attained a high level of understanding.[25] It is difficult now to feel that these are likely to be stages that develop in a step-like manner, like a ladder of growing wisdom. Most probably these different processes are braided together and we become better able to utilise them as we develop our emotional intelligence. While they may be tendentiously teleological and self-serving, they do map the major 'ways of seeing'[26] that we have consciously developed. These 'human givens',[27] increasingly understood through research into the relationships between our inherited capabilities and their unfolding in the world, still posit maturation through a sequence of learning that goes from arousal by a stimulus, to pattern-matching of the kind that we have discussed above, to emotional response to that stimulus, to a reasoned response.[28] Contemplating these, it is not difficult to appreciate how a strand of intelligence, its givens and the knowledge that we construct out of the interaction between those and our particular environments, could become submerged once mastered.

Today the battle lies between biologists who substantiate at ever finer levels of detail how selection – working both through and on environment (Steven Rose points out that the natural environment itself changes in response to the presence of faster-running antelopes: lion hunting selects for faster antelopes, faster antelopes means more intensive grazing, reduction in lion population …)[29] – has brought us to have the capacities that we have, and social philosophers who wonder how we can have a science of the mind that can explain how our values have evolved.[30] There is more and more evidence of selection for empathy, for example. As Jerry Fodor remarks in concluding his attack on evolutionary selection of values: 'Induction over the history of science suggests that the best theories we have today will prove more or less untrue at the latest by tomorrow afternoon. In science, as elsewhere, "hedge your bets" is generally good advice.'[31] Either way, as Nancy Mitford wrote in 1949, 'we are boiled'.[32] But either way the evidence[33] seems to move slowly in directions that support our being interested in why we have developed spatial intelligence, what we can know about its operations, how we deploy our spatial intelligence in the world, what that does to the world, and how we could use this knowledge when we wish to better design our environments.

A new basis for professionalism in architecture

What I think we now need is a profession that consciously investigates and cares for the ways in which our spatial intelligence helps us to be at home in the world. In his thoughtful book *Experiencing Architecture* (1959), Steen Eiler Rasmussen (1898–1990) proposed a developmental hierarchy of awareness around architecture, beginning with childhood playing at making houses and informed by multitudes of interactions with space – kinetic, aural, visual and tactile.[34] What has eluded us is a construct with which to connect these founding experiences, unique to each individual, yet shared through the templates we all inherit, back into the practice of Architecture and through design into the daily living of grown-ups who have lost their childhood awareness.

References

1 Nancy Mitford, *Love in a Cold Climate*, Penguin (London), 1954, p 132 (first published by Hamish Hamilton (London), 1949).
2 Henri Lefebvre was a member of the French Communist Party from 1928 until his expulsion in 1957. He published more than 60 books, the most relevant here being *The Production of Space*, published by Blackwell Publishers (Cambridge, Massachusetts and Oxford) in 1994.
3 Rupert Sheldrake, 'The rebirth of Nature', in Pavel Buchler and Nikos Papastergiadis (eds), *Random Access 2: Random Fears*, Rivers Oram Press (London), 1996, pp 100–21. Sheldrake argues that the universe is a learning system, that the colour blue is a recent – even historically recorded – invention, and that chromium has emerged as an element as the universe learns.
4 John R Searle, 'Consciousness: what we still don't know' (review of Christof Koch, *The Quest for Consciousness*, Roberts & Co (Reading, PA, USA), 2005), *New York Review of Books*, Vol LII, No 1, 13 January 2005, pp 36–9: 'the theory that we can never perceive the real world but only our inner pictures of it is the single most disastrous view in the past four

centuries of epistemology … this view leads from Descartes to Berkeley and then to Kant and eventually to Hegel … failure to make the distinction between content and object is part of (Koch's) failure to understand intentionality … often we are not conscious of our decision making, but often we are … the idea that all our consciousness is sensory is wrong' (p 38). John R Searle is Slusser Professor of Philosophy at the University of California, Berkeley.

5 See Andrew Hodges, *Alan Turing, The Enigma of Intelligence*, Unwin (London), 1986. Hodges' commentary explains how the Turing machine concept is related to Turing's philosophy of Mind, breaking new ground by relating Turing's thought to Roger Penrose's ideas about computability.

6 Roger Penrose, *Shadows of the Mind: A Search for the Missing Science of Consciousness*, Vintage/Random House (London), 1995.

7 Oliver Sacks, *An Anthropologist on Mars*, Pan Macmillan (Sydney), 1995, p 142. Oliver Sacks has made a study of what trauma and being 'differently abled' mean to our perceptual processes.

8 Ted Krueger, Associate Dean of Graduate Studies at Rensselaer Polytechnic Institute. See also Alison Motluk, 'Seeing without sight', *New Scientist*, Vol 185, No 2484, 29 January 2005, pp 37–9.

9 Oliver Sacks, *An Anthropologist on Mars*, op cit, pp 241–62.

10 See http://www.mftrou.com/multiple-intelligence-test.html (Beyond Classic IQ Tests: Howard Gardner's Multiple Intelligence Test), and Glenn Moore, 'Football: Science points oversize finger at true genius', *The Independent* (London), 18 March 2000: 'Boys exposed to high levels of testosterone *in utero*, said Manning, were likely to be gifted either musically, mathematically, or in terms of spatial awareness … . [B]etween 8 weeks and 12 weeks … in the development of the male foetus certain parts of the body become sensitive to testosterone. These are the heart and lungs … the right side of the brain, which controls spatial awareness and the perception of objects, and the fingers.' Beckham is cited as an exemplar.

11 I have tested this idea with Paul Carter in conversation. His work is the most profound exploration of these issues that I know of. See for example Paul Carter, *The Lie of the Land*, Faber & Faber (Boston, Massachusetts and London), 1996.

12 Graham Lawton, 'To sleep, perchance to dream', report on the 50th Anniversary of the Discovery of REM (Chicago), *New Scientist*, Vol 178, No 2401, 28 June 2003, p 31.

13 Daniel Goleman, *Working with Emotional Intelligence*, Bloomsbury (London), 1999.

14 Graham Lawton, To sleep, perchance to dream, op cit, p 33, on research by Terrence J Sejnowski, Salk Institute, California.

15 Jonah Lehrer, *Proust was a Neuroscientist*, Houghton Mifflin Company (New York), 2007, p 93: the author puts forward a hypothesis by Dr Kausik Si that the synaptic mark of memory is a prion, a protein that uniquely has two functional states: active or inactive. It 'holds' memory when inactive, but when memory is called upon it becomes active, and therefore labile. So the act of remembering alters the memory. This was Proust's key realisation.

16 Max Velmans (Professor of Psychology at Goldsmiths College, London), 'In here, out there, somewhere?', *New Scientist*, Vol 189, No 2544, 25 March 2006, pp 50–1.

17 Tomas Nollet to the author at a research seminar in Brussels, September 2007. See also Tomas Nollet & Hilde Huyghe, *Stills from a Design Process: Young Architects in Flanders*, Flemish Architecture Institute (VAI) (Antwerp), 2004.

18 Ignasi de Solà-Morales (translated by Graham Thompson, edited by Sarah Whiting), *Differences: Topographies of Contemporary Architecture*, MIT Press (Barcelona), 1995, pp 68–71: 'weak architecture', that strength that art and architecture are capable of producing precisely when they adopt a posture that is not aggressive and dominating, but tangential and weak.

19 Jessica Marshall, 'Future recall', *New Scientist*, Vol 193, No 2596, 24 March 2007, pp 36–40: 'It's as if, embedded somewhere in your brain, there is a time machine that can take you forwards and backwards at will. What if the thing we call memory works both ways, helping us to both recall the past and imagine the future? The brain areas that are active when you recall your personal past or think about the future are almost identical. Daniel Gilbert, Harvard Psychologist, 'Stumbling on Happiness'. Schachter – we recall the gist, not the detail. … It seems that unless called upon to do something specific, your brain is busy recalling the past or projecting into the future. So next time you catch yourself staring into space instead of getting on with your work, or drifting into reverie as you try to read a book, don't beat yourself up about it. Your daydreams will pay off in the long run.'

20 Gordy Slack, 'Found: the source of human empathy', *New Scientist*, Vol 196, No 2629, 10 November 2007, p 12.

21 'The power of music', *New

Scientist, Vol 180, No 2423, 29 November 2003, pp 38–49. The composer is known by his surname alone.
22 Iona and Peter Opie, *Children's Games in Street and Playground*, Clarendon Press (Oxford), 1963.
23 Alison Gopnik, 'The scientist in the crib, interviewed – what every baby knows', *New Scientist*, Vol 178, No 2395, 17 May 2003, pp 42–5.
24 An entire discipline of 'Spiral Dynamics' has been built on Clare Graves' observations. See Don Edward Beck and Christopher C Cowan, *Spiral Dynamics: Mastering Values, Leadership, and Change*, Blackwell (Oxford), 1996, p 28: 'Briefly what I am proposing is that the psychology of the mature human being is an unfolding, emergent, oscillating, spiraling process marked by progressive subordination of older, lower-order behaviour systems to newer, higher-order systems as man's existential problems change.'
25 Ken Wilber, *Integral Psychology: Consciousness, Spirit, Psychology, Therapy*, Shambhala (Boston), 2000.
26 John Berger, *Ways of Seeing*, British Broadcasting Corporation (London) and Penguin Books (Harmondsworth), 1977.
27 Joe Griffin, Ivan Tyrrell, *Human Givens: A New Approach to Emotional Health and Clear Thinking*, Human Givens Publishing (Chalvington, East Sussex), 2003. See also Joe Griffin, 'The dreamcatcher', *New Scientist*, Vol 178, No 2390, 15 April 2003, pp 45–7: 'We are all born with a rich natural inheritance – a partially formed mind containing a genetic treasure house of innate knowledge patterns … .'
28 Igor Aleksander, 'I, computer', *New Scientist*, Vol 179, No 2404, 19 July 2003, pp 40–3: 'Haikonen's work supports my own idea, which is based on an overwhelming body of evidence suggesting there are cells in the brain that compensate for motion, such as eye movement, in order to represent objects as they are in the real world. This allows us to get a sensation of the real world despite the constantly changing stream of sensory inputs, such as smell, vision, and so on that feeds our brain. To me this evidence implies that our brains contain some persistent representation of the outside world, encoded in the electrochemical impulses in their neutrons.' Aleksander posits a sequence that starts with a sense of place – the state of being conscious of our world and our place in it, proceeds to imagination – the state of being able to remember and construct hypothetical situations, from which arises the ability to undertake directed attention – purposeful interaction with the world through action and feedback, which in due course leads to planning – a process of learning and repeating sequences of sensory inputs in 'what if' scenarios, and finally to a decision/emotion stage – attaching qualitative values imagined through the imagination to hypothetical outcomes derived through 'planning'. The difference lies in 'human givens' asserting that emotional responses are primitive 'black or white' responses that need to be calmed for the many shades of grey that reasoning brings to bear. According to Rupert Sheldrake (*The Sense of Being Stared At, and Other Aspects of the Extended Mind*, Hutchinson (London), 2003), such encoding cannot be genetic but is part of an evolving series of templates that pervade the universe and to which growth is patterned.
29 Steven Rose (of the Open University, Milton Keynes), letter in *London Review of Books*, Vol 29, No 22, 15 November 2007, p 5.
30 Daniel Dennett (of Tufts University, Medford, Massachusetts) on Jerry Fodor's rejection of such a science, letter in *London Review of Books*, Vol 29, No 22, 15 November 2007, p 5.
31 Jerry Fodor, 'Why pigs don't have wings', *London Review of Books*, Vol 29, No 20, 18 October 2007, pp 19–22, on whether natural selection or adaptionism drive evolution.
32 Nancy Mitford, *Love in a Cold Climate*, op cit, p 132.
33 Frank J Sulloway, 'Parallel lives' (review of Nancy L Segal, *Indivisible by Two: Lives of Extraordinary Twins*, Harvard University Press (Cambridge, Massachusetts and London), 2005), *New York Review of Books*, Vol LIII, No 19, 30 November 2006, pp 39–42. Frank J Sulloway is a visiting scholar at the Institute of Personality and Social Research in the Department of Psychology at University of California, Berkeley.
34 Steen Eiler Rasmussen, *Experiencing Architecture*, Chapman & Hall (London), 1959.

2

How spatial intelligence builds our mental space

Each one of us should speak of his roads, his crossroads, his roadside benches; each one should make a surveyor's map of his lost fields and meadows. Thoreau said he carried the maps of his fields engraved on his soul. And Jean Wahl once wrote: the frothing of the hedges I keep deep inside me.

Gaston Bachelard[1]

As scientists carve their way through our neurones allocating functions to places, we may come to understand which parts of the brain relate to those capabilities and processes that support our spatial intelligence, just as linguistic intelligence is now being pinpointed: '… vocabulary is synthesised by the hippocampus early in the night during slow wave sleep, a deep slumber without dreams. The motor skills of enunciation are processed during "Stage Two, non REM sleep", and the auditory memories are encoded across all stages. Memories that are emotionally laden get processed during REM sleep.'[2] In due course we will have plausible accounts of how our distributed intelligence fits into such a mapping of our brains. We may come to know the links between the neurones and synapses[3] that enable us to assess the size and qualities of spaces and to navigate between them; and which parts of the mind code spaces emotionally, enabling us to empathise with how

Peter Lyssiotis, *Each one of us should speak of his roads, his crossroads, his roadside benches*, photomontage for *Spatial Intelligence*, 1998 – completed as part of an Australia Council New Media Arts Fellowship at RMIT, Melbourne, Australia.

others may experience and relate to spaces. Perhaps one day the 'wiring' (our every attempt at understanding is enmeshed in metaphors of machines, then computers) that enables a homing pigeon to return home unerringly from unknown locales hundreds of kilometres away will be exposed, and we will know something about an extreme form of spatial intelligence.

Holistic mapping of spatial intelligence

But as an architect I suspect that this mapping will only ever give us a version of the reality, one from which it will be difficult to derive strategies for designing spaces. While some parts of our human intelligence find

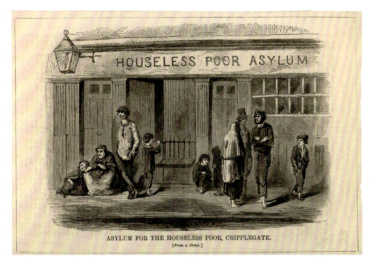

Asylum for the Houseless Poor, Cripplegate, from Henry Mayhew's *London Labour and the London Poor*, 1851. Mayhew interviewed 'everyone – beggars, street-entertainers (such as Punch and Judy men), market traders, prostitutes, labourers and sweatshop workers'.

comfort and derive effective solutions to problems in statistical analysis of complex situations, other parts wonder at what this dissection misses. Design necessarily reaches for wholes that reconcile many conflicting and contradictory forces – it is an unusual intelligence, as Russell L Ackoff[4] points out, that will deliberately weaken one part of a design for the sake of the best possible whole. We architects, in the pursuit of our spatial intelligence, are in a sense intimately aligned with Henry Mayhew (1812–87) – who in the 1840s collected anecdotes about the lives of the poor, enabling us enduringly to marvel at human ingenuity and courage – rather than with Friedrich Engels (1820–95) who collected the statistics that enabled social reformers to mount their case for radical change, because in designing we need to embrace the richer accounts of lives lived as well as the metrics that obscure individual realities at precisely the moment that they identify strategic pressure points in the underlying systemic engines of poverty. Henry Mayhew interviewed 'everyone – beggars, street entertainers (such as Punch and Judy men), market traders, prostitutes, labourers, sweatshop workers, even down to the "mudlarks" who searched the stinking mud on the banks of the River Thames for wood, metal rope and coal from passing ships, and the "pure-finders" who gathered dog faeces to sell to tanners'.[5]

When we go looking for spatial intelligence, we encounter novelist Marcel Proust (1871–1922) rediscovering the place of his childhood

A bowl of the famous madeleines, one of which provoked Proust's eidetic recall of his childhood.

as an 'involuntary memory' induced by dipping a madeleine in his tea,[6] and so describing a moment of eidetic recall: a flashback to a foundational memory, a moment in the construction of that character's mental space. What emerges from this reverie is a series of memories evoked by recalling a walk between two houses down hawthorn-hedged lanes. Gaston Bachelard (1884–1962) – that pioneer of systematic investigation into mental space – knows that literature captures our spatial histories; and, as if thinking of *Swann's Way*,[7] he cites Jean Wahl (1888–1974): 'The frothing of the hedges I keep deep within me'.[8] Those of us who have walked through the laneways in the twilight of a north European summer 'know' what is being described here. We are also transported directly back to some first experience of such a walk, its sensations and the emotions that caused this to be an eidetic moment for us. The soft breeze on our skins after the months of being covered up for warmth, the honeyed scent of the tiny white flowers that cover the new growth of the hedges in profusion, the blurring of that white into a 'froth' and the thought of our destination at the end of the lane, be it a pub where we are to meet friends, a study where – minds combed by the line of our walk – we are to continue writing, or some bower framed by the hedge itself which we will sleep beneath that balmy night.

Our earliest literature – the *Iliad* and the *Odyssey* – is about journeys between places, and scholars today still dispute the location of Ithaca, the site of the homecoming in that earliest of epic journeys, just as for so long they disputed the location of Troy, the besieged and then destroyed city that was the destination of the outward journey, and the departure point for the return. These 'journeys', whether accounted for by Proust or Homer, resonate with us because we are disposed to think of our lives as journeys on earth, with starting points and finishing points. Not that we are agreed that these journeys end on earth. As novelist Javier Marías (1951–) observes, we reassess our journeys from time to time and feel that they are, at every stage, somehow 'meant' to have run in the sequence that has eventuated, though as often as not that has mostly to do with chance.[9] If we are to grasp what our spatial intelligence does for us and could allow us to do, we must heed Bachelard's injunction: 'Each one of us then should speak of his roads, his crossroads (and) his roadside benches (for) thus we have covered the universe with drawings (that) we have lived'.[10]

We must do this because mapping neurones and synapses will not deliver us into the mental space that each of us builds in our life. While dissection may come to map what does what in our suite of tools (cells, neurones, synapses and so on) that enable us to grow our awareness, what dissection cannot do is record the way that the circumstances of our journey inflect that awareness at every stage, and colour it in our memories with sensate and emotional detail. We are born, not into abstract space, but into specific rooms. Well, some of us are born in the 'non-place'[11] abstractions of functionalist hospital wards, to be sure, but even these are nuanced. And we are soon taken to the haven of a home. Not that that is always a consolation. One of my designer friends was very late to start talking, and was about to undergo specialist treatment for autism when at the age of four he announced in a fully articulate sentence: 'I hate the wallpaper!'

Learning from our mental space

We build up a spatial history for ourselves composed of memories of room upon room, garden upon garden, street upon street, farm upon farm, field upon field. From the same capabilities we slowly construct diverging assumptions about the nature of the spatiality of the world, and differing preferences for how to inhabit it and move through it. Through our history in space we establish an individual 'mental space' of assumptions about space such that as adults we usually accommodate to new experiences of space by saying out loud: 'That's just like "X"!' – or, when with companions: 'Isn't that just like "Y"?' We are surprised and disconcerted when our expectations are

Mostly we are mired in our mental space, just as the character Winnie in Samuel Beckett's *Happy Days* (played here by Fiona Shaw in the National Theatre production) is buried up to her neck in a mound on the stage for most of the play.

not met – particularly when we are dealing with the duration of space. So many conversations compare experience of travelling familiar routes. Yet we only ever become aware of our 'mental space' through moments of eidetic recall, when some acute sensation triggers detailed recollection of an instant when one of our memories was laid down as a neural pathway – as our memory is constructed and reconstructed over and again.[12] Mostly we are mired in our mental space just as the character Winnie in Samuel Beckett's 1960 play *Happy Days* is buried up to her neck in a mound on the stage for most of the play.

Mapping the mental space of individuals is difficult, and the benefits to instrumental science seem elusive. So not much is done outside literature – to which we will therefore return. But some interesting work has been done. In the 1960s Terence Lee studied the way a sample group of people moved around Cambridge in England.[13] He plotted their daily routes from home to work, school, shopping and recreation. Then he compared these routes to the most direct routes between each departure point and each destination point. He found that we are very inefficient, and seldom use the most direct routes. When he interviewed his sample, he got this consistent response: 'But I prefer my route!' – and the reasons given were almost all to do with a preference for the 'pretty' over the utilitarian. This inquiry into what Lee termed 'spatial schemata' confirmed that people do make choices based on their preferences, but it was not able to go into what formed those preferences. What designers could learn from this, then, was rather limited.

Things have not improved that much. John Zeisel, interviewed in *New Scientist* in March 2006,[14] offered insights derived from a promising set of discipline areas – sociology, architecture and neuroscience. His work on space for people suffering from Alzheimer's disease has striking parallels with the work for cattle derived from the experiences of a person with an autistic condition that neurologist Dr Oliver Sacks records:[15] 'We ... ensure that all hallways and pathways have a destination visible from wherever you are in them ... and have plenty of familiar landmarks along ... them.' He worries about productivity in the abstract spaces of offices, classrooms and so on, and suspects that he could design spaces in these environments that could enable people to 'go off and think about something else', and in doing that solve 'offline' – as we now know is the usual way in creativity – the problems that they are struggling with. The suggestions for outdoor space design are a little disappointing: 'long vistas and few hidden areas', and 'lots of place names and signposting', both of which could fit some very soul-destroying places and would not work for most well-loved places in our cities and towns. Why is it so difficult to make sense of all of this on a parameter-by-parameter basis?

Consider the frothing hawthorn hedges above. Recently I worked with a highly cultivated translator whose home language was Chinese, and whose experience of the world was cosmopolitan but very urban, and only cursorily engaged with Europe. He found it almost impossible to grasp what Jean Wahl's phrase could mean. There were no bridges into his 'mental space' at all. We can talk about cognitive mapping as a process, but it is only in the fullness of its context, or of an imagined context, that we convey sense. In this instance the translator's first go was coloured with spikes and looming danger. We had to engage in a long discussion of our different mental spaces, and how they came to be what they were, before we could proceed. This is a familiar discourse wherever translation takes place. You are never simply conveying sense from one language to another. You are working alongside all the results of the unfolding of our capabilities in space and in place, often referred to as 'culture', and you are trying to convey mental space from one situation to another. As Charles Simic (1938–) writes on the poetry of Anne Carson (1950–), a poetry very much influenced by translating fragments of ancient Greek poetry: 'Translation … is that effort to convey in words of another language not only the literal meaning of a poem but an alien way of seeing things.'[16] The same can be said of designing in the full awareness of mental space in ourselves and in others.

Some years ago, when I was part of a team working on a garden design for a home for Alzheimer's patients, working very much along the lines described above, I encountered a 'regime of care' instituted by the nurses and a psychologist that seemed to take account of individual mental space. A patient who had been a hostess was encouraged to dress – as she wished to – in her evening gowns, and to act as a gracious hostess all day long. A patient in her nineties who had been a champion horse rider was taken riding everyday. As the staff found their way into the mental space of each patient, the distressing attempts to escape the home – mundane dangers like traffic await outside – diminished. This reveals some of the difficulty that we have in moving between the intellectual awareness that we can build up about 'cognitive mapping' as a human process, and using that mapping effectively when working with or for others. Too often we fail to become familiar with the mental space of those we are working with, while remaining fully aware of our own, and so we end by simply visiting our presumptions upon them.

Learning from literature

The examples above depend on intensive work between client and professional. Of course through much of history the works of art, architecture and landscape architecture, humble and great, that we admire have indeed resulted from such direct interactions between patrons and professionals. Yet in literature we enter quite fully into worlds at some remove from a personal dialogue. That insightful critic from the last century, IA Richards, developed a comprehensive way for us to test whether what we are receiving at second hand is the result of direct observation that can evoke in us our own eidetic responses, or whether the writer is using hand-me-down cliché, raising in us (annoyingly) the stock response of the sentimentally shallow 'tear-jerk'.[17] To be a serious reader seeking authentic engagements with the world still requires us to exercise our critical skills, and to be a designer working with this knowledge requires us to be able to critique every account of mental space that we can elicit in pursuit of an informed design, not least our own. In building we find this phenomenon in the standard plans of run-of-the-mill house-builders whose facades are described as 'Tuscan' on the strength of terracotta paint or 'Provençal' on the strength of mustard-coloured plaster, 'Georgian' on the strength of an applied portico or 'Spanish' on the strength of a row of tiles. These are very low-level congruencies with the originals that are evoked, and they fob the buyer off with a symbol rather than any actual experiential value. The plans of such houses are often interchangeable behind their facades, and rooms are labelled in the same symbolically suggestive way: 'family room', 'alfresco dining', 'entertainment centre' and so on. Author WG Sebald (1944–2001) has one of his characters describing living in such a house: 'there was something distinctly creepy about all of it, and at times I feel quite definitely that it did steady and irreparable harm to me. Only once, if I remember rightly, did I ever sit on the window seat in the drawing room, which was painted with foliage and tendrils like a festive bower ... .'[18]

How architecture might extend its influence

Late capitalism, and the re-emergence of the ideology of the 'hidden hand', of the 'self-regulating' market, has put us as architects and users of space in a position where large amounts of space – probably at least 80 per cent of it – are manufactured without engaging the mental space of the designer or future user. Supposing that designers (and their clients) had come to

The Church of St George at Voronet Monastery Romania. The designers of Romania's painted churches developed a genre of wide overhangs that protected the frescoes of biblical scenes painted on the external walls like huge wrap-around tattoos.

understand what is to be gained through engaging spatial intelligence at the outset, or even as a retro-fit; what tools are there that would enable them to work with the mental space of persons unknown and unknowable? How can we define a method so equipped? In Chapter Three I will discuss several designers who are 'precursors' of an approach that uses mental space skills, and in a later chapter I will discuss those architects who are 'pioneers' of new ways of doing this. Here I will come to the example of William Richard Lethaby (1857–1931), an architect who worked assuredly and consciously in the centre of a consciously understood 'mental space'. But first I want to sketch out what is to be involved if more designers are to operate in this way.

The first task would be for the designers to become fully aware of their own mental space, through an intensive excavation of their eidetic memories, and a careful mapping of those against their favoured canons in design. The means to this are well established, and architects who are acknowledged to have mastered architecture often prove to have followed the same paths towards consciously mastering it. Most designers know their mental space intuitively – intuition being the sum of their experience.[19] But as every educator knows, becoming aware of what is assumed requires that it be translated from the medium in which it is held into another medium that renders it consciously apprehensible and open to interrogation. There are ways in which we can do this, even though they demand the development in us of structured introspection and of new powers of description, making poets and translators of us all. This is fairly lonely work, involving individuals and creative partnerships that seldom consist of more than a handful of people.

As architectural theorist Dalibor Vesely (1934–) has long argued, there was a time when being unconscious of one's mental space was not a problem for architecture, because there was no escaping the unity of time, place and mental space.[20] The designers of Romania's painted churches developed a genre of wide overhangs that protected the frescoes of biblical scenes painted on the external walls like huge wrap-around tattoos. To us today these look extraordinary, but in the 13th century, locked up in their region and drawing inspiration from each other, this was simply how churches in Romania were done. They developed slowly, refining what their predecessors had done, each small shift in eaves design or fresco format a startling innovation because the architects were working within a completely understood and homogenous mental space – they and their communities shared one kingdom, one place, one mode of agriculture, one musical tradition, one literature and one form of religious belief.

In the late 19th century, WR Lethaby described the power of this situation in a way that is well summarised by the title under which his essays were eventually published as a book: *Architecture, Mysticism and Myth* (1892). In these he describes how in the pre-modern world architecture's principal purpose was to represent, within the belief systems of specific societies, their fullest understandings of the working of the universe. Egyptian art, architecture and life were a seamless continuity within a single shared mental space. The same can be said of all the ancient and medieval societies – Babylon is all of a piece, and the city states of Greece vied with each other through philosophy, military exploit, mercantile prowess and architecture. The Roman Empire can be summed up in one of its greatest surviving monuments: the Pantheon (AD 120–4). In this single domed construction we find evidence of the centralising power structures of that empire, of its engineering brilliance – the concrete structure of the Pantheon has survived two thousand years of wars, earthquakes and other calamities – and of its inclusive, eclectic approach to religion. The Romanesque, the Gothic and the Renaissance architectures of Europe can be dissected and classified region by region in ways that discernibly describe the mental spaces of each region. Lethaby's own design for Melsetter House[21] (1898) in the Orkneys is a superb example of designing within such a tradition, an approach that the Modern Movement in architecture was about to blast away.

How architecture was marginalised

What happened to disrupt this unity of mental space and creative endeavour, as Vesely brilliantly observed, was that the modern analytical empirical approach to knowledge led to taxonomic classifications of plants, insects and animals, to the dissection of the human body, and to the attempt to reassemble all of this separated knowledge in encyclopaedias. While the advances in medical understanding were palpable, there were – as complementary medicine acknowledges – costs associated with the loss of holistic approaches, and indeed the major advances in health are largely the result of epidemiology rather than of dissection. It was looking at the whole urban and social situation that led to the understanding that cholera, to take one example, was a water-borne disease. Architecture suffered greatly from being dissected, its parts described as 'features' and depicted as stylistic alternatives that could be recombined anywhere. Wrenched out of the mental space that gave it form and meaning, it lost in a sense its epidemiology. New understandings of the human spatial intelligence capability and the ways in which we use it to forge our personal histories and futures in space, as well as the ways in which these agglomerate into shared spatial cultures, give us the chance to reclaim this architectural unity. Or, rather, this new understanding gives us the chance to forge, in a world that constitutes its spatial understandings in such new ways – as I am sure Henri Lefebvre would have insisted – new kinds of unity between architecture and the communities it seeks to serve.

For example, few of us today have the privilege of living within a single homogenous mental space. But there are clusterings of mental space that we can work with. The analogy here is with our linguistic capability and the way in which it unfolds in response to the language of the place where we grow up, so that we all speak dialects that an expert like George Bernard Shaw's Professor Higgins could trace back to within a few streets of its origin.[22] How might such a spatial dialect appear to us? Eric Hobsbawm (1917–) gives us a clue when he grapples with his own identity.[23] He grew up in Bratislava, then a town in the Austro-Hungarian Empire, within easy reach of the Imperial capital city, to which he would travel as a child with his family to attend the Opera. As he grew into his teenage years his horizon expanded beyond his hometown, and he identified with the football team of Vienna, the metropolis. Then he was spirited away to live with relatives in London, which he grew to know from Hampstead Heath. And later in life he became a professor at the City University of New York, getting to know that great city from that base. 'What am I,' he asks, 'other than a Bratislava-Viennese, Hampstead-Londoner, Manhattan-New Yorker?' We are all in varying degree composed of such layers of mental space, rather like Gadamer's onion – his metaphor describing how successive descriptions of a phenomenon build our understanding, not by displacing earlier descriptions but by enclosing them.[24] In this metaphor, truth does not reside in any single layer, but each layer adds to those descriptions that have gone before, giving the description greater and greater acuity as the layers accumulate. We might regard Hobsbawm as multispatial, much as we would regard someone who spoke a number of languages as multilingual.

'Gadamer's onion' is Jonathan Rée's metaphor (following Hans-Georg Gadamer) for describing how successive descriptions of a phenomenon build our understanding – not by displacing earlier descriptions but by enclosing them.

Are architects today really unaware of their mental space? No one can escape their history in space, and I am sure all architects unconsciously build on their spatial memories when they project futures – that is when they design. But even those who one would expect to be very conscious of the role of mental space seem to work around this without an acceptable model beyond the very unsatisfactory 'identity' concept that occasionally bedevils architectural debate, leading people to look for national styles or traits. In the modern era, conscious identity formation might have operated at a national level – as an agent of nation building – when the English for example adopted the neogothic to differentiate themselves from Napoleon's neoclassical triumphalism. But the conscious investigation of mental space and the conscious use of spatial intelligence are only now emerging. There are,

The Houses of Parliament, London, UK, 1836–70. Architect Charles Barry's neoclassical plan was clothed in the more patriotic Gothic garb provided by architect AWN Pugin.

Leon van Schaik   047   Chapter 2 How spatial intelligence builds our mental space

however, architects who seem to operate as if they understand the concept and the processes it enables.

Reclaiming architectural reality through new understandings of mental space

In the coming chapters I will discuss architects and designers who were the precursors of a conscious use of mental space – figures like Ildefonso Cerdá (1815–76), whose plan for Barcelona was the first truly spatialised plan of the modern era, and who had to develop an understanding of spatial politics in order to implement his plan, an approach that resonates with the work of Colin Rowe (1920–99) and then with that of Mario Gandelsonas (1938–) (Chapter Three). I will discuss the work of architectural pioneers, showing how Peter Cook (1936–), Peter Zumthor (1943–) and Zaha Hadid (1950–) can be seen to exemplify three very different but mutually reinforcing viewpoints around conscious positions in mental space (Chapter Four). And then I will discuss the work of practitioners whose potential is dependent on a sophisticated involvement in the Internet-accessible technologies that are now determining an increasing proportion of the spatial histories of individuals, looking at the work of Asymptote, KOL/MAC and Kovac – which is also a triad of interlinked but distinctively different approaches (Chapter Six).

François Gérard, *Napoleon in Coronation Robes,* c 1804. The English sought to differentiate themselves from Napoleon's adoption of neoclassical imagery.

My own interest in mental space emerged directly from my experience as a migrant. I grew up until the age of fourteen (when my parents who were political radicals were forced to leave, settling in London) in the Anglophone world of the Natal midlands in South Africa – if surrounded every day by other languages – and after living on three continents I regard myself as 'English-speaking' when pushed into a tight definition of my identity. This is very much the result of my lifelong interest in literature, which I access through the English language. Much of what is spatial can be perceived of as seamless when our account of it is given through the printed word. Another designer friend tells of how she imagined all of the action in Jane Austen's novels taking place in her grandparents' modern, white-stucco villa when she read them as a child in Africa. We must all be making such transpositions when we read novels from places that we have not visited. Our lonely observer Henri Lefebvre would agree with 20th-century media theorist Marshall McLuhan (1911–80) that reality observed through screens is

David Hemmings in the film *Blow-up*, directed by Michelangelo Antonioni. Antonioni, who studied architecture, used spatial situations to change our understanding of space, and thus effect alterations to our mental space.

a slippery realm, lacking the barbs and burrs and stickiness of actual places, and our spatial consciousness is only partially extended through exposure to the visual media.[25] In the hands of film director Michelangelo Antonioni (1912–2007), who studied architecture, there is perhaps a sufficient density of observation of spatial situations to change our understanding of space, and thus effect alterations to our mental space – but such moments are rare in film, and even more fleeting in video and TV.

Thus it is that little in our daily lives disturbs the acquisition of our first layers of mental space that we acquire most intensely (eidetically) in childhood. Tourism sharpens for a moment the keenness of our understanding of our own cherished differences. But migration casts all our previous layers into doubt – even when there is no change of language involved. Paul Carter has written perceptively of how for the migrant everything is flattened, because 'living in a new country' the migrant has little access to the associations that give to all the components of any environment their full parts in the playing out of reality for those who have grown up in a place.[26] In my case, thanks to a shared language and literature, the flattening became apparent to me only very slowly. I recall a day four years after arriving in England when, idling in the architecture studios awaiting our results, a group of my colleagues were chatting about their plans for the summer. 'Oh,' said one, airily pointing down to my right, 'I am thinking of going to Turkey.' I was shocked. 'You mean Turkey!' I asserted, pointing up and to the right. My childhood mental space was still with me, and its Cape to Cairo view of the world was in direct conflict with my friend's English geographical sense. To me, Turkey simply could not be any variety of 'down'. This was one moment of collision amongst many that shocked me into awareness of the difference between my inner assumptions about the world and those of my new friends.

Later, when studying with Peter Cook at the Architectural Association School of Architecture, I found myself using early layers of my mental space when observing West London. Rather than looking at what was to be seen, I at first lapsed into musing about how miserable I would be to live in these streets, the hidden subtext being a comparison with the spectacular landscapes of my childhood. How could anyone bear it here? Almost at once I discovered how wrong I was to assume this, how delighted with this place those who

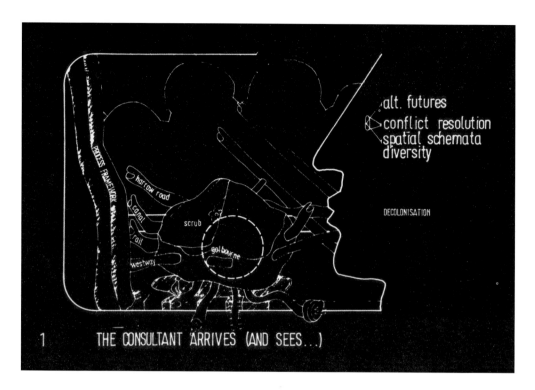

had grown up there were. I developed an ideogram, *The Consultant Arrives and Sees*, to keep me alert to the fact that observers need to account for the position from which they are observing if their observation is to be more than an unconscious projection of internalised assumptions.[27] In the ideogram there is a profile of a face framing a space for the recording of observations, a space I came to regard as a shoe-box theatre with curtains, drops and sets, all able to represent ideas, attitudes, facts and emotions about what was being observed, as well as holding (centre stage) evolving propositions about possible improvements. So I would become – as I argued we all should become – an observer observing myself observing. The French sociologist Jean Duvignaud (1921–2007) made a similar point in his insightful book *Change at Shebika*.[28] He and a group of researchers set out to study the arrival of modern life at this remote North African oasis. Assessing the research later, he decided that all that was discernibly of value was the way in which their work described how they, the observers, were changed by the process of observing.

Leon van Schaik, *The Consultant Arrives and Sees*, 1970 (from an unpublished Architectural Association Diploma thesis). I devised this ideogram to keep me alert to the fact that observers need to account for the position from which they are observing if their observation is to be more than an unconscious projection of internalised assumptions.

Even accepting that 'no two languages share identical associations',[29] we can conceive of communities that share large expanses of their mental space. In the early 1970s Ugo La Pietra (1938–), then editor of the Milanese journal *Progettare In Più*, ran a series of questionnaires[30] aimed at eliciting the attitudes of the citizens of Milan to the objects, spaces and places of their lives in that city. While the results were patchy, the returns on domestic space were rich, and revealed a palpable similarity of aesthetic preferences that seem to an observer from outside the city to reek of Milan. From time to time since that pioneering work, journals and newspapers have run quests to identify people's favourite places in their home cities, but these questionnaires have never subsequently penetrated beyond the pleasures of tourism. This is largely, I suspect, because the findings were obvious – 'the Milanese inhabit Milanese mental space' – and also because it was difficult to explain what one would do with such extensive mappings of communal mental space. Who would use them?

When Craig Bremner, then a PhD student at RMIT, became interested in these issues, he studied the *Progettare In Più* material and involved a commercial survey company in the quest of uncovering the mental space of a community. Through their extensive survey run through newspapers and including the use of disposable cameras, he devised a kit about the mental space of Glaswegians that was then used to inform the architects who were embarking on the design of a series of apartment buildings in that city during its tenure as European City of Culture. In analysing the results he was able to point to a number of instances where the designs that resulted were enriched by access to this material. There was no possibility in this research for a parallel investigation into the mental space of the architects, and the interchange was thus one-sided.

In the 1990s Akira Suzuki and Kayoko Ota ran a quest similar to (if less systematic than) that of *Progettare In Più* through the journal *Telescope*.[31] The journal went in search of 'the printed city', 'the edible city', 'the wild, wild city', 'the bubblicious (sic) city', and 'the big bad burb'. As these titles suggest, Tokyo in the 1980s was a very different place to Milan in the 1970s. The city and its citizens were riding an economic boom, nightlife was rampant and the emphasis was on the spectacular and the ephemeral whims of unpredictable fashion. Ultimately *Telescope* morphed into a web-based alternative guide to Tokyo – finding a use that the *Progettare In Più* investigation was also heading towards, but at a time when print technology confined the effectiveness of such a guide. Suzuki went on to observe the mental space of his daughter's generation in Tokyo.³² Perhaps because Japan is, thanks to its geographical and its linguistic separation from the world, a peculiarly homogenous culture, these investigations were of direct use to those designing there. The works of Nigel Coates (1949–) – such as Café Bongo in Tokyo Japan (1986) – seem to emerge from the pages of these journals. However, while examining at RMIT, Fumihiko Maki (1928–), that doyen of Japanese architects, rejected the notion that 'Ma' – conceived of in the West as a peculiarly Japanese form of spatiality³³ – has been isolated from the flattening and compressing impacts of technology first observed by Henri Lefebvre.

My conclusion in my West London Project (1971) was that we architects, intent on changing places for the better, had to become conscious of the layers of our own mental space, and of which layers we were using as we went about observing situations and proposing improvements. We needed a deliberate approach to ensure the outing of our preferences and assumptions, in order to avoid visiting on others only that which we knew and admired.

Nigel Coates, Café Bongo, Tokyo, Japan, 1986: drawing. This bar seemed to emerge from the investigations of the journal *Telescope*.

England at that time was being invested with large pieces of city that were the product of single layers of mental space, usually from the canon of Futurism or Modernism. These included several new universities such as York, Bath and Strathclyde, new towns such as Harlow and Cumbernauld, and tracts of housing such as that by Chris Cross and his partners in Fitzrovia and Milton Keynes. We had, I concluded, if we were to work with the riches residing in mental space, to engage with our own mental space *and* with that of the communities we were trying to work for. We had to put our preferences into a dialogue with the preferences of these communities, and adopt design strategies that allowed for the ways in which mental space evolves within us, and within communities. There is in this the seed of a conflict between the classical and the innovative approaches to architecture. Social radical Aldo Rossi (1931–97) believed that for architecture to have meaning for society it had to respect the deep language of that society; in his case this was the classical tradition of Greece and Rome, and he sought an 'Ur' architecture that resided, he thought, in the mental space of those who had grown up in the shadows of these architectures.[34] For social conservative Roger Scruton (1944–), English society needs to cleave to the same tradition – in its Georgian guise – in order to preserve its civic decency.[35] For Archigram, on the other hand (sharing as they do Scruton's mental space), or for Superstudio (sharing as they did Rossi's mental space), the issue is one of overturning the classical in order to provide access to the good things of life to a far wider audience than the classical tradition ever did.

Encountering mental space

For a while in Khutsong, South Africa in the late 1970s and early 1980s, working with an urban planner, another architect, an anthropologist and a number of social workers, I achieved something approximating to this. A thousand self-designed homes resulted from the process that we devised – all tailored to the mental space of the family that designed them. We began by helping each family to make a model of the shanty that they had built for themselves when they arrived as squatters. This was done using a baseboard cut with grooves into squares of 300 millimetres per side. Metal sheets could be inserted into these grooves, and magnetised doors and windows attached. Dolls'-house furniture was used inside. When everyone agreed on the model, a plan drawing of it was made on paper squared up to the same grid, and equipped with a few basic dimensioning rules; the families were left with a stack of paper and asked to come to the offices of the housing organisation with a plan in two weeks' time. The rules included a truss width and the information that every square enclosed represented a money value for their future loan repayment. A thousand houses, no two the same – a testament to the essential diversity of mental space – resulted.

Amongst my peers in the developed world, only Michael Sorkin (1948–) with his 'local code' has put his mind to how we might accommodate such dialogues within a micro-democratic framework that allowed differences in mental space to be developed and enjoyed,[36] while in the developing parts of Asia William Lim (1932–) points to the need for instruments that acknowledge differing mental spaces, respect them, and work for social justice in the light of that respect.[37] Some few of us have found careers in which the dialogue between architect and client approximates to that with patrons who are in full command of their mental space, and the results enliven our cities in the ways that the various manifestations of the Design City phenomenon illustrate, whether it is in the manner of Graz, Barcelona, the Randstad or Melbourne.[38] Others have been fortunate to work with patrons like Arata Isozaki (1931–) at the Kumamoto Artpolis (1988 onwards) (where Akira Suzuki of *Telescope* was – it is not surprising to discover – his adviser), Roland Paoletti on the Jubilee Line in London (1990 onwards), Fred Manson at Southwark (1990s) or the city planners of Vancouver.

Most architects are, however, not so fortunate, and in a world in which people are unaware of the workings of their mental space, and in which the profession of architecture has not played the role of custodian of the knowledge created by our spatial intelligence and embedded in our individual and communal mental space, they are engaged in the production of slabs of undifferentiated space defined by numeric quantum alone. In the following chapters I will give an account of how architects who have been concerned to deal with the mental space of others – first unconsciously, then intuitively and now interactively – have developed instruments that could be freshly marshalled, were architects to put working with our spatial intelligence to the fore in their understanding of the knowledge base of the discipline and thus of the profession.

References

1 Gaston Bachelard, *The Poetics of Space*, Beacon Press (Boston, Massachusetts), 1969, pp 11–12 quotes the American philosopher Henry David Thoreau and the French poet Jean Wahl.
2 Po Bronson, 'The lost hour', *Weekend Australian Magazine*, 24–25 November 2007, pp 30–6 (p 33) – reporting on the work of Dr Matthew Walker of the University of California.
3 Sue Halpern, 'Thanks for the memory' (review of Eric R Kandel, *In Search of Memory: The Emergence of a New Science of Mind*, Norton & Company (New York and London), 2006, and Katrina Firlik, *Another Day in the Frontal Lobe: A Brain Surgeon Exposes Life on the Inside*, Random House (New York and London), 2006), *New York Review of Books*, Vol LIII, No 15, 5 October 2006, pp 17–20 (p 18): 'the cellular mechanisms of learning and memory reside not in the special properties of the neuron itself, but in the connections it receives and makes with other cells in the neuronal circuit to which it belongs.' Sue Halpern is Scholar in Residence at Middlebury College, Vermont.
4 Russell L Ackoff, Professor Emeritus, Ackoff Center, Bryn Mawr, in a presentation to a Tallberg Workshop, Sweden, 2001.
5 Anne Humphreys, *Travels into the Poor Man's Country: The Work of Henry Mayhew*, University of Georgia Press (Athens, Georgia), 1977, p 203: 'Henry Mayhew, a chronology'. Mayhew wrote articles for the *London Illustrated News* from 1842, which were gathered together as a book in three volumes, *London Labour and the London Poor* (1851). Mayhew wrote in volume one: 'I shall consider the whole of the metropolitan poor under three separate phases, according as they will work, they can't work, and they won't work.' A fourth volume (co-written with Bracebridge Hemyng, John Binny and Andrew Halliday), taking a more general and statistical approach, was added in 1862.
6 Marcel Proust, *In Search of Lost Time, Volume One: Swann's Way*, The Folio Society (London), 2001, p 42 (first published in French as *A la recherche du temps perdu: du côté de chez Swann*, 1913).
7 Ibid.
8 Bachelard, *The Poetics of Space*, op cit, p 12.
9 Javier Marías, *Dark Back of Time*, Chatto & Windus and Vintage (London), 2004, p 316.
10 Bachelard, *The Poetics of Space*, op cit, pp 11–12.
11 Mark Augé, *Non-Places: Introduction to an Anthropology of Supermodernity*, Verso (London), 1995.
12 Jessica Marshall, 'Future recall', *New Scientist*, Vol 193, No 2596, 24 March 2007, pp 36–40.
13 Terence Lee's research circulated among students at the Architectural Association, London in samizdat form in the 1970s.
14 Michael Bond, 'A sense of place: interview with John Zeisel', *New Scientist*, Vol 189, No 2541, 4 March 2006, pp 50–1.
15 Oliver Sacks, *An Anthropologist on Mars*, Pan Macmillan (Sydney) and Picador (London), 1995, pp 241–62.
16 Charles Simic, 'The spirit of play' (review of Anne Carson, *Decreation: Poetry, Essays, Opera*, Alfred A Knopf (New York), 2005), *New York Review of Books*, Vol LII, No 17, 3 November 2005, pp 28–30, quotes Anne Carson: 'After all, texts of ancient Greeks come to us in wreckage, and I admire that – the layers of time you have when looking at sheets of papyrus that were produced in the third century BC and then copied and then wrapped around a mummy and then discovered and pieced together by nine different gentlemen and put back in the museum and brought out again and photographed and put in a book. All those layers add more and more life. You can approximate that in your life. Stains on clothing.' (in *Paris Review*, Fall 2004, p 202)
17 IA Richards, *Practical Criticism: A Study of Literary Judgment*, Harcourt Brace (New York), 1956 (first published 1929).
18 WG Sebald, *The Emigrants*, Harvill Press (London), 1997, p 210.
19 Sue Halpern, 'The moment of truth' (review of Malcolm Gladwell, *Blink: The Power of Thinking Without Thinking*, Little, Brown & Company (New York), 2005 and Elkhonon Goldberg, *The Wisdom Paradox: How Your Mind Can Grow Stronger as Your Brain Grows Older*, Gotham Books (New York), 2005), *New York Review of Books*, Vol LII, No 7, 28 April 2005, pp 19–21 (p 20): 'But in reality, intuition is the condensation of vast prior experience; it is analysis compressed and crystallized … It is the product of analytic processes being condensed to such a degree that its internal

structure may elude even the person benefiting from it … .'
20 Dalibor Vesely, 'Architecture and the conflict of representation', *AA Files*, No 8, 1985, pp 21–38; and for his definitive account: Dalibor Vesely, *Architecture in the Age of Divided Representation: The Question of Creativity in the Shadow of Production*, MIT Press (Cambridge, Massachusetts), 2004.
21 Trevor Garnham, *Melsetter House*, Phaidon Press (London), 1993.
22 George Bernard Shaw, *Pygmalion*, 1913. Professor Higgins is the philologer in Shaw's satire on class distinctions expressed in dialect.
23 Perry Anderson, 'The age of EJH' (review of Eric Hobsbawm, *Interesting Times: A 20th Century Life*, Allen Lane (London), 2002), *London Review of Books*, Vol 24, No 19, 3 October 2002, pp 3–7.
24 Richard Rorty, 'Being that can be understood is language' (review of a paper delivered in Heidelberg by Hans-Georg Gadamer on the occasion of his 100th birthday on 11 February 2000), *London Review of Books*, Vol 22, No 6, 16 March 2000, pp 23–5: 'As Jonathan Rée has suggested … objects are like onions: lots of layers made up of descriptions [the further into the onion, the earlier the description], but without a non linguistic core that will be revealed once those layers have been stripped off. … The deeper and more penetrating our understanding of something, so the story goes, the further we are from appearance and the closer to reality. The effect of adopting Gadamer's slogan [being that …] is to replace these metaphors of depth with metaphors of breadth: the more descriptions that are available, the more integration between these descriptions that are available, the better our understanding of the object identified by any of those descriptions' (p 24). Richard Rorty (1931–2007) taught philosophy at Stanford University.
25 Marshall McLuhan, *The Gutenberg Galaxy: The Making of Typographic Man*, Routledge & Kegan Paul (London), 1967.
26 Paul Carter, *Living in a New Country: History, Travelling and Language*, Faber & Faber (London), 1992; Paul Carter, *Migrant Musings: Christmas in Brunswick*, Agenda (Melbourne), 1992.
27 West London Project – AA Diploma Thesis, London, 1971. Translated into Italian and published as *I personaggi del 'Teatro Urbano', disegno 1972*, in Gillo Dorfles, *Dal Significato Alle Scelte*, Einaudi (Turin), 1973, figs 28–35.
28 Jean Duvignaud, *Change at Shebika: Report from a North African Village*, Pantheon Books (New York), 1970.
29 Charles Simic, 'The spirit of play', op cit.
30 Ugo La Pietra, 'L'uso dell'oggetto per un comportamento creativo nei processi di reappropriazione dell'ambiente', in Floriano De Angeli (ed), *Progettare In Più*, Jabik Editori (Milan), Vol 1, No 1, October/November 1973. This was the first of three issues. It was followed by: Ugo la Pietra, 'L'uso della città: per un comportamento creativo nei processi di reappropriazione dell'ambiente', in Floriano De Angeli (ed), *Progettare In Più*, Jabik Editori (Milan), 1973–4 and Ugo la Pietra, 'La guida alternativa alla città di Milano: per un comportamento creativo nei processi di reappropriazione dell'ambiente', in Floriano De Angeli (ed), *Progettare In Più*, Jabik Editori (Milan), 1974.
31 *Telescope*, edited by Akira Suzuki and Kayoko Ota (published by Workshop for Architecture and Urbanism, Tokyo): No 5, *The Printed City* (1990); No 6, *The Edible City* (1991); No 7, *The Wild, Wild City* (1992); No 8, *The Bubblicious City* (1992); No 9, *The Big, Bad Burb* (1993).
32 Akira Suzuki, *Do Android Crows Fly Over the Skies of an Electronic Tokyo?*, Architectural Association (London), 2001.
33 See also Frederic Jameson, 'Perfected by the Tea Masters' (review of Arato Izosaki, *Japanness in Architecture*, MIT Press (Cambridge, Massachusetts), 2006), in *London Review of Books*, Vol 29, No 7, 5 April 2007, pp 21–3.
34 Aldo Rossi's canonical books were *L'architettura della città* (first published 1966) and *Autobiografia scientifica* (first published 1981).
35 Roger Scruton, *The Aesthetics of Architecture*, Methuen (London), 1979.
36 Michael Sorkin, *Local Code*, Princeton Architectural Press (New York), 1993.
37 William SW Lim, *Asian Alterity: With Special Reference to Architecture and Urbanism through the Lens of Cultural Studies*, World Scientific Publishing (Singapore), 2007.
38 Leon van Schaik, *Design City: Melbourne*, Wiley-Academy (London), 2006.

3
The disruption of the unity of time, place and architecture, and some precursors of reunification

Any theory about the city will always be the product of one person's thinking from the vantage point of his or her experiences and convictions. These are its starting points. While it is true that genuine theory will manage to transcend them, it is also a fact, to a greater or lesser extent, it will still be coloured by them. In 1867 Cerdà opened his General Theory of Urbanisation by recounting those personal experiences that led him to develop an interest in cities …

Arturo Soria y Puig[1]

In preceding chapters I have sketched out the proposition that architecture is necessarily a product of mental space – the accumulated histories of individuals in space – and that there are great potentials for its future use to society were architects to operate with a consciousness of the new knowledge about the ways in which our spatial intelligence forms that mental space. I have suggested that there was a time before the modern era in which architecture operated seamlessly within the mental space of regionally distinct communities, and that one of the perhaps unintended consequences of early modernity was the disruption of the unity of time,

place and architecture – a disruption that has rendered the wonders of Egyptian, Chinese, Persian, Babylonian, Greek, Roman, Byzantine, Ottoman, Romanesque and Gothic architecture inaccessible to us today, except in the guise of the encyclopaedic wrenching of the elements of the 'features' of these great holistic works into compendiums of styles, of which Banister Fletcher's *A History of Architecture on the Comparative Method* (first published in 1896) is a surviving example. These encyclopaedias suggested the possibility of infinite recombinations – and this gave rise to the anomie of much 19th-century architecture, an ennui arising from the very ubiquity of the styles that the encyclopaedias enabled.

Architecture and the city: integration and separation

Intuitively we all know that architecture grows in cities – which are the tangible manifestations of the mental space of their citizens, buildings superimposed in layers by generation after generation. If in our mind's eye we were to imagine a time-lapse record of a city's growth through the centuries, we would see spaces being formed by jostling ranks of buildings. A sequence on Alnwick, a town in the border country in the far north of England, would begin with it being laid out as a Roman *castrum* on a simple grid with a main street running north–south. As the sequence moved forward to the present, we would see many encroachments on this street from the narrow lots abutting – often simply a stall at first, later built in with a permanent roof, later still built over with an upper storey, until today the street has an 'S'-bend so pronounced that you cannot see from north to south. Archaeologists understand this phenomenon better than most of us, digging as they often do down through the many layers of the ancient site of an abandoned city like Troy, starting with what seems to be a small hill, and paring away skin after skin until they find the stratum that relates to the historical moment they are studying. Much more difficult is to look around us in our own city and see that this is what is happening: we are laying down a stratum that records our culture; but if we adopt an archaeologist's eye for a moment, we will begin to see that the architecture and the artefacts of our time are indeed all of a piece, and tell the story of our present culture. Modernity has created the illusion that we can be free from this process, and has led us to design as if we – and our mental space – will not become the past. Once we realise the folly of this view, the question is: how can we have come to regard architecture as something independent of

Peter Lyssiotis, *Architecture grows in cities...*, photomontage for *Spatial Intelligence*, 1998 – completed as part of an Australia Council New Media Arts Fellowship at RMIT, Melbourne, Australia.

our cities and the culture that each one manifests? How have we come to regard architecture as independent from our spatial intelligence?

Part of the answer lies in the separation of architecture from the matrix of the city, a process of self-consciousness that slowly ended the tradition of the usually anonymous master builders who both designed and constructed the buildings of those cities – including the great cathedrals up to and including the Gothic – and replaced it with the architects as designers and arbiters of taste.[2] In the 19th century, architecture was formalised as a profession – around (as we shall see in a later chapter) the knowledge embedded in master building. In a process that was coterminous with the rediscovery of the knowledge of ancient Greece and Rome, architects (first in Renaissance Italy, later in 18th-century Britain) began to endow buildings with a status derived from overt connections to the exemplars of classical architecture, and this referencing burst apart the integuments that held architecture and place together so powerfully in Tudor England, for example. In the Veneto, Andrea Palladio (1508–80) styled the often fairly humble farmhouses of his patrons as small palaces, using large gables and colonnades to link everything into a grand composition rather like a stage set. In the early 19th century, John Nash (1752–1835) styled the terraces around Regent's Park in London in a very similar way, providing large numbers of moderately well-to-do tenants with the sense that they were living in a palace; and in his Brighton Pavilion (1815–22) he provided a stage-set symbol of the Empire's domination of India – all symbol. Earlier, in Kew Gardens near London in 1762, suitably sited within a collection of exotic plants, Sir William Chambers provided his clients with the immensely tall Pagoda – a sign more Chinese than its original inspiration. These are all symptoms of the disconnect between architecture and place that has slowly rendered architecture itself an exotic art, which means that in the public mind – even in Australia, that long-urbanised country (80 per cent of the population have lived in the main cities for more than a hundred years) – those architects who build in the wilderness are the ones who are most often illustrated. Architecture happens in isolation, while the cities are expressions of power either by design – as in Tiananmen Square in Imperial Peking (Beijing), or Red Square in Moscow – or in the graph-paper skylines of the corporate cities of the USA.

Modernity opened up so many possibilities that it is churlish to regret the enthusiasm with which the imitation of the styles was embraced – ironically nowhere more enthusiastically than within the glazed shelter of the Crystal Palace that housed the Great Exhibition of 1851. While Joseph Paxton's

Joseph Paxton, Crystal Palace, Hyde Park, London, UK, 1851: hand-coloured lithograph by Philip de Bay. The wonderful Crystal Palace that housed the Great Exhibition in 1851 was in itself largely a work of exquisite engineering derived from the pragmatics of glasshouse design; it contained, however, a plethora of hybridised products that combined the fake with the new.

wonderful structure was in itself largely a work of exquisite engineering derived from the pragmatics of glasshouse design, it housed a plethora of hybridised products that combined the fake (like synthetic ormolu) with the new (old materials cast in new ways). Amongst these products were carpets woven with such persuasive trompe-l'oeil effects that people tripped when walking across their perfectly flat surfaces. One can deplore the loss of spatial unity these amazing, mostly kitsch works displayed as they 'denied the unacceptable' and 'excluded the uncomfortable', aiming to 'give emotion (sentimentality IA Richards would have called it) its head and draw people together by offering images that keep the real world at bay'; or, one can argue – as Venezuelan cultural historian Celeste Olalquiaga does, with her stake in the periphery – that these popular forms were the means for those on the periphery of industrialisation to regain some influence over the centre. That centre itself recoiled at first, seeing the solution in a return to the past of handcrafted arts that manifested a unity of space, time, facture and place. Leading this reaction was William Morris (1834–96). Allied was Lethaby, whose design for Melsetter House in Orkney (1898) revealed the power of

William Richard Lethaby, Melsetter House, Orkney, UK, 1898. The design worked from an ancient farmhouse towards an Arts and Crafts ideal.

the approach in a work of architecture. Robin Evans[3] proves, however, that – as was revealed in Philip Webb's (1831–1915) earlier plan for Morris's marital home, the Red House in Bexleyheath, Kent (1859), which retains the partition of social classes, ensuring (as indeed does the Melsetter plan) that servants and family do not mix – this was a superficial reform; its benefits were made available only to a moneyed elite. What kitsch promised, however, was what Archigram argued for in the 20th century – access to the good things in life for all, not simply for the rich. Sadly the Arts and Crafts movement became and remained the toy of a wealthy few. Kitsch went on to service the masses.

Reintegrating architecture into our mental space

One strand of mature modernism in architecture, that championed by Hannes Meyer (Head of Architecture at the Bauhaus, 1927–30), who pursued Walter Gropius's 'Existenzminimum'[4] – an approach to design that would support the simple decencies of life for all – sought ways to distil out (of the styles that the encyclopaedias enabled) the essences of good form and functionality, and to deliver these to all. The ultimate failure of this noble aim lay in its denial that architecture at least (industrial design may be different) is place and time specific – not, except at great risk, generalisable and transferable.

This was fundamentally an error engendered by the analytical dissections of the encyclopaedic method – as argued in the previous chapter. There was, however, in early modernism a precursor for the integration of place, time and space that emerged within a shared mental space and found – after many years of struggle – an implementation strategy through a politics that worked within that particular community. It is a precursor rather than a pioneer because, although both the proposition and the solution to its implementation depended on a harnessing of a very local politics of space, the players were not specifically aware that they were operating within a mental space. This is the history of the plan devised by architect, engineer and mathematician Ildefonso Cerdá for the extension of Barcelona, a plan that brought together the thinking of thirty years when submitted to the Madrid government in 1859.

This remarkable story is not much known in the Anglophone world, nor even in the Spanish-speaking world, because it arose in Catalonia in the 19th century and was specific to the city state centred on Barcelona and forged in that region's often fraught peripheral relationship to Madrid, from which it has long sought a degree of autonomy. So particular is the design itself that it is seldom discussed outside Catalan scholarly circles, and within these the particularity to a shared mental space is so taken for granted that the originality of the design and the implementation is somewhat obscured. Ironically, the very closeness of the fit to the spatial history of Catalonia of this project has made its message difficult for the outside world to grasp, and this has rendered local analysis largely in technicalities. Yet this is surely one of the clearest examples of the benefits of consciously using spatial intelligence in design – one that, understood in the context of 'mental space', has a huge significance for us as we move away from the 'one size fits all' ideologies of modernism.

Ildefonso Cerdá's proposition for the extension of Barcelona arose from a spatial analysis of the longevity of the citizens of the ancient city. This epidemiological approach revealed that the higher up in the buildings of the old city people dwelt, the longer they lived. The pioneering spatial distribution of statistics then cross-referenced to adjacency to sunlight and fresh air, and distance from sewage and refuse. From this arose the proposition to extend the city across its coastal hinterland on a grid that enshrined, in its very shape, spatial relationships between sunlight and air and propositions about transport that were the logical consequence of seeking to enshrine equality of access to the goods of city living for all of its inhabitants, not only for those rich enough to live in the top storeys. The chamfered corners of the grid allowed for the threading of cables and tramcar turning circles through any part of the grid. And streets were wide enough to allow for the parking of individual vehicles, Cerdá observing that as technology advanced, individual ownership of (he thought steam-driven) vehicles was a certainty. In a part of the design that was overwhelmed by development pressures resulting from its own (ultimate) success as a

Barcelona, Spain: aerial view showing the distinctive chamfered grid of Ildefonso Cerdá's 1859 plan for the city. Critics argue that development pressures subverted the design, and yet its success in moulding a diverse architectural expression for the city is evident.

development process, the plan specified that neighbourhoods would be built up of a set of grid pieces configured to enshrine markets, schools, pocket parks. Yet, brilliant though the design was agreed to be, and endorsed though it was by parliament, it stalled. Its egalitarian principles engendered the hostility of landowners and speculators. The issue was that the plan spread across the ancient field system around the city covering a myriad of ownerships of different parcels of land. This complexity made it very difficult to find an acceptable way of apportioning shares in the new development plan for the existing owners. The reduced land areas available for development in the new grid once the new streets and squares were laid out exacerbated this, and there was dismay at the fact that the plan required some compulsory purchase of existing property in order to connect to the old city. Baron Haussmann's contemporary scheme (1852–70) for Paris – that major transformation of the ancient city that was completed as Proust was born in 1871, but is nowhere mentioned in his writing – benefited from a canny development process that allowed different sizes of investment (one bay, two bays, more) behind a continuous facade. This softened the blow of compulsory purchase by giving in return a ladder of opportunity for investors large and small. Such a mechanism eluded Cerdá's scheme for twenty years, during which parliamentary committees made report after report, but no parliament ever had the conviction to act – until, in almost a last gasp for the concept, Cerdá realised that the plan areas of ownership could be transferred into volumes of development rights proportional to those numerous different areas. On this spatialised basis the plan was approved and enacted.[5] Much of the picturesque appeal of Barcelona today stems from this solution, because as a consequence no block was developed by one owner using one architect. All the blocks have different patterns of ownership, different designs by different architects – a mosaic that is a built representation of the mental space of city and citizens.

Taipei is a city that shares this manifesting of its mental space with Barcelona. Taiwanese capitalism takes a very particular form, rather like Jane Jacobs' description of pre-Second World War Birmingham.[6] This mode of capitalism is characterised by myriads of small firms in family ownership, capable of forming alliances in response to any challenge and any opportunity. The city has a fine grain of development reflecting this ownership pattern, and families vie with each other through architectural invention and – as RMIT-based architectural educator Sand Helsel has shown[7] – through novel encroachments on the public realm, not however unlike those I have mentioned in Alnwick. Helsel and her students made figure-ground plans

Sand Helsel et al, figure-ground plans of the legal structures of the Yong Kung community in Taipei, Japan, and of the legal and illegal structures combined, 2004. These reveal in the comparison a 'swollen rice' effect as the actual boundaries of the spaces were constricted by the expanded profile of each small building.

of the legal structures of the Yong Kung community, and of the legal and illegal structures combined, revealing in the comparison a 'swollen rice' effect as the actual boundaries of the spaces were constricted by the expanded profiles of each small building. This is not simply a plan effect. They also documented add-on structures for storage and laundry that encroach on the space of laneways above street level. Whether in Taipei or any other city where they occur, these individually crafted but strangely homogenous additions to the streetscapes take a form particular to each city in which they occur and are what give them their distinctive flavours. We often marvel at the phenomenon, but do we appreciate that we are looking at the popular manifestation of spatial culture? It is easier for us to read the mental space of societies other than our own – especially when they are as distinctive as Barcelona became, as Taipei has become.

One might have thought, therefore, that awareness of 'difference' lay at the core of observation of the city and of attempts to prescribe programmes for their improvement – as indeed it does in the work of Sand Helsel and her student teams. There is, however, here again, a tension between the 'scientific' generalising approach of Friedrich Engels, harbinger of 'Social Science', and Henry Mayhew,[8] the interviewer and recorder of the stories of specific attempts to adapt to what may very well have been general conditions (see Chapter Two). Cerdá's work stands in a clear contradistinction to the urban proposals that resulted from the 'scientific' approach (an approach that we will see was more abstractionist than scientific, and that is better described as 'rationalist'). The urban hygiene movement, heralded by MP Joseph Chamberlain proposing bylaws for the city of Birmingham (1876), was one such outcome. The movement was so called because these bylaws laid down minimum standards for insolation with a ratio of window area to floor area, cross-ventilation, and room ventilation – requiring air-venting bricks in all habitable rooms to prevent asphyxiation from open braziers, as well as demanding twin-pipe plumbing systems to prevent cross-infection of potable water, vent traps to sewers, and so on. They also proscribed 'back-to-back' developments (to ensure cross-ventilation was possible), defined the minimum requirements for 'party walls' (fire walls dividing dwellings in terraces), and introduced 'set backs' – minimum distances between developments and boundaries of sites. These – or close variants of them – were applied abstractly across the British Empire, regardless of whether in the tropics, in the highlands or in deserts. They undoubtedly achieved their goals, but have had many irrational and unintended consequences. Think for a moment about the rigid

Black Country Living Museum, Dudley, West Midlands, UK. Bylaws passed in 1876 proscribed the back-to-back housing that occurred in the rapid urbanisation following the Industrial Revolution (here preserved at the Black Country Living Museum outside Birmingham).

application of the vent brick rule in other than temperate climes, particularly as technology changed, and the problem will become apparent.

Problems of urban theory that lacks an overt spatial intelligence concept

Cerdá had worked with the same life-saving intent, but his solution was a design specific to his city and its mental space. Its success, even when subjected as it has been to massive overdevelopment – the average height of Barcelona's hollow blocks exceeds 10 storeys, and all sides of blocks have been developed, where in Cerdá's rules many blocks in a neighbourhood should have been developed along two sides only – is due to the specificity of the solution. Lacking a concept of 'mental space', the architectural world has largely ignored his achievement as an unscientific quirk, not replicable and therefore not instructive. The lack of an understanding of mental space has caused urbanists of many persuasions to write general theories (even Cerdá thought he was doing that, titling his work a 'general theory',[9] hence he is a precursor rather than a pioneer). Whether that most influential Italian urbanist of the late 20th century, Aldo Rossi (whom we have already encountered in Chapter Two), formulated his 'Rationalism' as a generally applicable system, or whether we have – thanks to our lack of an appreciation of the necessary spatial boundaries of such ideas – imbued his work with a universalist quality, is an open question. Architects in general took Rossi's Rationalism – a culturally specific revival of a tradition that his predecessor and fellow countryman Giuseppe Terragni (whose most celebrated built work is the Casa del Popolo, Como, 1932–6) also mined in a radical manner – to be a movement that need acknowledge no mental space boundaries, even though its key formal proposition was based on the belief in a deep popular consciousness of the classical architecture of ancient Greece and the Roman Empire that was necessarily bounded geographically to those communities still living in the shadow of the great monuments of those ancient states.

The 18th-century Picturesque movement in landscape in England – as evidenced in the grounds of great houses like Stourhead or Blenheim – has been widely influential, as if a general movement; but it was the creation of a handful of landowners, writers and gardeners within a tightly shared and even socially circumscribed 'mental space', forged by a common interest in the improvement of large properties. It was informed by a shared academic background embracing the classics, concepts of Arcadia derived from the classics and interpreted by a set of fashionable painters, and an education that culminated in a Grand Tour to Rome – something only the wealthy could afford. Gentleman theorist Uvedale Price (1747–1829) wrote as if he was addressing the known world; Lancelot 'Capability' Brown (1716–83) designed as if for the known world; Humphry Repton's (1752–1818) before and after images invented a marketing approach that addressed specific potential clients – and in due course the movement attracted from within its own 'mental space' its falsifiers (see discussion of Rowe and Popper below), who criticised Brown's strategy for converting formal avenues into natural-looking copses as 'clumping'.[10] But the movement reveals that a concept developed within a 'mental space' is not doomed to irrelevance as the 'Rationalists' believed. Rather, what has emerged from the intense hothouse concerns of an elite has come to have an impact on every other suburban garden in the world. As a householder lays the garden hose in a sinuous curve along a lawn preparatory to cutting out a garden bed, that householder is paying homage to Uvedale Price, even if only in a 'dimly resonant'[11] way. We might in fact see the Picturesque as a model for working with 'mental space', except that the people involved inhabited a 'little life' (as Ingmar Bergman put it in his

Humphry Repton, trade card, 1780. The landscape gardener Humphry Repton understood the mental space of his potential clients very well, presenting them with 'before and after' images of their estates, and signalling on his trade card both his own agency in design, and the probable outcome!

1983 film *Fanny and Alexander*, which concerned life in a multi-generational family of provincial theatre owners and actors unified in space, place and time, and united by a shared repertoire), and were so unified that the 'little life' could seem to be the whole world to its inhabitants. Little need then to consider that there were other 'mental spaces' beyond our own – though in his fable Bergman uses the Jewish family friend to point to the existence of other mental spaces and to their uses. It is hard to find such geographical and cultural unity anywhere today, although – as we shall see in a later chapter – we humans have an exceptional capability for forging communities of interest and we are embracing Internet-accessed experiences to create them; and this is why a conscious approach to 'mental space' – now possible thanks to advances in our understandings of our spatial intelligence and its operations – is both possible and needed.

Observation informed by the Picturesque sensibility might seem to be a promising route into observing, describing and working with mental space; but everyone who has ventured down this path has, bereft of the concept of mental space, vitiated their argument by accepting the rationalist need to make their findings generally applicable everywhere. Camillo Sitte (1843–1903) studied a relatively small number of European town centres in his bid to counter the sterile effects of symmetry and geometry in Beaux Arts city planning. The venture was informative, but with spaces reduced to diagrams its proposal was merely formal – curiously mirroring the desiccation of what it was attacking, lacking as it did a theory of mental space. As we shall see, Colin Rowe did much to introduce such a theory into the connoisseurial approach pioneered by Sitte, and he did this because it was the difference between cities and city districts that fascinated him. Gordon Cullen, for many years the 'Outrage' columnist in the London-based journal *Architectural Review* (1946–56), pursued a vision of what specific places could be like, if they were cleaned up – surfaces given their integrity and the bones revealed.[12] A politic that could have sustained this persuasive vision eluded him and his readers, perhaps because he was so embedded in the mental space of one class of taste, and he failed to find a way to the 'popular' that artists like Richard Hamilton (1922–) (whose famous collage of all things consumable and American heralded in Pop Art) and Eduardo Paolozzi (1924–2005) – members of the 1950s Independent Group with architects Peter and Alison Smithson – were signalling.[13]

Two further 'precursors' merit discussion: Kevin Lynch (1918–84)[14] and Christopher Alexander (1936–).[15] Lynch's picturesque approach pioneered its application to the scale of the car much as if he had anticipated in a small way the thinking of Henri Lefebvre, with persuasive analyses of Washington and other East Coast cities as picturesque systems that operated at the speed of a driver. His sketches of the swirling motions between landmarks are a breakthrough, even if they speak of a time with less urban congestion. However, his work is sadly bereft of a sense of particularity, and his 'solution' is proposed as a general system, applicable anywhere. I suspect that his diagrammatic summations influenced Robert Venturi, Denise Scott Brown and Steven Izenour's book *Learning from Las Vegas*, which as we shall see, while it embraced the 'dirty reality' of popular urbanism, also rationalised this into a general system. Alexander's interest in creating a notational system that captured what people actually did when unselfconsciously building their settlements over many generations and incorporating into their form the means to subtly moderate the microclimate and support their social rituals was very promising, but it slipped into a taxonomy of partial solutions at the scale of individual daily functions – bed alcoves, bay windows, entrance thresholds and so on, garnered from every corner of the world and classified. These results are fascinating, but they resist re-combination into designs because they are deprived of their life force by the act of cutting them away from their surrounding fabric, and the mental space within which they were formed.

Towards the application of spatial and cultural specificity in urbanism

A scholar whom I claim as a true precursor of the conscious use of mental space in architecture is Colin Rowe, whose figure-ground studies of cities across the world, conducted with generations of postgraduate students at Cornell University, pioneered a connoisseurship of the spatial configuration of cities.[16] Based on the work of Camillo Sitte[17] and on Giambattista Nolli's 1748 plan of Rome, Rowe was able to demonstrate how certain kinds of 'grain' predicated certain ranges of use and cultural behaviour, proving over and again to sceptics that he was able to read the specifics of the mental space of many cities from such abstracted representations. The plans that his graduate students made of their home cities were produced in complementary pairs, one showing all the built fabric in solid black, the other rendering black all the open space. The 'black as space' figure ground of Wiesbaden c 1900 featured on the cover of *Collage City* is an extreme example demonstrating a dramatic difference between the 'grain' of the inner city – where all is white save for the narrow streets and small squares – and the 'grain' of the suburbs – where all is black except for the white spots of suburban villas.[18] (The method is still in use to great effect – see the discussion of Sand Helsel's work on Taipei above.) Rowe also proposed a theory of 'collage' to account for the way in which generations of mental space succeed each other, enriching cities through time. He argued that a fundamental role of the architect was to reveal in their designing the palimpsests of ideas about the city that every site contains, and called on designers to respect the process of collage, which always relies on the retaining of enough of what previously existed for it to enter into dialogue with the imported new. Like Cerdá, he came to argue the politics of this spatial respect, demonstrating how collage and total redevelopment were antithetical, and suggesting that totalitarianism was the enemy of the civic in architecture as well as of human rights in politics.

Rowe was much influenced by Karl Popper (1902–94), whose concept of 'falsification' was an important moment in the understanding of scientific process. For Popper, there is no 'final' truth in science, only a cascade of propositions that are tested until 'falsified' and thus replaced by another proposition that is in turn scrutinised, challenged and so on.[19] When Rowe's concept of the city is seen in this light, we can see that he is criticising the totalising implications of those modernists who sought to treat the old world as dispensable, replacing it with a tabula rasa on which their ideal future prevailed. This put Rowe in a difficult position as a critic, because while he greatly admired Le Corbusier (1887–1965) as an architect whose work grew out of past traditions – as he demonstrated by comparing the Villa at Garches (1927) with a Palladian villa (the mathematics of the ideal villa)[20] – he saw the same architect's Ville Radieuse (1933–5) as a totalitarian vision which had to be rejected because of its political relationship to the final solutions of fascism and its denial of what Rowe saw as the enriching dialogue between the utopian visions of one generation and the next.

Rowe's critics argued that his analysis failed to account for the city of the automobile age.[21] Though this work was never published, he and his colleague Fred Koetter (1938–) were certainly very interested in the utopias

Fremont Street, Las Vegas, USA, 1954 – an image of the city not used in the book *Learning from Las Vegas* by Venturi Scott Brown, but capturing the exuberant spirit that attracted the authors to this focus for a new mental space.

Leon van Schaik   073   Chapter 3 The disruption of the unity of time, place and architecture

of the automobile experience, and at the International Institute for Design summer school at the Architectural Association in London in 1970, Koetter described how Rowe and he were thinking about ways to intensify the differences between the experience of driving into New York along the Hudson freeway and along a suburban strip. The desire was to make the Parkway more park-like, the strip much more strip-like. I imagine that the latter was influenced by the work of those other precursors of the deliberate use of mental space, Denise Scott Brown (1931–) and Robert Venturi (1925–). Their seminal *Learning from Las Vegas* was published in 1972,[22] and is almost a casebook for how to engage with the mental space of a city. I write 'almost' because while it argued that what was being produced by the popular imaginary should be examined, it tended to frame that examination in terms of an architectural argument external to what was being observed. This drove too rapidly to a generalised position, applied haphazardly all around the globe by people who have never been to Las Vegas, and in cities that have no functional relationship to that desert tourism centre. Thus observation became all too immediately an encyclopaedia of stylistic devices, much as his influential book *Complexity and Contradiction*[23] begat pale imitations of classical devices on tilt-slab factories all around the world. The best of their own work – and I claim the Sainsbury Wing of the National Gallery in London (1988–91) as a high point – combined acute observation, respect and wit.[24] Architects who were influenced by their arguments, and who were also acute observers, have made a major contribution to enhancing the spatial – and amongst such pioneers of conscious mental space design that I will discuss in a following chapter are Edmond & Corrigan (1976–) of Melbourne, and Sean Griffiths of FAT in London (1995–).

Perhaps, though, the most telling response to the critique of Rowe has come in an almost perfect 'falsification' by Mario Gandelsonas, whose work on the form of the American city used a higher level of abstraction than did Rowe's. Where Rowe's analysis was conducted at walking pace (Grahame Shane recounts how in 1970 Rowe looked at his drawings of London for 10 minutes, and then walked around the key sites comparing the drawings to what they could see as they walked)[25] Gandelsonas's analysis[26] is conducted as it from a moving car, even if at a maximum speed of 50 miles an hour! Faster, scenographic analyses have been conducted by subsequent generations of students. Thus in the wonderful drawings of cities that emerged from Gandelsonas's laboratory, we see vectors and grids and blockages in different colours and with the permeabilities of one direction separated from the permeabilities in another.[27] Gandlesonas then can point to shifts

Mario Gandelsonas, *Invisible Walls* (in *X-Urbanism: Architecture and the American City*, Princeton University Press (Princeton, New Jersey), 1999, pp 146–7). In the wonderful drawings of cities that emerged from Gandelsonas' laboratory, (opposite and overleaf), we see vectors and grids and blockages in different colours and with the permeabilities of one direction separated from the permeabilities in another.

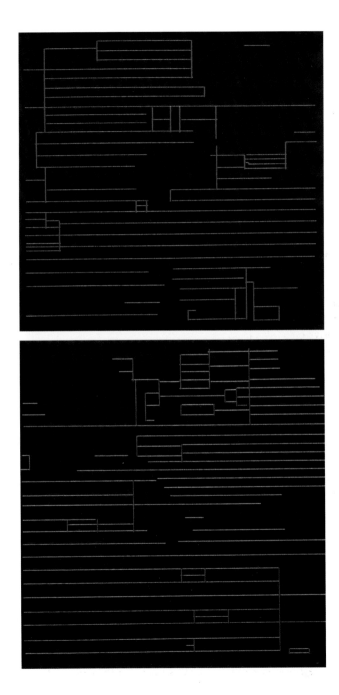

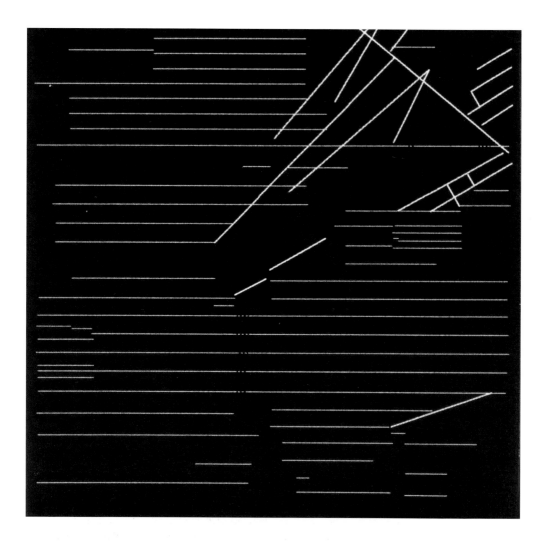

in grids where traffic is radically impeded, and show how some of these relate to concentrations of retail opportunity (shops), while others mark the boundaries between communities of different socioeconomic groups.

The architectural proposals of Agrest & Gandelsonas,[28] originating in Buenos Aires but one of New York's most engaging practices, are manifestly influenced by this work, and suggest new ways of designing in American cities, using American mental space from a well-researched base. Luckily for them, and unlike Venturi, Scott Brown, the world has not attempted to adopt their work as a style. Perhaps this is because Gandelsonas's approach has been based on an analysis that abstracts rather than represents the experience of the automobile city. It is also because it does not regard architecture as a single unified field of ambition. The work is presented as an alternative, not as a truth. This makes it easier to work with as part of a propositional system, essential to cultures that promote intellectual change[29] and to falsification, while *Learning from Las Vegas* owes much to the totalising approach that Le Corbusier has bequeathed to architecture in his disarming but prescriptive title *Towards A New Architecture*.[30] So it is that what was learned from Las Vegas was encyclopaedic and strategic. The book poses a bipolar future for architecture: choose between the building as a simulacrum of what it houses (illustrated with a building shaped like a duck) or the building as a 'decorated shed' in which the decoration signifies what the building houses.

And yet one looks in vain for the influence on architecture and urbanism as practised in the USA of Gandelsonas's sophisticated research, or for a physical realisation of the propositions Agrest & Gandelsonas crafted from this research for their 'Vision Plans' for Des Moines, Iowa. They have yet to find the spatial politics that would make the ideas implementable, and it is worth remembering that it took Cerdá 20 years to craft these within the parliamentary system of Catalonia. Is such a politics likely in the USA? Not in all probability in the general development process that, as Chicago-based historian Robert Bruegmann has shown in his entertainingly entitled book *Sprawl: A Compact History*,[31] is best left to the dynamics of micro-democracy. But the quest for solutions to the collapsing central cities of Detroit and other 'rust-bucket' towns across Middle America may lead to the development of just such a politics. In the context of the explosive growth of Asian cities, architect William Lim has advocated a reverse engineering approach that backfills social justice through post-planning interventions on sites that the growth has swept past. Bruegmann shows how such sites are often where dense urban fabric emerges in the untrammelled sprawl of most USA cities. These insights are dependent on analyses that have a sophisticated approach to the spatiality of cities. Unfortunately the generation succeeding Gandelsonas, characterised by its belief in collective creativity, has been swept up into the Engels approach, fascinated by statistics and – as the Venice Architecture Biennale of 2006 demonstrated – lost in them. It is after all easier to agree on statistics than on a creative spatial proposition …

My account of precursors cannot conclude without a look at Rem Koolhaas's *Delirious New York*.[32] Few books in the 20th century are so interested in the mental space of a city, and few have such novel insights into its dynamics. I think that the observation that, as in fashion, one generation's playground is the next generation's workplace is an inspired understanding of the workings of spatial intelligence and mental space. The book also reveals how the futurist romance of Hugh Ferriss's (1889–1962) projections of a Manhattan built up to the boundaries of sun-angle-determined development envelopes promoted a popular understanding of the city as a 'city of congestions' – in this way rendering demand desirable rather than deplorable (Bruegmann's argument is the suburban equivalent – stop trying to inhibit sprawl, work out how to make a virtue of it!). So too are the images by Madelon Vriesendorp (1945–) that are used to capture perceptions of the heyday of Manhattan's mental space, a period now clearly locked in the past much as is that of Paris,

Madelon Vriesendrop, *Flagrant Délit*, 1975. This painting was used on the first-edition cover of Rem Koolhaas's *Delirious New York* (published 1978) to capture the heyday of Manhattan's mental space.

which was Manhattan's alter ego during the late-19th- to early-20th-century modern period. Sadly OMA (the practice of Rem Koolhaas (1944–)) has since taken the statistical path, delivering reductively smart but essentially empty analyses to support its proto-modernist aesthetic.

The Situationists[33] were a group (existing in some form from 1957 to 1972) who were the precursors to all the current collectives that, inspired by Koolhaas's analytical work, are engaged in statistical epidemiology of our world – some clustered around Stefano Boeri (editor of *Domus*, 2004–7), some around Richard Burdett.[34] The Situationists concocted a series of procedures that were used to probe beneath the surface reality of the city and 'derive' (their term for the core procedure) from this encapsulations of the mental space that they regarded as being more substantial than the physical material of the city itself. Immensely subtle formulations resulted, many of them succumbing to the pathetic fallacy and being envisaged as physical networks above the existing city fabric. Related to these are Yona Friedman's 1957 megastructures for Paris,[35] a weave of space above the city allowing for new occupations and inhabitations freed from the constraints of the current fabric, resonating with Konrad Wachsmann's giant space frames (of whom more later). More closely allied to the Situationists' own work however is much that NATO (Narrative Architecture Today) did in the 1970s under the leadership of Nigel Coates, beginning with the placing of eternity-reflecting mirrors on sticks in mudflats, and concluding in a psycho-orgasmic polymorphic cloud that floated over the city and connected everything to everything.[36] These procedures can certainly be seen to 'derive' from what was being observed, but they have not gained traction as operative systems for architecture. Perhaps this is because they were rooted in a projective form of observation, objective in intent, but failing to account for what they as individual observers brought to the act of observing. As I have argued, such second-order awareness of one's own spatial history is crucial to understanding the ways in which we share mental space.

Konrad Wachsmann (1901–80),[37] subsequently in the 1950s designer for the American government of an aircraft hangar with unsupported projections of over 50 metres, was on the other hand so able to operate at a simple functional level that he was the architect for Einstein's disarmingly simple house at Caputh outside Berlin, where the theory of relativity was written.

So my precursors are all people who have tried to work with the epidemiology of the city in a spatially intelligent way. Their work sits within the mental spaces of particular cities, and achieves effective implementation through inventing a spatial politic specific to those cities and within their mental space – even though this last requires the discovery ways to awaken a conscious awareness in the citizens of their mental space, and demands the introduction of new possibilities for action through that awareness. Now in the next chapter we will consider individual works of architecture that force us to confront our own spatial intelligence by moving us so much that we recall the eidetic origination of our own mental space.

References

1 Arturo Soria y Puig (ed), *Cerdà: The Five Bases of the General Theory of Urbanisation*, Electa (Madrid), 1999, p 53.
2 Professor Jonathan Hill of the Bartlett School of Architecture, University College London, argues that this first takes place through the assertion of 'disegno' as an act of conception separate to and prior to construction. He has presented this argument in lectures that I have attended at his school, at the University of Westminster and at RMIT.
3 Robin Evans, *Translations from Drawing to Building and Other Essays*, Architectural Association (London), 1997, pp 77–82.
4 Existenzminimum or minimum-existence housing in terms of minimally acceptable floor space, density, fresh air, access to green space, access to transit, and other such resident issues.
5 In a catalogue for an exhibition at the Architectural Association, it was argued that the plan was then subjected to 'speculative destruction' – which is, though, the process that created what we see, and admire, in the city today. Architectural Association (London), 'Ildefonso Cerdá: Egalitarian Planner', exh cat, February 1978.
6 Jane Jacobs, *The Economy of Cities*, Vintage Books (New York), 1969, pp 86–94.
7 Sand Helsel with Kuang Chien Bee, *Taipei Operations*, Human Environment Group (Taipei), 2004: pp 56–65, swollen rice effect; pp 104–5, the add-on structures.
8 Anne Humphreys, *Travels into the Poor Man's Country: The Work of Henry Mayhew*, University of Georgia Press (Athens, Georgia), 1977.
9 Arturo Soria y Puig (ed), *Cerdà*, op cit. Cerdá graduates in 1840 as an engineer; devotes himself to the city from 1849 onwards (p 25); his plan is adopted by the city in 1859, and he rails that the life expectancy of workers is half that of the upper classes (p 15); his concept of mobility predates the motor car by 50 years (p 16); communications end centrality (p 16); he invents the term 'urbanisation' in 1860–1 (p 23); he integrates housing and traffic into a single theory in 1864–7 (p 33); he tackles the city and its outlying regions as a whole in 1866–76 (p 34); 'in twenty years of feverish activity while under aggressive harassment by powerful local interests, Cerdá turned Barcelona into a major modern city' (p 35); he nurtures the Barcelona extension project from 1855 onwards (p 36); he dies in poverty in 1876.
10 Christopher Hussey, *The Picturesque: Studies in a Point of View*, Frank Cass & Co (London), 1967, p 141: 'The remnants of an avenue, that is, could be formed into clumps.' (Hussey's book was first published in 1927.)
11 This term emerged from the studies of the extensive suburbs of Melbourne which I conducted with postgraduate students at RMIT in the 1980s under the heading '38 degrees South'.
12 His approach is illustrated in Colin Rowe and Fred Koetter, *Collage City*, MIT Press (Cambridge, Massachusetts and London), 1978, p 35.
13 Richard Hamilton, *Just what is it that makes today's home so different, so appealing?*, 1956, collage, 260 x 250

mm, millimetres, collection of Edwin Jans Jr, Thousand Oaks, California. Printed in the catalogue for the exhibition 'Richard Hamilton', Tate Gallery (London), March 1970, p 21.
14 Kevin Lynch, *The Image of the City*, MIT Press (Cambridge, Massachusetts and London), 1968.
15 Christopher Alexander, *Notes on the Synthesis of Form*, Oxford University Press (London), 1971.
16 Colin Rowe and Fred Koetter, *Collage City*, op cit.
17 George R Collins and Christiane C Collins, *Camillo Sitte: The Birth of Modern City Planning*, Rizzoli (New York), 1986. Sitte's essay 'City Planning According to Artistic Principles' was published in Austria in 1889.
18 Colin Rowe and Fred Koetter, *Collage City*, op cit, p 82: Wiesbaden c 1900.
19 Karl R Popper, *The Logic of Scientific Discovery*, Hutchinson (London), 1980.
20 Colin Rowe, *The Mathematics of the Ideal Villa and other essays*, MIT Press (Cambridge, Massachusetts and London), 1976.
21 George Baird, 'Urban Americana: a commentary on the work of Gandelsonas', *Assemblage*, No 3 (edited by K Michael Hays), MIT Press (Cambridge, Massachusetts), 1987, pp 60–2.
22 Robert Venturi, Denise Scott Brown and Steven Izenour, *Learning from Las Vegas*, MIT Press (Cambridge, Massachusetts and London), 1972.
23 Robert Venturi, *Complexity and Contradiction in Architecture*, MOMA (New York), 1968.
24 Venturi and Scott Brown devised a vista 150 paces long (100 of these in the pre-existing building). Shaped on the altarpiece at the end of the vista by Cima da Conegliano, *The Incredulity of Thomas* (1502–4), their section is a constructed perspective that neutralises the seeming distances. See the criticism of Richard Hamilton for the compromised detail this entailed: *Encounters: New Art From Old*, National Gallery (London), 2000, pp 140–51: 'It is a diminishing perspective, in which the prominent pillars are shorter, and placed closer together, to Hamilton, the idiosyncrasy of the vista needed to be corrected' (p 145).
25 Grahame Shane in conversation with the author, 27 September 2007.
26 Mario Gandelsonas, 'The order of the American city: analytic drawings of Boston', *Assemblage*, No 3 (edited by K Michael Hays), MIT Press (Cambridge, Massachusetts, 1987, pp 63–71.
27 Mario Gandelsonas, *X-Urbanism: Architecture and the American City*, Princeton Architectural Press (New York), 1999.
28 Diana Agrest, Mario Gandelsonas and Anthony Vidler, *Agrest and Gandelsonas Works*, Princeton Architectural Press (New York), 1995.
29 See my discussion of Randall Collins's work on this topic in *Mastering Architecture: Becoming A Creative Innovator in Practice*, Wiley-Academy (London), 2005, p 106.
30 Le Corbusier, *Towards a New Architecture*, Architectural Press (London), 1946 (first published in French in 1923).
31 Robert Bruegmann, *Sprawl: A Compact History*, University of Chicago Press (Chicago and London), 2005.
32 Rem Koolhaas, *Delirious New York: A Retroactive Manifesto for Manhattan*, Monacelli Press (New York), 1994: Madelon Vriesendorp, *Flagrant Délit*, 1975, p 160. (*Delirious New York* was first published in 1978.)
33 Simon Sadler, *The Situationist City*, MIT Press (Cambridge, Massachusetts and London), 1998.
34 Richard Burdett, Centennial Professor in Architecture and Urbanism at the London School of Economics, is chief adviser on architecture and urbanism for the London 2012 Olympics. He was Director of the 2006 Architecture Biennale in Venice on 'Cities: Architecture and Society'.
35 Sabine Lebesque and Helene Fentener van Vlissingen, *Yona Friedman: Structures Serving the Unpredictable*, NAI Publishers (Rotterdam), 1999: pp 29–33, La Ville Spatiale (1958–62); pp 33–5, Paris Spatiale (1959).
36 Nigel Coates, *Ecstacity*, Architectural Association (London), 1992.
37 Jürgen Joedicke, *A History of Modern Architecture*, Architectural Press (London), 1961, pp 151–2.

4
Intuitives: confronting spatial intelligence – tracing the use of spatial intelligence

We usually fall into much error by considering the intellectual powers as having dignity in themselves, and separate from the heart; whereas the truth is, that intellect becomes noble or ignoble according to the food we give it, and the kind of subjects with which it is conversant.

John Ruskin[1]

Peter Lyssiotis, *The spaces that we first use as surrogate houses as we form our spatial histories and our mental space*, "Draws, Chests and Wardrobes, Nests, Shells, Corners". photomontage for *Spatial Intelligence*, 1998 – completed as part of an Australia Council New Media Arts Fellowship at RMIT, Melbourne, Australia.

As we have seen, our cities are the product of the layering of particular cultural points in time and mental space. This is even more the case with the buildings and spaces of which cities and their regions are composed. Despite the manifest lack of awareness of this interdependence between architecture and the mental space that gives rise to it, the world is peppered with places and spaces that have the power to move us. Over the centuries, beginning 2,000 years ago with Vitruvius and his identification of three poles of architecture, translated into English in 1642[2] as 'firmness, commodity and delight', there have been attempts to define what makes such architecture. Most of these are insightful to a degree, but very few acknowledge at their core – or even peripherally – that architecture is the product of our spatial intelligence, of its workings in establishing the mental space of every individual, and of the spatial values shared by groups. They tend – as we shall see – to universalise their propositions either because they (like Cao Xueqin in the 18th century) have no conception that there are mental spaces other than their own, or because they subscribe (like Kenneth Frampton (1930–))[3] to a general theory of architecture independent of any local articulation beyond adaptations to meet the needs of local climatic conditions.

This is not surprising because the processes of spatial intelligence – although suspected – have not been validated with substantial evidence heretofore. One of those few who have argued intuitively for the inseparability of architecture and context is Dalibor Vesely, an architectural theorist who has spent his teaching life demonstrating that in the modern era the unity of time, place and culture that is essential to architectural reality has been fractured.[4] As a consequence in architecture today our spatial knowledge is either buried deep within our unconscious, or it is surfaced in a highly simplified form. For architecture this has become problematic. Because of this disjunction with our spatial intelligence, architecture has no ready connection to the daily expectations of citizens, but is seen rather as a brutal instrumental servant to corporate or governmental interests; or as the purveyance of esoteric spatial luxuries to domestic elites. In the anglophone world for example, for the last few decades, statistics reveal that architects design less than eight per cent of houses and housing.[5] The remainder is derived in a dimly resonant way from these designs. Conditions elsewhere in Europe are very different, as we shall see, but almost always in far less cosmopolitan circumstances with few challenges to the unity of space, place and architecture.

Architectural theories: architectonics, poetics, narrative and 'terrain vague'

Attempts to understand what architectural principles underpin the kinds of spaces that move us are reductively taxonomic in the encyclopaedic manner that has failed Christopher Alexander (see Chapter Three). In the 1970s there was a determined push to import systems engineering approaches being used in the 'space race' into architecture – a movement that was headlined as 'Design Methodology'. Bristol University opened an architecture programme which emphasised mathematics in its curriculum, the founding professor certain that his graduates would be designing space stations. This parameter-by-parameter approach has since been seen to be problematic even at NASA, where its shortcomings have been exposed by the tragic failure of a space shuttle mission. The approach (endorsed at a notorious Heads of School meeting in Oxford in the 1970s) fostered a formulaic, teaching-by-numbers approach that was radically challenged by Peter Cook and then by Alvin Boyarsky (1928–90) through their idea-based pedagogies at the Architectural Association in London. These latter were not (unless accidentally) conscious of differing mental space: they were – and possibly still are – in the vanguard of an internationalism in architectural discourse. If we dig into the charismatic debates about architecture – some enshrined in the ANY (Architecture/New York) conferences in the early 1990s – and consider why certain works of architecture move some of us some of the time, we are confronted by an evasion of the architectural experience as such.

When we allow ourselves to seek out and dwell on spaces that cause wonderment, we find that there is a continuum of spatial experience, between the intimate and the immense, with stops that can be celebrated all along the scale. Past research into these propose that powerful spaces act on us through three levels of expression: the architectonic, the poetic and the narrative.[6] Working between the wars on understanding London,[7] Steen Eiler Rasmussen lectured at the RIBA in 1958 on his distillation of the fundamental architectonic qualities[8] that he had identified through his decades of research and thinking. These include our appreciation of: whether a space has been carved, moulded or surfaced;[9] scenographic procession through colour planes; scale and proportion; rhythm, texture, light and shade, colour and sound. They include propositions about the ontology of architecture in caves, huts and tents, and derive from these antecedents arguments about what is proper and satisfying. And these arguments do resonate with what we now know about our deep histories of spatial intelligence; but only up to a point, because the theory presumes – despite exemplars from a wide range of countries – a universal set of qualities for architecture, and does not consciously account for differences in mental space between individuals and communities, although it often argues from very specific situations. Rasmussen does seek to ground his universals in our shared human capabilities, reminding us (for example) of our tendency – even if we are not boat-minded – to knock on the hulls of boats to hear whether they are sound, at the same time as he inadvertently points to their particularity by arguing (for instance) that the boys playing ball on the steps of S Maria Maggiore in Rome are learning about space in the abstract, when he should be arguing that they are learning about it in the concrete particularity of that space.

What Rasmussen does incomparably describe is the way in which we build our architectural intelligence kinaesthetically using all our senses – touch, sight, sound and, implicitly, taste and smell. He argues that we construct our understanding of rhythm, scale and proportion, texture and colour through our childhood play: getting dirty in the vegetable garden, playing with balls and rackets, and generally exposing ourselves to the world. He makes an early connection with film to prove his case, citing the scene in *The Third Man* (1949) in which there is a chase in the sewers of Vienna, footsteps echoing behind the escaping hero. In his claim for the engagement of all the senses in architecture he presages Juhani Pallasmaa's 1996 book *The Eyes of the Skin*,[10] which implores us to understand how damaging to architecture is the age of information's excessive emphasis on the visual form of communication. Not all the senses or intelligences are helpful in architecture, however. Oliver Sacks (1933–) gives some thought to this, arguing that, while we 'have to construct a visual world for ourselves, and a selective and personal character infuses our visual memory from the start – we are given pieces of music already constructed'.[11] In music, replication is vital; in architecture, it is deadly. Every musical performance is judged by its respect for or defiance of its origin; while in architecture replicas always ring hollow, because their substance is built up out of their context – place, time and culture. Rasmussen's world of architecture is a lost world of decorum – a lost mental space in the terms of my argument. Much of what inspired his thinking was bombed out of existence in the Second World War, and he would perhaps have been dismayed at the surrealistic disruption of his 'rules' by the architectures of what was called 'Deconstruction' by Mark Wigley, or – even more tellingly – 'Violated Perfection: Architecture and the Fragmentation of the Modern' by Aaron Betsky.[12]

The phenomenology of space – the matter of how we experience it – has preoccupied many thinkers, but most pertinent to my quest has been French philosopher of science Gaston Bachelard's investigation into the 'poetics' of space and reverie and the 'psychoanalysis' of fire.[13] This research concerns speculations about the first shelters that we used in our distant history, about the rooms into which we are born and about the taboos and shibboleths that permeate our ideas of the house, the relationship between our home and the universe, about the spaces that we first use as surrogate houses as we form our spatial histories and our mental space: drawers, chests and wardrobes, nests, shells and corners, as the most famous collecting of these to date has it. It is about the contemplative effects of the miniature, about the paradoxical way in which the scale of many of our most cherished monuments can switch in our minds from large to minute – the quality of 'intimate immensity'; it is about the complex relationships between inside and outside and the surface between, and about the phenomenology of roundness.[14] Again, these propositions resonate widely, but misleadingly. The foundation work has been embraced everywhere without understanding that this is the account of a phenomenology of one country, possibly of one region in that country. We have not taken to heart the author's injunction: 'Each one of us then ...' should make a record of our spatial histories.[15] The 'poetics' approach has the incidental merit, however, of acknowledging that the environment changes, and that it consists not only of place and space, but also of what is written about it – if especially by poets. It is implicitly an evolving system, and we can imagine our lonely observer, Henri Lefebvre, adding to this understanding, whereas the architectonic approach attracts radical conservatives like Roger Scruton[16] or Kenneth Frampton[17], who believe that a civil society depends on a 'civil' or classical order in architecture, with everything in its correct place, and – as Rasmussen argued – never allowing something solid and heavy to seem to rest upon something febrile and made of particles. Rasmussen illustrated this with a photograph of a granite column resting implausibly on thin brick pavers. Although Frampton is rightly concerned to argue for the collective in architecture, his dismissal of the 'merely individual' is at odds with what Henri Lefebvre observed: what may seem to conservative eyes to be spurious novelty, may well be an early response to the ever changing nature of a world that is – as climate change forcefully reminds us – inherently fungible. The very rocks upon which Frampton's admired Nikos Konstantinidis argued that architecture is bedded are a shifting plate, and will not endure.

The issue of how you learn from great works has concerned all cultures. Perhaps the most sophisticated account of the conservative position described above is found in a depiction of a poetry club set up by some precocious teenagers, in a novel based on the family life of the Commissioner for Textiles in Nanking in the 18th century[18] by Cao Xueqin (c 1715–63). The youngsters vie with each other to produce a poem about a chrysanthemum. In discussion they consider the form of the poem, and issues of originality, character and depth. They assess each other's efforts with reference to the canon of poems about chrysanthemums, dismissing any lines that do not add to the description of the flower a quality not previously captured. The novel is almost hermetically sealed within the mental space of a Chinese elite. We peer into this world, and are guided through it by an inmate. There is no hint of an awareness that mental spaces other than that of the Imperial Chinese court exist, although at the end the world of the peasants crashes violently into the idyll.

The narrative in architecture has a long history, beginning perhaps with *architecture parlante* ('speaking architecture') in the 15th century,[19] with Francesco Colonna's *Hypnerotomachia Poliphili*, a novel in which the main characters are buildings, and manifesting itself in many different ways in many different cultures. Outlawed during the Modern period in architecture, it returned – as we have seen in Chapter Three – with the pioneering work of Venturi, Scott Brown, who in their seminal book *Learning from Las Vegas*[20] studied the narratives of that city, and inspired by spontaneous signage of the city applied this in their designs as 'super graphics', thus creating a new 'speaking architecture' in the late 20th century. But, as we have seen, this civic narrative expressionism faltered because the theory lacked an accommodation with the spatial dialects of different cities, different psycho-islands within cities. Nevertheless, as we shall see in the next chapter, there are those who have applied the theory

The Hollywood sign, Los Angeles, California, USA, 1923. Super-graphics entered architecture via signs such as this.

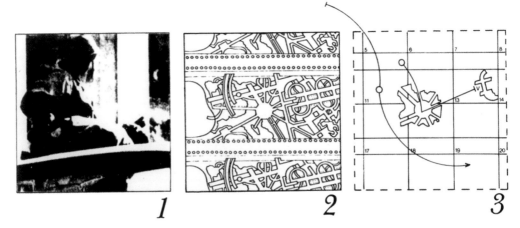

Bernard Tschumi, Manhattan Transcript 1: The Park, 1977 – the choreography of events elevated into a 'frozen music' architecture.

within consciously defined spatial communities. There have been attempts to win back for architecture the narrative role that it had when temples and cathedrals were, as Lethaby argued, the most advanced expressions of our conception of the universe. Some of these involved the appropriation of film director Sergei Eisenstein's (1898–1948) cinematic notation system, and projects such as Bernard Tschumi's 'Screenplays' of 1978 elevated the choreography of events (in one instance of a murder) into a 'frozen music' architecture that proved very soon to be a dead-end.[21] Today 'hypersurface' enthusiasts have embraced new opportunities to imbue the surfaces of buildings with digitised information, a self-defeating approach as every commercial building adopts the same strategy and Times Square is spread thinly throughout cities.

There is a counter culture to this focus on fine architecture from the pre-modern past, and it has grown out of an increasing consciousness of the accidental circumstances which give rise to undesigned spaces that are aggressively adopted by adjacent communities, who spurn so often what designers have presented them with, appropriating rather abandoned industrial sites in particular in preference to spaces devised according to rules of design that owe nothing to understanding or working with the mental space of these adopters. Such spaces have been described by thinkers as different and as geographically separated as Barcelonan Ignasi de Solà-Morales (1942–2001) (who uses the term 'terrain vague')[22], Melburnian and (then) Mancunian Nikos Papastergiadis (1963–) ('para-functional space')[23] and New Yorker Andrea Kahn ('mobile ground')[24]. The soon-to-be-developed ruins of Potsdamer Platz in Berlin, appropriated as summer camps, were an origin for the theorising of 'terrain vague'. These theorists have grappled with

'Terrain vague': in Penang, Malaysia an empty site has been coopted by the dramatic use of colour.

understanding the phenomenon, and what it means for designers. What they agree is that these undesigned spaces meet a deep need that current approaches to design do not. This critical movement is in a sense descended from the influential book *Architecture without Architects*,[25] which is packed with examples of works that have a very close relationship to the material culture of places isolated from the commerce of globalisation and thus 'all of a piece' with the people who made them and whom they serve. There are sleights of hand in that account – the observatories of Jantar Mantar at Jaipur in Rajasthan are clearly the product of sophisticated specialist design, and many of these works are, by a definition of architecture that includes sophisticated specialist expertise. But the appeal of this book points to an awareness of what has been lost, just as the perplexity of designers at the manifest success of specific examples of 'terrain vague' points to their need to find their way back to understanding and working with mental space. Land artist Robert Smithson (1938–73) called these places 'ruins in reverse';[26] and that master of landscape space, John Brinckerhoff Jackson (1909–96),[27] gives many accounts of how what seems permanent to us today is an inversion of what was permanent to previous generations: the verdant Arcadian valleys of New England were dense forest in the early days of settlement, and the wooded hills that we see today were scalped and grassed then – each an island fort against incursions by the indigenous population.

Jantar Mantar Observatory, Jaipur, Rajasthan, India, 1728. Each construction for viewing a particular zenith or azimuth of the solar system is clearly the product of sophisticated specialist design.

Leon van Schaik   091   Chapter 4 Intuitives: confronting spatial intelligence – tracing the use of spatial intelligence

Reed & Stem and Warren & Wetmore, Grand Central Station, New York, USA 1913. Grand Central haunts the mental space of New Yorkers.

This grappling with the unintended appeal of the poetic of the ruins of our cities brought into being by war, industrial obsolescence and failed development[28] nudges in the direction of research carried out by Marc Augé (1935–)[29] into the departure lounges of our world: airports, hospitals and other – he argues – infrastructural spaces that are so determined by instrumental concerns that every last vestige of architectonic, poetic or narrative content has been wrung out of them. Personal experience can invest even the most drably undesigned of them with emotion, and when the new Euston station was opened in London in the 1960s, painter David Hockney (1937–) cited it in a weekend supplement as his favourite space, describing how, after being cooped up in a train for hours, its broad expanse of granite floor invited him to pirouette through the vast top-lit space (difficult to envisage this today when the concourse is cluttered with kiosks, every column obscured by a pavilion, its vaulted ceiling is a dirty downward-pressing cream, and its walls are covered in billboards). People love[30] Grand Central Station in New York (1817–1913), which unusually in this context is an architectural space, dressed in the orders of classical architecture, unlike most of the great train sheds of Britain – engineering structures created without architectural intent. Grand Central haunts the mental space of New Yorkers, appearing as an emotive force in the novels of Edith Wharton (1862–1937) and memorably in the book *By Grand Central Station I Sat Down and Wept* by Elizabeth Smart (1945). The Champagne Bar that features as 'the longest in Europe' in the restored, altered and extended St Pancras Station in London expressly aims to capture the minds and emotions of travellers to the Continent and to the suburbs. In the redesign the duality of the amazing engineering of the

Ernst Sagebiel, Tempelhof Airport, Berlin, Germany, 1936–41. This airport has a huge cantilevered roof under which aircraft nestled, looking for this reason like toys.

Leon van Schaik   093   Chapter 4 Intuitives: confronting spatial intelligence – tracing the use of spatial intelligence

Eero Saarinen, TWA Terminal, JFK Airport, New York, USA, 1956–62 – a carefully crafted work of architecture affording a sense of the romance of travel, in contrast to the inflated 'non-place' idiom of today's massive airports.

single-span arched shed and the fantastical Scottish Baronial romance of the Hotel abutting it (Scotland being a destination reached from this terminus) are dynamically linked by new spatial cuts and insertions.[31] I list Tempelhof Airport in Berlin for its huge cantilevered roof under which aircraft nestled, looking for this reason like toys. The departure ritual of walking through glass doors onto the tarmac and up into the sheltering aeroplane before it climbed into the skies that could be glimpsed beyond is a pleasure those who have experienced it remember always. Early visitors to Eero Saarinen's (1910–61) TWA Terminal in New York (1956–62) or to Paul Andreu's (1938–) Terminal 1 of Paris's Charles de Gaulle Airport (completed 1974) also talk of the romance of travel that these carefully crafted works of architecture afforded before they became dwarfed by other terminals in the inflated 'non-place' idiom that Marc Augé has identified as the ubiquitous spatial form of these facilities today.

Architectural principles applied: holidays, spiritual and secular exemplars

What makes these architectonic, poetic and spatial propositions superficially persuasive is that they can be applied to both categories of space under consideration here: unselfconsciously integrated architecture from the pre-modern past, and the unselfconsciously adopted spaces of the 'terrain vague' of the present. In the next chapter we will see how these analyses relate to the work of contemporary architects like Peter Zumthor who work self-consciously integrated into the spatiality of their own fairly closely defined communities. We will then see how a return to this integration is emerging through the networked communities of our information age. Here, in theory, I could now establish a matrix of these architectonic, poetic and narrative qualities, and subject a comprehensive range of architectural types to an evaluation against that matrix. There are pattern books that have attempted to do this taxonomic act through the ages. Colen Campbell's three-volume *Vitruvius Britannicus*[32] (1715–25) was a hugely influential vehicle for the exportation of the Palladian style. John Claudius Loudon published exemplary cottages for use in picturesque landscapes in *An Encyclopaedia of Cottage, Farm, and Villa Architecture and Furniture* (1833). More recently, generations of students have imbibed a formulaic modernism through the manuals of Francis DK Ching. That insightful critic, Geoffrey Baker, has published books of analytical drawings of Le Corbusier[33] and others – critiques of considerable interest to some of the architects he unpicked in his meticulous abstractions

Leon van Schaik, analytical drawing, 1985. This exploded diagram shows the principles by which Sir John Soane inserted 'ideal rooms' into existing buildings.

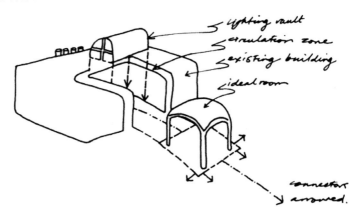

5. *Exploded diagram illustrating the principles of insertion: Single lighting vault and 'ideal' room*

This exploded diagram shows the relationship of the lighting vault to the circulation zone in the tartan grid and the location of the 'ideal' room on its axial connection to the house. Note that the integrity of the 'ideal' room combined with its location in a tartan grid leads to access-ways at the corners of spaces.

(there is a testimony from James Stirling)³⁴, although these analyses do not seem to help architects to improve their own work.

One of the disappointments of life today, enforced by the weakness of our critical and theoretical framework for accounting for the impact of space on us, is how cut off we are from architecture – opening ourselves to it in the main only when on holiday, and failing to demand its presence in our everyday lives. As we have seen in the previous chapter, much of this is to do with that disconnect between our mental space and the way in which architects have come to design, treating cities as if they were interchangeable.

The cathedral of Trani, Italy, consecrated 1143. The bell-tower arch affords back to the town views that make the painter Giorgio de Chirico's distorted perspectives seem mere reportage.

Missing from the theories above is a means of being conscious of the differing spatiality of individuals and communities, real and virtual. But there is much to be learned from examining the spaces, designed and made by people fully integrated into the communities for which they were created in pre-modern times or, in postmodern times, adopted by communities in a revulsion at being designed for by technocrats from anywhere. What we await, and what the next chapters explore, is a profession that is based on the understanding that our spatial intelligence creates a spatial memory in each of us: one that never stops evolving, for sure, but one that – if we are not conscious of its early origins – lies in wait for us in surprising corners, as Proust so memorably revealed with his madeleine dipped in tea.[35] As we have seen, we are the inheritors of a deep spatial capability, evolving over millennia, and changing even in our own time, as Henri Lefebvre has demonstrated through his thinking about what seeing the world through screens is doing to our perception of space. Like the language capability, we share our spatial intelligence as a capability with all other humans, but we 'speak' a spatiality that is specific to our history in space, and we share our spatiality with everyone in the abstract, but read it best in our own regions.

When on holiday we encounter or seek out spaces that we find arresting, places that move us, we return from these experiences somewhat gasping for air. What (for example) could be more stupendous than the Romanesque

Giorgio de Chirico, *Piazza d'Italia*, c 1917, showing de Chirico's typical use of exaggerated perspective.

cathedral at Trani in southern Italy, sitting in front of its city on a little promontory in the Adriatic, silhouetted against a mountain range across the bay to its north, its bell-tower arch affording back to the town views that make the painter Giorgio de Chirico's (1888–1978) distorted perspectives seem mere reportage? But what do we do with this experience? Where do we park it in our critical framework when we rely on architectonic, poetic or narrative accounts of wonder in architecture?

We tend to reduce them to symbols, freestanding mental images, like a postcard of the Taj Mahal in the moonlight, or the Eiffel Tower in spring, or the Sydney Opera House on its promontory. These iconic buildings have a powerful graphic quality; they have in our mind's eye the qualities of a good poster. Our attempts to understand their power have thus far tended to assume that what we have seen is – if recorded and analysed – transportable into our own design practice and into other mental spaces. Literal translation happens: Las Vegas[36] or Disney World[37] replicate iconic exemplars from around the world, making veritable zoos of architecture. But, as with zoos, there is something as hollow about seeing Venice indoors in the middle of a desert, as there is in seeing a polar bear sweltering amidst concrete representations of an iceberg. That hollowness spreads through our cities when those cities fail to cultivate their own architectural culture, emanating from their own clusters of mental space, and compete with each other through the importation of iconic works by a handful of internationally recognised stars.

And yet the spaces that move us, do so surely by resonating with our unconscious spatial histories, built up from those first years of playing house under tables, in cubbies, in the shelter of hedges, in treehouses and in dolls' houses or in model buildings made for us or by us, and it is that resonance that we take away when we leave. We are innately wired to respond to domestic spaces, given the ways in which our spatial consciousness has been built up through inhabiting a series

A polar bear at San Diego Zoo, California, USA, sweltering amidst concrete representations of an iceberg.

Treehouse designed by Paul Neuhaus.

of rooms. As we grow up, we begin to experience other spaces: solemn, celebratory and functional – school halls, theatres and airports or stations. We are also possibly exposed to spaces that are designed to lift our spirits to the heavens. Spaces that resonate with our spatial unconscious can be large, as are cathedrals, or they can be small, as are chapels. The Sainte Chapelle in Paris (1239–41)[38] is a space designed to express the ethereality of matter and the eternity of heavenly light. The architecture of continuously flowing ribs presenting their narrowest profile to us makes a space that seems drawn rather than built, and in our wonder we are rendered alone even in the midst of the tourist crush that bedevils experience of it today. The soaring, delicate stone ribs and vaults defy gravity; the chapel seems to be all glass, and glows with light even on the darkest winter day. I know this – I spent afternoons there, first as an impressionable teenager, later as an adult pondering life choices. King's College Chapel in Cambridge (1441; fan vaults commenced 1508) with its mathematical vaulting – so pure and rational, and yet so spiritual – is a space that is heard as much as seen, a musical instrument

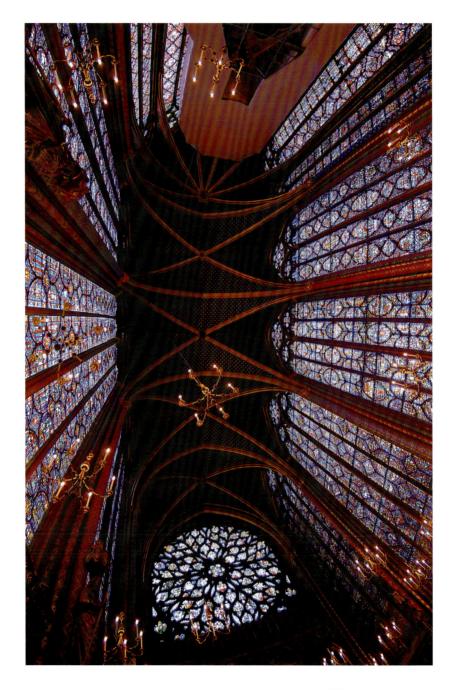

King's College Chapel, Cambridge, UK, 1441 – a space that is heard as much as seen.

Sainte Chapelle, Paris, France, 1239–41 – a space that expresses the ethereality of matter and the eternity of heavenly light.

played by the choir that has evolved over the centuries in response to its very particular acoustic properties, and the long reverberation time that only the voices of boys can break through into clarity. Spaces that burr on one's memory can be sacred or secular; and spiritual spaces can be occidental like these above, or oriental like the temples of the Forbidden City in Beijing,

A temple of the Forbidden City, Beijing, China, 1406–20. The temple sits athwart the processional axis, in contrast to the Western tradition of entry on the long axis.

similar in their rectangular form, but sitting – due to a radically different mental space – athwart the processional axis along which the Western examples are aligned.

The design of spiritual spaces is not accidental: substantive architectonic strategies underpin these spaces that have been created with a conscious intent of moving us. Guy Underwood believes that there is a continuity in sacred sites in Europe, transcending the presence on any site of a temple for any particular religion.[39] He argues that these sites are 'blind springs' – places where magnetic forces act to lighten the impact of gravity. Water diviners holding hazel switches find that these flip upright over such blind springs. Walking down the nave of cathedrals these diviners find themselves under compressive forces until they reach the crossing – usually located on ancient pagan sacred sites – when the forces reverse. Underwood believes that the designers of these sacred buildings understood these forces, and used them to create spatial progressions that took people towards a moment of magnetic 'lift', a progression mirrored by the movement from dark to light in ritual passage through these buildings, a model most expressly evident in the hipped churches of France's Massif Central, like Romanesque Orcival (12th century) in the Auvergne, where the transept is raised above the nave

The church of Orcival, France, 12th century. The raised transept allows light to stream in over the crossing from concealed clerestory windows.

to allow light to stream in over the crossing from elevated and concealed clerestory windows.[40]

Their secular counterparts are often also basilican in form, drawing on an ancient Roman tradition for working buildings – as is (for example) Trinity

Gordon Bunshaft, Beinecke Rare Book and Manuscript Library, Yale University, Connecticut, USA, 1960–3: interior and exterior. The granite-faced concrete frame filled in with grey marble slabs makes it appear heavy and solid in daylight

College Library in Dublin (1712–1723), which on the other hand, seen on a dark winter day, when the panelled vaults and book stacks melt into blackness and the white busts of the scholars at the end of each stack punctuate the miasmic darkness in a long avenue of enlightenment, has a poetic atmosphere equally impressive as its lateral flow. Also basilican, but more temple-like in its conception, is former SOM (Skidmore, Owings & Merrill) partner Gordon Bunshaft's (1909–90) Beinecke Rare Book and Manuscript Library at Yale University (1960–3). This building is a rectangular, granite-faced concrete frame five bays high, 15 long and 10 deep sat upon squat columns; the frame is filled in with grey marble slabs so that in the daylight it appears heavy and solid. Some office blocks of the period, like Richard Seifert's (1910–2001) Centre Point at the corner of Oxford Street and Tottenham Court Road in London (1963), used this exoskeletal frame, and so you expect layers of floors inside. However when you enter you discover that you are in a single high volume, the full extent of the rectangular frame, the space seemingly approximating to a golden rectangle, and that the marble, one-and-a-quarter inches thick, admits a soft golden light into that cube. Having entered, you also discover that the frame contains a glass rectangle, inside which rise the book stacks. The spines of the books are predominantly red and they give to the centre a warm glow, a poetics of colour planes – both Rasmussen and Bachelard at work, perhaps. The impact of the building is powerful in an abstract formal sense, but it has a look – sitting on those squat columns that so resemble the mushroom-capped, rat-proof stumps that elevate granaries from the ground – that also resonates with a medieval granary store from any part of the Old World, European or Asian, and it connects, possibly deliberately, to long cultural memories of protective storage. It works on us both as an abstract form with surprising transitions from external appearance to internal experience, and it has narrative associations with ancient traditions of conserving precious resources. Whether current generations recognise this narrative allusion is, however, doubtful: only a small elite will have travelled and seen these granaries, and be in a position to avail themselves of the association.

In modern times the use of progressions from darkness to light was popularly understood to be architect Sir John Soane's (1753–1837) leitmotif, and he certainly used light in the delineation of his 'ideal rooms';[41] so much so that his contemporaries regarded this as his chief skill. The use of divining has not been replicated in the present; although, as a student in the 1960s when 'vibes' were understood to be observable phenomena, I heard of a Polish architect who camped out on sites and laced them with strings, the vibrations of which he recorded as he profiled the 'soul' of the site. In the 1960s, Carlos Castaneda (1925–98), who may or may not have been an inspired hoaxer, described how Yaqui shamans could sense which hollows in a landscape were benign, and which malevolent.[42] So it is possible that these spaces that move us do so not only by association, nor by triggering sentimental 'stock responses'[43] in us, but by the actual effect of surface tectonics, used by designers who are conscious of them to heighten or graduate our spatial experience; achieving designs that engage our emotional attention such that we become conscious again of the eidetic origins of our spatial intelligence and thus actively engage with and extend our mental space. Outside the sacred, however, little is said about the ways in which we can design spaces that 'magic' us. But some architects do just this by combining associations with well-known building types and an abstract replication, in the forms and spaces of their work, of the compression and release that characterises sacred architecture through the ages.

Architecture and its origins: ontologies of cave, hut, tent and tattoo

If we engage with architectural wonder using our current critical apparatus, we need 'to begin at the very beginning', or at least to acknowledge that much thinking about architecture attempts to construct its logic on a beginning. In this we may well adopt the approach posited by the philosopher Hans-Georg Gadamer (1900–2002) in which, instead of rejecting seemingly superseded understandings, we stitch them together, accepting that our knowledge grows in layers, with each era of description resting upon its forbears, superficially supplanting them, but containing them.[44] Indeed, in his account of how we deal with the wonder of rare experiences, critic Philip Fisher argues that every attempt at a description aids our appreciation of the wonder, and that our wonder is sharpened as the descriptions of their object sharpen through time.[45] This ontological approach is usually the beginning of an argument about what is right and proper in architecture – as in the cases of theoretical historians Joseph Rykwert (1926–) and Kenneth Frampton(1930-), both reasoning that their mode of the classical is better and more authentic than the Gothic; or vice versa, as Ruskin, who regarded the Renaissance as a disease, would have had it. For me these are dry intellectual positions, readily interchangeable, for the reason that Ruskin gives in the quote at the beginning of this chapter. What is our proper object in this terrain? It is indeed to join all of these theoretical accounts at their margins,

A Maori tribesman with tattoo.

and build anew on the basis of the knowledge available to us today. There is something in the ontological scholarship that we do have to consider, because we have a very deep history in space, and in that history there were aeons of finding caves and working out how to use them, aeons of making temporary shelters and huts, and working out how to create secure thresholds between the wilderness and where we would sleep – that so vital time for the workings of our intelligence, as we have seen. And there were aeons of weaving fabrics and cording ropes and inventing the intricate structures of tents that could withstand sandstorms in deserts, and so on; and we cannot assume that these experiences have not become part of our inherited spatial capability.

There is a strand of ontological thinking that claims precedence over all others: it sees architecture beginning with tattooing and leading through self-decorating to an architecture in which inscribed pattern is the prime mover. This school of thought has persistent appeal for Anglo-New Zealanders, settlers as they are in a land where the tattoo has a primary cultural role for the indigenous. A noticeable number of architectural scholars from Auckland are concerned with ornament in architecture. But it has Western origins too. The late-11th- and early-12th-century cathedral of Durham, sitting on its inland peninsula far to the northwest in England, was – perhaps like all cathedrals – built to awe us into awareness of the fleeting nature of our individual lives and the enduring of the spiritual.[46] At Durham the massive, crudely scored columns speak of ancient rituals of tattooing, and reverberate possibly with our deep histories of skin decorating, awakening emotions that we find it difficult to rationalise. These can be troubling, if we are not aware of their origin. Durham haunts me because a lithograph of its interior hung in my bedroom at my grandparents' house. At both ends of the scale, how we react depends on our individual histories in space, and the way those always growing histories nest with the spatiality of our group, network or community.

The cathedral of Durham, UK, late 11th and early 12th century: interior. The massive columns suggest ancient rituals of tattooing, and perhaps reverberate with our deep histories of skin decorating, awakening emotions that are difficult to rationalise.

When we engage with the notion that architecture originates in caves, huts and tents, we need – again – to be wary of making generic claims. There are, for instance, caves of many kinds, and the deep cavernous spaces of Lascaux in France evoke cathedral-scale architectures, and may indeed underpin the European search for spiritually engaging space. Other caves – those in the cliff faces of the Great Rift Valley of Africa, for example – could be argued to drive to more domestic outcomes. And in both cases we need to account for – as ontological theorists do not – the specific playing out of these deep histories in the specific architectural realities of given communities. My experience of caves, for instance, is limited to those fairly open overhangs in the sandstone cliffs of the Drakensberg in South Africa, where I spent my childhood. The Game Pass Cave[47] is on a spur that juts out at right angles to the main range of the mountain, and it overlooks the Game Pass Valley, so named because it was a migratory passageway for that most stately of antelopes, the eland, from the plains to the tops. The cave is reached up the steep catenary curve of the grassy flank of the valley, or it can be descended to from the tops through a defile worn into the cliff by a stream (that also provides water). Here in the dry created by a huge cantilevered overhang, flints were chipped, fires were made, pigments were crushed and sinuous flowing images of eland were

Game Pass Valley, South Africa – a migratory passageway for the eland.

Game Pass Cave, South Africa: entrance.

Game Pass Cave, South Africa. In the cave, flowing images of eland were painted.

painted. Sun came obliquely into the cave in the morning, and left it obliquely in the evening, warming the rocks at its base. It is hard not to believe that our common enjoyment of a protected overview, our backs secure (and warm), did not stem from centuries of seeking out such inhabitable caves. When Beatriz Colomina describes the way in which the front door, the entry hall and the more public reception rooms of a house by Loos are overlooked from a boudoir raised above those spaces,[48] I cannot help but recall a Drakensberg cave. There is to me a sense of deep comfort and security that I never have in a glass pavilion, sitting on the sofa with my back to a wall of glass. In those circumstances I rise often to check what is behind my shoulder, become restless, anxious.

The 'hut as origin' argument has been used to validate the classical tradition in architecture. From the assemblage of poles around a tree trunk to the elaboration into a wooden temple form in which all of the stone elements of the Parthenon – the apogee of the type – are prefigured, be they columns, column bases, capitols, metopes and so on, in the necessary elements of a timber construction system which has become so *de rigueur* that it is transferred *in toto* into stone construction, where the elements are in fact redundant. Whether this is a plausible argument or not, it encapsulates

Ludwig Mies van der Rohe, Barcelona Pavilion, Barcelona, Spain, 1929 (reconstructed 1986). This iconic structure is imbued with an ideology of purist neoclassical tectonics.

the ongoing debate about whether science is an enquiry that brings forth techniques to further its hunches, or whether new technologies open the way for new hunches. Perhaps the most famous 'huts' of modern times are Mies van der Rohe's (1886–1969) Barcelona Pavilion (1929) and his Farnsworth House (1950), and both are imbued (one dynamically, one statically) with an ideology of purist neoclassical tectonics that seems inherent to the lineage. The foremost Australian hut – also widely influential in the world at large – is Glenn Murcutt's (1936–) Fredericks Farmhouse in Jamberoo, New South Wales (1981–2) which quite extraordinarily marries the Miesian tradition, in which Murcutt started his practice with the glazed pavilion of the Laurie Short House in Sydney (1972–3), to the peeled bark hut of Aboriginal tradition,[49] known as a 'humpy' because of its shape – a catenary hump resulting from hanging the flattened bark sheets over a pole. This connects the most extreme modernist form back to a tradition that is between 60,000 and 40,000 years old. I admire this feat intellectually, but I am uncomfortable in Murcutt's interiors in part because of that over-the-shoulder sense that plagues me. Am I alone in this? I think not, but perhaps a new spatial sensibility is emerging in the world that will supplant my unease?[50]

Glenn Murcutt, house for an Aboriginal client, Yirrkala, Australia, 1994 – connecting the most extreme modernist form back to an ancient tradition.

Ontologies derived from our oldest tradition, the African experience, emphasise the threshold in architecture, the framing of experience in serially arranged spaces of increasing security and privacy. The African huts that I visited as a child and that I later studied for ten years often interposed as many as a dozen thresholds between the prairie on which they were situated and the inner space where everyone slept. It was as if many layers of protection had to be established between the wide world and the domestic, with outer walls – sometimes made of wattle and daub – and with a seat at their base from which that world could be surveyed across a number of lower walls and platforms, a narrow opening into a courtyard open to the air where domestic chores could be carried out, and within which there were often separate storage huts, a larger central thatched rondavel with projecting eaves affording some shelter when it rained, often an outer ring of space for looser storage, and then a central space where a fire was lit at night, around which the family slept.

Thresholds: our oldest tradition, the African experience, emphasises the threshold in architecture.

It has seemed to me that in the temperate forest climes of Europe, a similar process was at work, not so much in the building of thresholds, but in the carving of rooms – and vistas – out of the forest. These created open, surveyable spaces around the hut, and pushed out a threshold made all the more insistent by being orthogonal and thus very man-made. That such strategies are still with us is evident in modern times in Gerrit Rietveld's (1888–1964) Schröder House (1924), in which he replicates, condensed into the entry hall, stairs and moveable walls of the

little suburban house, the dozen or so thresholds that his widowed client had been accustomed to between the estate gateway, the driveway, the portico, the entrance hall and stairs of the country mansion she had lived in when her husband was alive.[51] In the context of the carving of controlled space out of forest thickets, a glass house in a walled garden – unlike its counterpart riding ridges in open country – is a reassuring precept, moving in its contained fragility. I think we respond to the contrast for reasons deeply embedded in our unconscious. Perhaps beyond the brick walls, the Green Giant still prowls. For me this contrast creates a reverie about the differing time cycles of the wall of an estate, and the technical conveniences with which the inside is periodically graced. And without the glass house the walled garden can be a little grim. Maybe, given what we are uncovering about the way in which we build our mental space, this is because as a schoolboy in England I worked for pocket money in the conservatory in a walled garden tucked into the estate wall at Cliveden – of which stately house more later. Perhaps too that is why the little glass house by Peter (1923–2003) and Alison Smithson (1928–93) designed around a wall of such a garden haunts my imagination as an ideal retreat.[52] You rise up into its glazed upper storey with views over the rolling hills beyond and perch atop the wall on the edge of a threshold space carved

Peter and Alison Smithson, Upper Lawn Pavilion, Wiltshire, UK, 1959. This country retreat presents as a glass box, but is grounded by its relationship to the pre-existing masonry of a walled garden (*Architectural Design*, Vol 77, No 2: *Landscapes*, May 2007, pp 4–5).

out of the woods, or remove yourself from the view, sink down to the ground and sit with your back to the wall.

Much is made of the tent as an origin in architecture, often because the weaving tends to be done by women, and this ontology goes some way to redress the silence of the histories where women are concerned. There is a specific romance of the tent, leading to those lightweight structures by Frei Otto (1925–) that are often cited as descendants of the tent. I am drawn to the 'Nuage' ('Cloud') structure that floats between the towers of Johann Otto von Spreckelsen's (1929–87) Grande Arche (1982–90) at La Défense in Paris, I suspect because of the strong contrast between its cloud form and the sturdy pillars between which it rides. The effect for me is poetic rather than tectonic, with a reverie induced by the contrasts and by the imagery. Architects who espouse this ontology can be people who are utterly fascinated by Bedouin tents, who know the names of every part, their reputed origins, their roles in the organism that is the tent at work resisting gravity and wind, and who are absorbed by the specific ways in which each kind of tent folds away when packed up and placed on a camel. For me the weave that resonates is more a planning concept – that special grid that is often referred to as a 'tartan grid' that surrounds squares of open space with double or treble tram lines which can be circulation or structure, or ancillary storage space. It fascinates me that Gottfried Semper (1803–79), that ardent 19th-century advocate of an architectural ontology of weaving, was a master of tartan grid planning – as in his ETH building in Zurich (1858–63). So clear is its organisation that when

Johann Otto von Spreckelsen's, Grande Arche de La Défense, Paris, France, 1982-1990. The 'Nuage' floating between the towers expresses the ontology of the tent.

Traditional Bedouin tent, Negev Desert, Israel.

Gottfried Semper, ETH building, Zurich, Switzerland, 1858–63 – an example of 'tartan grid' planning.

I walk through the building I feel as if my mind has been combed. And that is a sensation that is spatial and poetic rather than architectonic.

It is a short step from the Ur-world of caves, huts and tents to their most direct modern successors. These are a class of building that impact on us through the poetic of their 'intimate immensity'. The temples I am thinking of here aspire to express the completeness of the world, and they assert an in-the-round symmetry of form – which is purely expressed in the little Temple of Vesta in Tivoli (c 80 BC) with its a circle of columns surrounding the drum

Temple of Vesta, Rome, Italy, late 2nd century BC – a form you can imagine holding in your hand like a saltcellar.

Bramante's Tempietto (S Pietro in Montorio), Rome, Italy, 1502: also a form you can imagine holding in your hand like a saltcellar.

The Pantheon, Rome, Italy, AD 120–4 – a large monolithic dome with an open oculus admitting a taste of the vastness of the universe.

of a cylindrical *cella* 7 metres in diameter[53] and just as compelling in the much larger Pantheon in Rome (AD 120–4), a circular rotunda surmounted by a dome and with an internal height and diameter of 43 metres each.[54] Both play on the phenomenology of roundness that for Bachelard has much to do with a small bird pressing the fibres of its nest into the form of a cupped hand, a gesture that signals a taking of care. These round temples have a singularity of form that is scaleless. Daydreaming, you can experience them as a large monolithic dome like the Pantheon with an open oculus admitting a taste of the vastness of the universe with a traversing ray of sunlight or a shower of rain, or you can imagine holding them in your hand like a saltcellar. Bramante's tiny Tempietto (S Pietro in Montorio) in Rome (1502) works in the same way – you can imagine it in silver on a cardinal's dining table, or inflated into a Pantheon.

The games children play and architecture

Some of us know about the Pantheon and the Tempietto, because, like the children Rasmussen[55] depicted in a photo (dated 1952) playing on the steps of S Maria Maggiore in Rome, they were part of our mental space. Others, like antipodean architects in my father's generation, have learned it the hard way, tracing the drawings out of Sir Banister Fletcher's key work *A History of Architecture on the Comparative Method* (first published in a single volume in 1897). But we have all had the experience of the souvenir, the miniature Eiffel Tower, the Golden Gate in a snow-dome, the Big Ben pencil. However haltingly, these invite reverie, a going into one's own history in space … Something in this phenomenon appeals to many of us, it seems to resonate with the way in which our toys are so often miniatures of items in use in the adult world. If this is the case, one way of ensuring that children build mental space that links to the pleasures of great architecture is to ensure that the toys they play with are miniatures of architecture. (Sir John Soane

Souvenirs like the miniature Eiffel Tower or the Golden Gate Bridge in a snow-dome, or the Big Ben pencil – however haltingly – invite reverie.

thought so – he constructed a play-space at Pitzhanger Manor in Ealing (1802) that was designed to teach his children the history of architecture, but he forced them to play, and they hated it! Soane's architecture pursued the toy-like in its facade articulations which give the impression that his buildings were made by placing the elements, each whole in itself, one upon the other in such a way that the building could be demounted.)[56] In the past, sets of wooden building blocks used to introduce children to architectures of arches, pediments and walls with textures of warm wood and primary colours; many architects today talk fondly of the ways in which the plastic, clip-together forms of the construction toy Lego first introduced them to the joys of designing. Jan Kaplicky (1937–) of Future Systems has kept the toys that lured him into architecture, and his Meccano set may be responsible in part for his systems approach to design.[57] The delight in the toy, and the daydreaming reverie that this delight induces, are a direct route into our mental space, and one that – very rare, this – we all share. In the 1960s Iona and Peter Opie published their research into the games that children play, and revealed some astonishing continuities that certainly support the notion that we are born with inherited capabilities and tendencies.[58] They describe how street games played in England can be traced back to accounts of similar games in ancient Greece. They also show how the rhymes sung by children are assumed by each generation of children to have been invented by them, when in fact these too have ancient lineages. Discernible in their wonderful accounts are differences that are the result of changes to the morphology of the street, but these distinctions – of import to my argument – are sidelined by the extraordinary commonalities that they had uncovered. Nevertheless, perhaps one part of a conscious 'mental space' programme would be that we architects design toys that induct our future communities into the shareable delights of our architectures?

Juhani Pallasmaa's (1936–) fear that such play has been banished from architecture by the pushing of architectural thinking into visual abstraction through the agency of digital modelling on the screens of computer terminals becomes very understandable when you consider what is lost from 'play' if it is confined to the world of the 'game engines' that power computer games. The most experimental architects in my city work in a manner that adds the digital model to the range of modes of creative play that their design engages. I recall visiting ARM (Ashton Raggatt McDougall) when they were designing the Great Hall of the National Museum of Australia in Canberra (2001).[59] The spatial concept evolved from a Boolean topological figure that traced the path of a knot through space. The computer screens on their

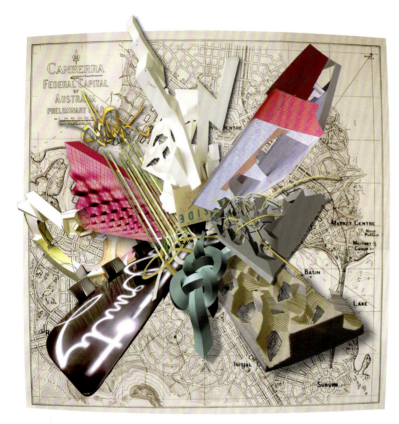

ARM (Ashton Raggatt McDougall), Great Hall, National Museum of Australia, Canberra, Australia, 2001. ARM used concepts derived from the axial plan of the city, the cursive script of a famous Sydney street artist who inscribed 'Eternity' in chalk on pavements every day for decades, Boolean knot geometries, and paper, card and computer-drafted models and reconciled these over and again within the digital environment of the computer as the design advanced.

tables were surrounded by a litter of working models in card, clay, rope and plastic; the walls are covered in print-outs from the computer, altered by hand using crayon, felt-tip pens, and collages of images from other mediums. To play in one domain only is to become rapidly bored. Good architects play in every arena available to them.

Pavilions as an ontology, on the other hand, while small, resist miniaturisation. They incorporate a valency, a direction. Perhaps they descend from the Parthenon or the Roman basilica. Like the basilica, they have work to do. As we saw in the Introduction to this book, work takes place in socio-spatial structures that, when they are not real, reassert themselves in virtual networks. In our mind's eye they are grounded in their particular circumstance; they do not float from being a baptistry in a cathedral precinct to being a biscuit tin in a nursery. Pavilions represent us in World's Fairs, asserting our version of spatiality. Konstantin Melnikov's (1890–1974) designs for the Paris 'Exposition Internationale des Arts Décoratifs et Industriels Modernes' (1925)[60] depict Russia rising from its slumber. Mies's Barcelona Pavilion (1929) is the last gasp of the Weimar Republic and its designer's dreams of an industrially perfectible future. Toyo Ito's (1941–) Serpentine Gallery Pavilion (2002)[61] invites a post-digital future of woven composite fibre structures. Every pavilion is a work apart, divorced from site and from city. Every pavilion is a propaganda poster. Like successful posters, they have a strong graphical quality. Like posters, we collect them for their imagery rather than for their spatiality. In my own architectural community pavilions act as manifestos: Sean Godsell's (1960–) Future Shack (2001) asserts that architects can say something about emergency shelter and homelessness. Tom Kovac's (1958–) Virtual Australian Pavilion at the 2004 Venice Biennale was an outcry against the mediocrity of the beach house pavilion that represents Australia today. Terroir's Canberra lavatory pavilion (2008) caters to the needs of the living in avenues of memorials to the dead. Richard and Michelle Black's

Toyo Ito, Serpentine Gallery Pavilion, London, UK, 2002 – inviting a post-digital future of woven composite fibre structures.

Shack for a Potter (2008) fits into the Henry David Thoreau-like tradition of the idealist living lightly in the country.

Tom Kovac, Virtual Australian Pavilion, Venice Biennale, Italy, 2004. Pavilions act as manifestos.

The house 'holds childhood in its arms'[62]

Very seldom do researchers mention domestic spaces when considering what constitutes good architecture.[63] Perhaps this is because they feel that what gives houses their quality is what the inhabitants have done to them in the course of making them into homes, and that these are not architectural spaces. Here architecture suffers for spurning the decorators who service these domestic needs. Or perhaps it is just that my dream house is not your dream house – as, for example, I find Salvador Dali's (1904–89) lovingly elaborated house at Port Lligat in Cadaqués, Spain (1930–70) simply creepy.[64] It is not in any way related to the ways in which I 'construct … (my) ideal domestic universe'.[65] I find the profusion of objects, built-in furniture and the swags and drapes curious rather than appealing – as no doubt Dali intended. He did not seek to make us comfortable. Perhaps, however, he was comfortable here! The house has become a museum and seems suited

Terroir, lavatory pavilion, Canberra, Australia, 2008.

Richard and Michelle Black, Shack for a Potter, Green Gully, Castlemaine, Victoria, Australia, 2008.

to its role as a collection of cabinets of curiosities. We architects do have to be very careful in this territory. What we regard as comfortable could very easily be disconcerting to clients from another mental space. I recall my shock at reading in Gaston Bachelard's chapter 'The house, from cellar to garret …' the dictum 'a house is imagined as a vertical being'.[66] Houses where I grew up were horizontal beings – if indeed they had being at all.

They were bungalows, ranch houses or derivatives from the 'prairie houses' of Frank Lloyd Wright. Thinking about this in the African savannah, I could reconstruct Bachelard's argument by reference to the thresholds (see above in Caves, etc) that the ancient occupancy of this terrain had wrought. Where his vertical house has an attic and a cellar, I understand what is being said when Bachelard cites psychologist Carl Gustav Jung's (1875–1961) claim that 'a man hearing noises in the cellar who looks for rats in the attic is avoiding the cellar',[67] but I understand this description of someone avoiding their unconscious with my rational waking mind, not through my deeply internalised spatial history. The horizontal house is zoned, of course: bedrooms to the east, living rooms to the west, perhaps, and entrance hall and service rooms interposed. There are many patterns. Where is the unconscious? Well, thinking back to specific houses of my childhood, it is in many different places: in a thicket of hydrangeas against the bathroom wall, in one instance; or at the bottom of the garden and behind a shed in another. Intriguingly, when I was measuring up indigenous houses in the savannah in the 1970s I encountered a village which was composed of individual dwellings each with its own beautifully wrought and cared-for thresholds, all facing the sun, and – untrammelled by the adjacency of a town – this little village had its own graveyard (to the west) and its own herbalist and herb garden (to the east). I already knew that people preferred to lie with their heads to the west so that the spirits of their ancestors (thought to follow the setting sun) could not enter their facial orifices as they slept. But here was a deliberate structuring of life-saving elements to the east! Maybe a horizontal being is evident in the ancient housing traditions of Africa?

When (as I described in Chapter Two) I worked in a team on a self-help housing project at Khutsong near Johannesburg, we did not expect great diversity in the designs. Indeed, superficially the houses looked similar, but when I studied the plans of a thousand of the houses, I could find no two quite the same, though there were ten persistent themes – which could be traced to ancient tribal preferences for spatial arrangements. I suspect that every one of us has a preferred pattern, built up individually and shared through our common capabilities with some but not with all others. This is I think where Christopher Alexander's taxonomic technique fails. The idea of the house has roots in our deep mental space, and we cannot prescribe what will be successful. But we architects must begin by making a full account of our own spatial history – individual, communal and historical – before we can be sure that we are not unconsciously visiting our unconscious preferences onto others.

Mark Robbins's book *Households* (2006) is a rare visual account of that intimate relationship between people and their spatial intelligence.

Mark Robbins's book *Households* (2006) is a rare visual account of that intimate relationship between people and their spatial intelligence.[68] Using carefully composed portraits of people, their partners and their spaces, it shows how people's mental space is revealed by the way they occupy their own spaces. Such capturing of mental space seems to be growing. In the *China Now* exhibition at the Victoria & Albert Museum in London in 2008 there was a photocollage installation by Chen Shaoxiong entitled *Homescape* (2002). The interiors of many homes were photographed and rearranged in individual boxes, animated with cut-out figures. Space and the objects with which people fill them became evident, with rooms filled with electrical goods, or occupied by an exercise bike. These glimpses into other people's spatiality are fascinating. Home and garden magazines are enormously popular because they allow people to daydream about the way they could be, were they able to shift their mental space. The magazines fail people because they suggest that you can shift your lifestyle by purchasing symbols of a desired state – a terracotta pot standing for all of Tuscany – when in fact the changes that we seek are not symbolic but experiential, and can only be attained through immersion. When we encounter lesser villas, we can daydream that we might indeed have inhabited or could one day inhabit these 'lush situations'.[69] These are always particular to specific communities, moulded by their politics, their economics, and the spatiality of their 'popular imaginary'.[70]

In England 'lush situations' have had many manifestations – as many as there are psycho-islands within that culture, and there are (and have been) many. Some – particularly the country houses of the early-20th-century Edwardian heyday of British power and wealth – play into a fantasy of a deep connection to the land, a fantasy captured by fabulist author JRR Tolkien (1892–1973) in his description of the hobbits.[71] English architect Philip Tilden[72] (1887–1956) was a designer of such houses, and his long low rooms harked back to the first Elizabethan era, as was the fashion in Edwardian England – a tendency wittily parodied by contemporary satirical writer EF Benson (1867–1940) in his Lucia novels, the heroine of which added to her house so authentically that the new wing seemed much more ancient than the original cottage.[73] Tilden's designs, such as his house for the Baring brothers on a cliff at Prussia Cove in Cornwall (1911–14), nestled into their landscapes as if they had always been there, but provided far wider expanses of leaded windows with internal window seats than any Tudor cottage would have featured. This was a period of supreme power in which the English elite adopted a Marie Antoinette-like passion for the Arcadian past, a passion that belied the fact that their wealth arose not from the land but from commerce. As an architect, Tilden was unusual in that he both pandered to the search for faux authenticity that prevailed, but also – out of a realistic concern for comfort – made innovations that included internal guttering to collect the condensation that dripped down along the base of the reproduction leaded windows and eject it to the outside through handcrafted copper spouts. I include Tilden here as an intuitive because we do not have evidence that he was conscious of doing more than extending a tradition, while Lethaby, his predecessor in seamless connection to the past, wrote about how the sacred worked, demonstrating a conscious awareness of how sacred architecture

Sir Edwin Lutyens, Deanery Garden, Sonning, Berkshire, UK, 1899–1902 – a fantasy of Tudor grace.

at least related to the mental space of the societies that designed and built it. Despite this, Lethaby did not seem conscious of the boundaries of his mental space when it came to domestic work, achieving strangely in what he extrapolated from the ancient farmhouse at Melsetter in Orkney a design (1898) that seems more 'authentic' than the old buildings it amplified. Sir Edwin Lutyens's domestic work is also in the fashionable Edwardian, high imperial, neo-Elizabethan mode – perhaps the finest of these, and the most in the spirit of Benson, is the Deanery Garden in Sonning, Berkshire (1899–1902).[74] Completed one year before the wealth and power of Great Britain peaked,[75] it is a fantasy of Tudor grace, with a dreamlike garden by Gertrude Jekyll (1843–1932), who collaborated with Lutyens (1869–1944) on many of the gardens for the villas he designed and has had a deep impact on everyday English living, perhaps because her reinvention of the herbaceous border was an innovation that can inspire any gardener. The houses, despite their approachable looks, enshrined in their planning – as we saw in Chapter Three – the separation between servants and family that then prevailed, and that has limited their ongoing influence.

Charles Francis Annesley Voysey (1857–1941) did his share of country houses, but they are somewhat uncomfortable. He was at home in a different, much more pan-European, bourgeois and urban psycho-island, and he set out to invent a new architecture that reflected an urban mental space, designing many modest suburban houses like his studio for the artist WEF Britten at West Kensington (1891) and the three-storey Forster House in Bedford Park (1891), and two townhouses for Grove in Kensington (1891–2). This concern with urban living sets him apart – a fact acknowledged by German critic and theorist Hermann Muthesius (1861–1927), whose book on domestic architecture introduced this new approach to Europe.[76] Recognition by someone from another mental space, thanks to their shared bourgeois values in this case, is one sign of consciousness in this realm. In the same vein of recognition, a recent review notes how Russian Imperial architecture was strongly influenced by Edwardian country house building, and notes that once again today books on these houses are selling well in Russia![77] One could rewrite the history of these times, a history that some have suggested is that of an alternative tradition, that works to extend existing traditions of mental space rather than to invent new architecture – a tradition suppressed, it now seems, only temporarily by Modernism.

Across the Atlantic the Romanesque flourished in the domestic works of Henry Hobson Richardson (1838–86), designer of the Marshall Field Store

Frank Lloyd Wright, Frederick C Robie House, Chicago, Illinois, USA, 1908–10 – perhaps the most iconic of Wright's 'prairie houses'.

in Chicago (1885–7), but later Frank Lloyd Wright (1867–1959) was to consciously construct architectures designed to accommodate and enhance the mental space of specific zones of the continent, 'reading' – in the sense that Lethaby read Melsetter – prairie, desert and Californian littoral with superb clarity. Wright even transcended his Midwest origins and Usonian ethos (he coined this term for the 'Broadacre' property owning democracy that he saw as the very Midwestern future for his country) when he designed the Imperial Hotel in Tokyo (1923), 'reading' in this instance the intense hierarchical nature of Japanese society at that time. Wright's Robie House in Chicago (1908–10) is perhaps the most iconic of his 'prairie houses'. The long horizontal lines of the roofs are pushed down low around the reception rooms of the house, creating a tightly compressed ring of space around them, occupied by the tightly compressed spaces of entry halls and service areas, and with window seats tucked under bands of windows that barely interrupt the eaves as they flow inwards until they reach the core spaces, when clerestory lights announce the layering of another higher set of eaves and roofs, into the crown of which the main rooms rise. This seemingly open expression afforded many degrees of privileged overlook of the surrounding suburb (that was) with its egalitarian sweep of lawn across lot after lot. The deep eaves offer shade in the hot prairie summer, and in winter light is reflected off snow and bounces into the house – a dual function that reveals intimate knowledge of place. At 'La Miniatura' in Pasadena, California (1923), a house he built for Mrs George Madison Millard, Wright turns to the temperate dreams of living in orange groves near the sea. This house is one of several built in purpose-made blocks, an approach resulting from Wright's desire to create affordable houses for the wider middle class of his libertarian dream. As at La Miniatura, the dream usually found expression in exquisite little palaces for the wealthy, and afforded Wright the occasion to use all of his tricks of compression and release alongside the familiar creation of a sense of the immense through deflecting any easy reading of internal volumes from the outside. Addressing a wilderness, Wright's Taliesin West at Scottsdale, Arizona (1937–8) slumps local slabs of stone and cement into formwork that makes a tectonic extension of the rocky desert floor, and surmounts this with a skeleton of imported timber that holds up a folded tent of canvas, an

Frank Lloyd Wright, Mrs George Madison Millard House ('La Miniatura'), Pasadena, California, USA, 1923. Here, Wright turns to the temperate dreams of living in orange groves near the sea.

Frank Lloyd Wright, Taliesin West, Scottsdale, Arizona, USA, 1937–8. Wright slumps local slabs of stone and cement into formwork that makes a tectonic extension of the rocky desert floor.

awesome invention poetically. Wright's many followers have concentrated on replicating the forms of his work, and in so doing have produced many hollow and unsatisfying derivatives – as empty to experience as a Disney World castle. He left many clues: he constructed an overt spatial history for himself through his study of his Welsh ancestry – his many concepts for his home and studio Taliesin in Wisconsin (built in three stages: Taliesin I in 1911, and Taliesin II and III in 1914 and 1925 respectively, after consecutive fires) illustrate this, and he was explicit about the mental space of a broadly based property-owning democracy. Close study of Wright's mental space would have been more rewarding; it would have revealed his mental space, and the ways in which he created with it utterly grounded architectural realities. Perhaps the aura of the great border king – so played to by his partner – overpowered his egalitarian message. What one wonders is: what is the prevailing type in the houses for the elite in the world's most powerful state today? And how conscious are the clients of the mental space that they are manifesting through the realisation of their desires? We have to look at the few houses that have become public, like that of Bill Gates … but perhaps this should be classed more as a stately home?

Collectors of mental space: stately homes

Stately home visits are another popular form of daydreaming about altered states – a pursuit increasingly available to us, as across the world many of the grandest houses have become publicly accessible galleries. Architects encounter clients who want to replicate some aspect of such places, often seen only in magazines. Can we distil some abstract principles that could evoke what has been so particularly wrought in these great estates, often over – as we shall see – long periods of time? We wander through them, imagining what it would have been like to live in them; but, as Raymond Williams has written, we are deluded in this.[78] When the powerful families who created these estates occupied them, very few of us not in their service would have had access to them. We would have been confined beyond the elegant wrought-iron gates, locked into a subject-object contemplation of the power of the inhabitants and the distance from their grandeur to our humble estate. Every such house has a story, and much of their fascination for us lies in their narratives. Blenheim Palace (1704–25), designed by the successful playwright Sir John Vanbrugh and completed by his protégé Nicholas Hawksmoor, was in some accounts designed as a theatrical recreation of the battle after which it is named. It was never enjoyed by the man for whom it was built as a monument: he 'spent the last six years of his life wandering disconsolately through his huge and as yet unfinished palace' while his wife 'would have infinitely preferred a medium size house by Wren'.[79] Nevertheless, the arrival through the massive wrought-iron gates into a hard and urban room echoes the parti of Versailles; and the emergence up stairs into the long gallery overlooking the gardens, which were modified in 1764–74 into a magnificent faux-natural landscape by 'Capability' Brown, is to experience the full theatricality of the type. One recalls, however, that Winston Churchill was born in a small room under these same stairs – how one lived in these places was very different to what we imagine as we do the tours today. I too would have preferred the mid-16th-century Loire chateau of Vaux-le-Vicomte, set placidly within its moats, and with a much more manorial intention, so that one could imagine setting out with the dogs for a morning stroll on one's own.

The great house Cliveden, in Berkshire, perched above the wooded cliff of the valley with its extended vista down along a reach of the Thames, affords a case study of how a site has been crafted over a long period of time, within a singular but evolving mental space. This magnificent site has attracted a few distinctive shifts in the mental space of England, and enshrined them in architecture. Here, in the last stages of absolute monarchy, the restored King's favourite, the Duke of Buckingham, made rich in his role as Chancellor of the Exchequer, set out to build a palace bigger than Versailles. A huge platform of vaulted basements was constructed (1666 by William Winde)[80] before he was assassinated at Portsmouth cathedral – circumstances immortalised in John Dryden's satire *Absalom and Achitophel* (1681). The site defied improvement for a hundred years – its grounds set out with a picturesque inland valley, the cliff terraced with long walks punctuated with 'two little 18th C conceits by Giacomo Leoni (the Octagon Temple and the Blenheim Pavilion)',[81] the woodlands cut with vistas running west and east, a venue only for masques, and in an open amphitheatre cut into the flank of the cliff, the gardens witnessed the premiere of 'Rule Britannia', the signal of a nationalistic, imperialistic Britain. Later, in 1851, Charles Barry (1795–1860) designed an exquisite neoclassical house sitting upon the Duke of Buckingham's platform, and using its wide expanse as a terrace on the eastern face, looking grandly out over the vista along Cliveden Reach. That the platform had defied generations of potential builders by the very ambition of its scale is evidenced by Barry's triumphant Latin legend around the house, just below its cornice, stating that this house had been made possible by the grace of God, by the patronage of the Duke and Duchess of Sutherland and by the genius of the architect.[82] Barry occupies a very significant place in the evolution of English mental space, being one of the

Charles Barry, Cliveden, Berkshire, UK, 1851 – an exquisite neoclassical house.

two architects of the Houses of Parliament (1840–60), the other being the Gothicist architect Augustus Welby Northmore Pugin (1812–52). Barry's plan captivated the jury for the competition for the rebuilding of the Parliament, but his neoclassical architecture was too much associated with French Imperial ambitions, and he was forced to work with Pugin in devising the look of the buildings. The collaboration resulted in a masterpiece of architecture and of political symbolism, as Barry's approach was idealist and Whig in spirit, while Pugin's was incrementalist and realist in alignment with Tory sentiment – a marriage thus of the prevailing politics of the country, as Li Shiqiao has shown.[83] Cliveden's reflection of shifts in mental space does not end here, however. As the USA emerged from civil war and began to take a prominent role on the world stage, the house passed into the hands of the Astor family, and they recast it somewhat in the High Italianate manner then fashionable, adding a clock tower and service wing in this romantic mode, as well as importing – as their compatriots were doing to mansions in their homeland – the entire balustrade from the Villa Borghese in Rome, and locating this, complete with its warm Italian brickwork, along the leading edge of the Duke of Buckingham's platform. Nancy Astor, an early feminist Member of Parliament, ran her salon here between the World Wars, dangerously flirting with fascism. And down the sylvan glades of the picturesque valley inland which terminated in a high Edwardian, Tudorbethan boathouse and a pool, the British establishment seemed to succumb to a terminal sleaze of frivolity after the Suez debacle, as Government minister John Profumo was caught up with osteopath Stephen Ward and his friends Mandy Rice-Davis and Christine Keeler. These are almost operatic caricatures of the mental space of England over a few centuries, and indeed the parallel story of the divorce of the Duke and Duchess of Argyll has been enshrined in *Powder Her Face* (1995), an opera by English composer Thomas Adès (1971–). The sensitivity to the mental space is exquisite, but intuitive, because an unselfconscious reflection of it from within. Cliveden itself, however, was pickled in aspic as Britain shrank back from its Imperial position after the Second World War – a process of selecting and archiving through the agency of the National Trust that is minutely documented in the 1942–7 diaries of James Lees-Milne (1908–97).[84] As the quintessentially English satirical history *1066 And All That* put it: 'America was thus clearly top nation and history came to a full stop.' Had it not, we could have expected to find further improvements to the estate – perhaps a pavilion by David Chipperfield (1953–), one of whose rare commissions in England is the River & Rowing Museum (1998) up river at Henley, or by Zaha Hadid, who has yet to build in England. Instead these 'firsts' are commissioned by the Serpentine Gallery in Kensington Gardens,

David Chipperfield, River & Rowing Museum, Henley on Thames, Oxfordshire, UK, 1998 – a rare English commission.

London – the public institution having taken up the role of patron that the landed wealthy have largely abandoned, and Hadid features in 2008.

Workplaces reveal us …

Workplaces can reveal mental space, especially when their users have designed the interiors. An illustration of this is *Barcelona Lab*, a clever book on the studios of designers (graphic, industrial, fashion, architectural and so on) in this Spanish city.[85] Two books are bound into one cover; one book contains numbered photos of the studios with no one in them, while the other book contains numbered portraits of the individuals or teams that work in the spaces. You can flip through the two books, wondering who belongs to which space, and then, using a third removable key, check if your guesses are right! Surprisingly often they are. This reveals that we are able to make judgements about people's mental space, even without being fully aware of the science behind it. Both Mark Robbins's *Households* (mentioned above) and the Barcelona book owe much to the work of artist and photographer Ed Ruscha (1937–), whose collections of infrastructural pieces (car parks,[86] gasoline stations) and deadpan records of famous streets (Sunset Strip) show an artist at work consciously isolating evidence about mental space. The car parks, all viewed from above, throw up an unsuspected patterning of oil slicks, elegant and fanned out from the entrances of the facilities they serve. The Sunset Strip book predates any architectural interest in the dirty realism of the city, including *Learning from Las Vegas*.[87] What Robbins has discerned, and *Learning from Las Vegas* perhaps did not, is that our visual intelligence far outstrips our rational mind's grasp of the nuances of mental space.

Unpicking the threads of intuitive ability to make space that awakens our spatial intelligence by resonating with the eidetic moments through which we form our mental space could be a way back to a continuum between architectural expertise and popular awareness of the joys that architecture can give. Can we design consciously in this way without turning the understanding into a recipe? Forty per cent 'intimate immensity', 20 per cent allusion, so much compression, a touch of magnetic release, a hint of the toy? Some architects, as the following chapter describes, do now work conscious of their mental space; in the past many have done it intuitively. Intuition is not itself a mystery – it is the internalised sum of our knowledge. If architects have been able to 'magic' us using their intuition, can we not rely on that to continue? If it happens anyway, whether the architects are conscious of it or not, why pursue a conscious articulation of the processes by which spatial intelligence enables us to build personal histories in space and partake in shared mental spaces? The reason we must pursue this consciousness now is that intuition 'is the product of analytic processes being condensed to such a degree that its internal structure may elude even the person benefiting from it,'[88] and while this works – as we have seen in the Picturesque movement – when clients, theorists and designers share the same mental space and are often interchangeable in role, that is not the case in the modern industrialised world, and is certainly not the case in the global information culture that we inhabit today. To be effective now, we need to unpack these intuitions and be aware of our own mental space as a constructed realm, not as a given understood by all.

References

1 John Ruskin, *The Stones of Venice*, Folio Society (London), 2001, p 318. (*The Stones of Venice* was first published in 1851–3.)
2 For Vitruvius, see: Geoffrey Scott, *The Architecture of Humanism: A Study in the History of Taste*, University Paperbacks (London) 1961, p 1: 'Well-building hath three conditions: Commodity, Firmness and Delight.' Scott is citing Sir Henry Wotton, *Elements of Architecture*, 1624, who is adapting Vitruvius, *De Architectura libri decem*, 33–14 BC. See also Hanno-Walter Kruft, *A History of Architectural Theory, From Vitruvius to the Present*, Princeton Architectural Press (New York) & Zwemmer (London), 1994, pp 233–4, Christopher Wren Tracts I–IV, 1632–1723 (first published in *Parentalia* by Stephen Wren, 1750): 'Architecture has its Political Use; public Buildings being the ornament of a country; it establishes a Nation, draws People and Commerce.' He believes in the

validity for architecture of the laws of Nature, and in timeless principles of architecture taking over Vitruvius' principles of 'Beauty, Firmness and Convenience', and adding like the scientist he was: 'the first two depend upon geometrical Reasons of Opticks and Staticks; the third only makes variety' (Tract I, the Wren Society, 1942).
3 This, at least, is my interpretation of the latitude allowed to regions in his 'critical regionalism' (see Kenneth Frampton, 'Towards a critical regionalism: six points for an architecture of resistance', in *The Anti-Aesthetic: Essays on Postmodern Culture*, edited by Hal Foster, Bay Press (Port Townsend, Washington), 1983), an argument that cements in place a north-western metropolitan control over architectural manners.
4 His findings were first published in Dalibor Vesely, 'Architecture and the conflict of representation', *AA Files*, No 8 (edited by Mary Wall) (London), January 1985, pp 21–38. They are now available in book form: Dalibor Vesely, *Architecture in the Age of Divided Representation: The Question of Creativity in the Shadow of Production*, MIT Press (Cambridge, Massachusetts), 2004.
5 This is discussed in Robert Gutman, *Architectural Practice – Critical Review*, Princeton Architectural Press (Princeton, New Jersey), 1988. The *RIBA Journal* has reported similar statistics, as has the RAIA.
6 Aaron Betsky, *Violated Perfection*, Rizzoli (New York), 1990.
7 Steen Eiler Rasmussen, *London: The Unique City*, Pelican (London), 1960 (first published 1934).
8 Loosely based on Steen Eiler Rasmussen, *Experiencing Architecture*, Chapman & Hall (London), 1959.
9 In *Experiencing Architecture*, op cit, p 46, Rasmussen outlines an ancient duality of architecture: 'Building material is the medium of architecture … can there be any other? Yes … instead of letting his [sic] imagination work with structural forms, with the solids of a building, the architect can work with the empty space – the cavity – between the solids and consider forming the space as the real meaning of architecture.' The information age has architects adding a third term to this duo: the surface. Techno-nomads, we float above the ground surveilling the terrain through screens, wind-, computer-, TV … The hard-won tactility of architectural reality fades for us into an undifferentiated array of surface effects all brought to comfort by air conditioning and piped music. An architecture of expression has emerged, competing in its coding with film. I want to demonstrate that in contrast Kovac is making an architecture out of this third term, and that he does so by engaging us in conflicting expectations that his work is concerned primarily with the poles of the duality. I want to argue that it is precisely by making it impossible for us to incorporate either into our mental space that we come to fully experience a spatiality of the present rather than the caverns or objects of the past.
10 Juhani Pallasmaa, *The Eyes of the Skin: Architecture and the Senses*, Academy Editions (London), 1996; revised edition, Wiley-Academy (Chichester), 2005.
11 Oliver Sacks, *Musicophilia: Tales of Music and the Brain*, Knopf (New York), 2007, p 47. A visual or social scene can be constructed or reconstructed in a hundred different ways, but the recall of a musical piece has to be close to the original.
12 Aaron Betsky, *Violated Perfection: Architecture and the Fragmentation of the Modern*, Rizzoli (New York), 1990.
13 Gaston Bachelard, *The Poetics of Space*, Beacon Press (Boston, Massachusetts), 1969 (first published in French in 1958); *The Poetics of Reverie*, Orion Press (New York), 1969 (first published in French in 1960); *The Psychoanalysis of Fire*, Beacon Press (Boston, Massachusetts), 1987 (first published in French in 1938).
14 These 'poetic' qualities are derived from Gaston Bachelard, *The Poetics of Reverie*, op cit, p 13.
15 Bachelard, *The Poetics of Space*, op cit, pp 11–12: 'Each one of us, then, should speak of his roads, his crossroads, his roadside benches; each one of us should make a surveyor's map of his lost fields and meadows. Thoreau said that he had the map of his fields engraved in his soul. And Jean Wahl once wrote: "the frothing of the hedges I keep deep inside me". Thus we cover the universe with drawings we have lived.'
16 Roger Scruton, *The Aesthetics of Architecture*, Methuen & Co (London), 1979.
17 Kenneth Frampton, *Studies in Tectonic Culture*, MIT Press (Cambridge, Massachusetts and London), 1975, p 373 cites Konstantinidis citing Leger: 'Architecture "is a natural function, it grows out of the ground, like animals and plants",' , p 375: 'One may argue that the tectonic resists and has always resisted the fungibility of the world. Its tradition is such that it has constantly sought, at one and the same time, both to create the new and to reinterpret the old.'
18 Cao Xueqin, *The Story of the Stone*, also known as *The Dream of the Red Chamber*, translated and edited by David Hawkes, Penguin (London), 1973, *Vol 2: The Crab Flower Club*, pp 213–58 (chs 37 & 38).
19 Robert Harbison, *Eccentric*

Spaces, Secker & Warburg (London), 1989, pp 74–5: 'The moaning issues from the mouth of a fallen Colossus whose head rests on pieces of marble as on a pillow, a noise made by wind finding its way into rents and tears in the bronze … .'
20 Robert Venturi, Denise Scott Brown and Steven Izenour, *Learning from Las Vegas*, MIT Press (Cambridge, Massachusetts and London), 1972.
21 Bernard Tschumi, *Architectural Manifestoes: Manifestoes 6, 7, 8*, Architectural Association (London), February 1979. The murder is documented in Manifesto 6, Transcript 1, 'The Park'.
22 Ignasi de Solà-Morales Rubio, 'Terrain Vague', in Cynthia C Davidson (ed), *Anyplace*, MIT Press, (Cambridge, Massachusetts and London), 1995, pl 18–123.
23 Nikos Papastergiadis and Heather Rogers, 'Parafunctional Spaces', *Architectural Design*, Profile 50: *The Dream of Urbanity*, Academy Group (London), 1996, pp 76–88. Ugo La Pietra was early to identify such spaces: in Gillo Dorfles, *Dal Significato Alle Scelte*, Einaudi (Turin), 1973, figs 16–18, Ugo La Pietra's 1973 photographs of parafunctional space are illustrations of Milanese mental space.
24 Andrea Kahn, *Mobile Ground*, Transition RMIT (Melbourne), 1992, insert Folded Poster, 1992.
25 Bernard Rudofsky, *Architecture without Architects*, Doubleday (New York), 1964.
26 Robert Smithson, 'A tour of the monuments of Passaic, New Jersey', in Nancy Holt (ed), *The Writings of Robert Smithson*, New York University Press (New York), 1979; first published as 'The monuments of Passaic', *Artforum*, December 1967.

27 John Brinckerhoff Jackson, *American Space, The Centennial Years 1865–1876*, Norton (New York), 1972. See also John Brinckerhoff Jackson, *A Sense of Place, a Sense of Time*, Yale University Press (New Haven, Connecticut), 1994.
28 We must however remember that Gaudí's Park Guell (1899–1908), a wonder of Barcelona, is a 'failed development', its structures being the carriageway that was to lead to the villas of the subdivision on the steep hillside. Only the gatehouse was built. The irony of this being a wonder through failures when the city is a wonder through the overdevelopment of Cerdá's grid (see Chapter Three) gives pause for thought.
29 Marc Augé, *Non-Places:, Introduction to an Anthropology of Super-Modernity*, Verso (London), 1995.
30 A recent manifestation of this love is in Frank Moorhouse, *Martini – a Memoir*, Knopf (Sydney), 2005, pp 66, 76, 103.
31 'Action station: St Pancras enters the 21st century', *RIBA Journal*, The Builder Group (London), January 2008, pp 26–41.
32 Hanno-Walter Kruft, *A History of Architectural Theory: From Vitruvius to the Present*, Princeton Architectural Press (New York) and Zwemmer (London), 1994, p 237: Colen Campbell (1676–1729).
33 Geoffrey Howard Baker, *Le Corbusier: An Analysis of Form*, Van Nostrand Reinhold (London), 1987.
34 Geoffrey Howard Baker, *Design Strategies in Architecture: An Approach to the Analysis of Form*, Van Nostrand Reinhold (London), 1989.
35 Jonah Lehrer, *Proust was a Neuroscientist*, Houghton Mifflin Company (New York), 2007, p 93: the author puts

forward a hypothesis by Dr Kausik Si that the synaptic mark of memory is a prion, a protein that uniquely has two functional states, active or inactive. It 'holds' memory when inactive, but when memory is called upon it becomes active, and therefore labile. So the act of remembering alters the memory. This was Proust's key realisation.
36 See Karin Jaschke & Silke Ötsch (eds), *Stripping Las Vegas, A Contextual Review of Casino Resort Architecture*, Verso (London), 2004.
37 David Grahame Shane, *Recombinant Urbanism: Conceptual Modelling in Architecture, Urban Design and City Theory*, Wiley-Academy (Chichester), 2005, pp 145, 212 & 269. Grahame Shane is Adjunct Professor of Architecture at Columbia University, Graduate School of Architecture and Planning.
38 Rose windows added in 15th century, restored 1855 by Viollet-le-Duc after despoilation in the French Revolution.
39 Guy Underwood, *The Pattern of the Past*, Abacus (London), 1972, p 39.
40 Marie-Claire Ricard, *Orcival, The Basilica of Notre-Dame*, Lescuyer (Lyons), 1992.
41 Leon van Schaik, 'Walls, toys and the ideal room, an analysis of the architecture of Sir John Soane', in Mary Wall (ed), *AA Files*, No 9 (London), 1985, pp 45–53.
42 Carlos Castaneda, *Don Juan: A Yaqui Way of Knowledge*, University of California Press (USA), 1968.
43 IA Richards, *Practical Criticism: A Study of Literary Judgment*, Harcourt Brace & Company (New York), 1956, p 228–40 (first published 1929).
44 Richard Rorty, 'Being that can be understood is language' (review of a paper delivered in Heidelberg by Hans-Georg Gadamer on the occasion

of his 100th birthday on 11 February 2000), *London Review of Books*, Vol 22, No 6, 16 March 2000, pp 23–5.
45 Philip Fisher, *Wonder, the Rainbow, and the Aesthetics of Rare Experiences*, Harvard University Press (Cambridge), 1988, p 119: 'there is a part secured within the process of explanation for the same triggering mechanisms that brought on attention in the first place. These wonder-preserving features of explanation can now be summed up: First, when we undo the rarity of an experience we do so by surprising means and in unexpected directions' etc – enumerating seven reasons.
46 Leon van Schaik, 'Spatial intelligence and place making', in Paul Brislin (ed), *Arup Associates: Unified Design*, John Wiley & Sons (Chichester), 2008, pp 129–47.
47 AR Willcox, *Rock Paintings of the Drakensberg*, Max Parrish (London), 1956, p 16, pl 2, 'A view from a Bushman's Shelter, Site 20'. 'Looking Eastwards out of Game Pass Valley; the conical mountain is the Kamberg', pp 56–7, pls 41–4. Plate 44 is cited by Nigel Spivey (via Lewis Williams) as the key to understanding that these paintings – like those at Altamura and Lascaux – record images seen in trance states. This solves the problem of the ontology of image making, explaining that what was depicted was a two-dimensional image projected by the mind in sensory deprivation states. The power of these images led to the first sacred architecture 12,000 years ago in Anatolia, rings of 'T'-shaped columns inscribed with such images, the making of which is accompanied by agriculture and the earliest domestication of wheat. (Nigel Spivey, *How Art Made The World*, BBC Books (London), 2005, pp 34–9.)
48 Beatriz Colomina, 'Intimacy and spectacle: the interior of Adolf Loos', in John Whiteman, Jeffrey Kipnis & Richard Burdett (eds), *Strategies in Architectural Thinking*, MIT Press (Cambridge), 1992, pp 68–89.
49 Philip Drew, *Leaves of Iron – Glenn Murcutt: Pioneer of an Australian Architectural Form*, Law Book Company (North Ryde), 1994. Reviewed by Rory Spence in *Architectural Review*, Vol CLXXVIII, No 1066, December 1985, pp 96–8.
50 Having written this I stroll across the lawns outside to have a coffee with architect Tom Kovac (whose work we will encounter in a later chapter) in the café in the State Library in Melbourne. I select a seat, and Kovac observes: 'You always select that seat if you can, with its back to the wall, with views into the two lobes of the café each side, overlooking the entrance and the terrace outside!' And indeed that is the seat where I do feel most comfortable in this space.
51 Paul Overy, Lenneke Büller, Frank den Oudsten and Bertus Mulder, *The Rietveld Schröder House*, MIT Press (Cambridge, Massachusetts), 1988. You will need to count these yourself, but they are quite evident in the markings made for construction.
52 *Architectural Design*, Vol 77, No 2: *Landscapes*, Wiley-Academy (London), March 2007, pp 4–5.
53 Banister Fletcher, *A History of Architecture on the Comparative Method*, Athlone Press (London), 1963, pp 194–5.
54 Ibid, pp 197–8.
55 Rasmussen, *London: The Unique City*, op cit, pp 16–17.
56 Leon van Schaik, 'Walls, toys and the ideal room: an analysis of the architecture of Sir John Soane', in Mary Wall (ed), *AA Files*, No 9, London, 1985, pp 45–53.
57 Jan Kaplicky, 'Future forward', in Jan Kaplicky (ed), *Architectural Design*, Vol 71, No 5: *Looking Back in Envy*, Wiley-Academy (London), 5 September 2001, pp 6–15.
58 Iona and Peter Opie, *Children's Games in Street and Playground*, Clarendon Press (Oxford), 1963.
59 Dimity Reed (ed), *Tangled Destinies: National Museum of Australia*, Images Publishing Group (Melbourne), 2002.
60 S Frederick Starr, *Melnikov: Solo Architect in a Mass Society*, Princeton University Press (Princeton, New Jersey), 1981, pp 96–7.
61 Toyo Ito and Cecil Balmond, *Serpentine Gallery Pavilion 2002: Toyo Ito with Arup*, telescoweb.com, 2002.
62 Gaston Bachelard, *The Poetics of Space*, Beacon Press (Boston, Massachusetts), 1969, pp 3–37, Chapter 1: 'The house, from cellar to garret'.
63 An amateur exception is Michael Pollan, *A Place of My Own: The Education of an Amateur Builder*, Bloomsbury (London), 1997.
64 The house is illustrated in Gustau Gili Galfetti, *My House, My Paradise: The Construction of the Ideal Domestic Universe*, Editorial Gustavo Gili (Barcelona), 1999, pp 104–13.
65 Ibid.
66 Gaston Bachelard, *The Poetics of Space*, Beacon Press (Boston, Massachusetts), 1969, p 17: 'A house is imagined as a vertical being. It rises upward. It differentiates itself in terms of its verticality. It is one of the appeals to our consciousness of verticality.'
67 Ibid, pp 18–19.
68 Mark Robbins, *Households*, The Monacelli Press (New York), 2006. See also my review 'Home Body', in *Architectural Design*, No 189: *Rationalist Traces*, Wiley-Academy (London), September–October 2007, pp 146–8.
69 The term comes from the title of the painting *Hers is a Lush Situation* (1958) by Richard Hamilton, under

whom I studied in 1964. In the picture a pair of glossy lips floats above the body of a Buick Electra, in the wrap-around windscreen of which the United Nations building is reflected. This is an encapsulation of a specific mental space.
70 I was introduced to this useful term by cultural historian John Welchman, *Modernism Relocated: Towards a Cultural Studies of Visual Modernity*, Allen & Unwin (St Leonards, New South Wales), 1995.
71 JRR Tolkien, *The Hobbit*, Allen & Unwin (London), first published 1937.
72 James Bettley, *Lush and Luxurious: The Life and Work of Philip Tilden*, RIBA (London), 1987, p 7: Prussia Cove (1911–14) at Porth-en-Alls, for TT and Brian Behrens: 'They (Philip and Brian) first built a little curved cottage set into the hillside, partly to test out their techniques and materials, before embarking on the house itself .... With teak used for external woodwork and gunmetal for the window frames, it has proved to be an extraordinarily resilient building, the only weak element being the Forest of Dean slates on the roof – an unfortunate instance of sticking too closely to the Cotswold tradition. Its most curious feature is a door covered in rhinoceros hide, so unyielding it had to be sent to an army steel mill to be rolled flat and then fixed to a steel framed door.'
73 EF Benson, *Queen Lucia* (1920), *Miss Mapp* (1922), *Lucia in London* (1927), *Lucia's Progress* (1935), Penguin Books (London). See *Queen Lucia*, p 7: 'She had persuaded him to buy three of these cottages that stood together in a low two-storeyed block, and had, by judicious removal of partition walls, transmuted it into a most comfortable dwelling, subsequently adding on a new wing at the back, which was, if anything, a shade more blatantly Elizabethan than the stem onto which it was grafted, for here was situated the famous smoking-parlour, with rushes on the floor, a dresser ranged with pewter tanks, and leaded lattice windows of glass so antique that it was practically impossible to see through them.
74 *The Work of the English Architect Sir Edwin Lutyens 1869–1944*, exh cat (exhibition designer Piers Gough, catalogue designer Roger Huggett), Arts Council of Great Britain (London), 1984, pp 92, 105.
75 Sir George Cox points out that the GDP of that year was equalled by the GDP of the first six weeks of 2003! Conference lecture, RMIT University (Melbourne), 8 March 2008.
76 *Hermann Muthesius 1861–1927*, exh cat, Architectural Association (London), 1979, pp 6–15 contains a lecture given by Professor Julius Posener at the AA and published in AA paper No 5, *From Schinkel to Bauhaus*, 1972.
77 Clementine Cecil, 'Far formed pavilions' (review of Dmitry Shvidkovsky, *Russian Architecture and the West*, Yale University Press (New York), 2007), *Times Literary Supplement*, No 5472, 15 February 2008, p 20.
78 Raymond Williams, *The Country and the City*, Hogarth Press (London), 1973, p 106: 'where so many admirers ... have stood and shared the view finding its prospect delightful ... the other effect, from the outside looking in ...'.
79 John Julius Norwich, *The Architecture of Southern England*, Macmillan (London), 1985, pp 479–80.
80 Ibid, p 63.
81 Ibid, p 63.
82 The inscription runs: 'AEDIFICATA-FUNDAMENTIS-A-GEO-VILLIERS-BUCKINGHAMIAE-DVCE-OLIM-LOCATIS-REGE-CAROLO-SECUNDO-INSTAURATA-DOMM-II-PIUS-IBIDEM-IGNE-ABSUMPTIS-A-GEO-DVCE-SUTHERLANDAE-ET-HENRIETTA-UXORE-EXSTRVCTA-AD-MDCCCLI-ANNUM-JAM-XIV-DEO-AUSPREGNANTE-VICTORIA-POSITA-INGENIO-OPERA-CONSILIO-CAROLI-BARRY-ARCHITA-D-MDCCCLI'.
83 Li Shiqiao, *Power and Virtue: Architecture and Intellectual Change in England 1660–1730*, Routledge (London), 2007.
84 Five volumes concluding with James Lees-Milne, *Midway on the Waves*. Faber & Faber (London), 1985.
85 Ramon Prat, Anna Tetas and Carles Poy (eds), *Barcelona Lab*, Actar (Barcelona), 2003.
86 Edward Ruscha, *Thirtyfour Parking Lots in Los Angeles*, Edward Ruscha Editions (Los Angeles), 1967 and Edward Ruscha, *Every Building on the Sunset Strip*, Edward Ruscha Editions (Los Angeles), 1966.
87 Robert Venturi, Denise Scott Brown and Steven Izenour, *Learning from Las Vegas*, MIT Press (Cambridge, Massachusetts and London), 1972.
88 Sue Halpern, 'The moment of truth' (review of Malcolm Gladwell, *Blink: The Power of Thinking Without Thinking*, Little, Brown & Co; and Elkhonon Goldberg, *The Wisdom Paradox: How Your Mind Can Grow Stronger as Your Brain Grows Older*, Gotham Books), *New York Review of Books*, Vol LII, No 7, 28 April 2005, pp 19–21: 'But in reality, intuition is the condensation of vast prior experience; it is analysis compressed and crystallized ... It is the product of analytic processes being condensed to such a degree that its internal structure may elude even the person benefiting from it' (p 20). Sue Halpern is Scholar in Residence at Middlebury College.

5

Pioneers of mental space – tracing the use of spatial intelligence

> I mean an architect is wonderful when he is in his own house, maybe beyond this he is terrible?

Romaldo Giurgola[1]

So what do we need if we are to break away from the atomising effects of the encyclopaedic dismemberment of the place, space and culture unity of architectural reality? How do we set a course away from the old-fashioned linearity of architectural discourse, its 'one true path' fallacy, its myopic focus on its canon and its lack of contact with the spatial intelligence of everyone? How do we heal the disruption of the continuum between the spatial intelligence of us all and those whom we charge with the custody and development of our spatiality? We cannot go back, we need to find a dynamic way to heal the divisions that have marginalised what architecture has to offer; ways to overcome the divisions that have facilitated architecture's decay from its role in meaningfully adjusting particular environments to shifting understandings of the universe we inhabit into a branded consumable. Let us look at the output of some radical architects whose work is inextricably bound up in the architectural reality of the places in which they operate … even if they are not expressly aware of this, and even if they are not always designing in this mode. I regard these works as pioneering design using spatial intelligence.

Peter Lyssiotis, *I mean an architect is wonderful when he is in his own house, maybe beyond this he is terrible?*, photomontage for *Spatial Intelligence*, 1998 – completed as part of an Australia Council New Media Arts Fellowship at RMIT, Melbourne, Australia.

The pioneers I will discuss in this chapter were working without the benefit of the advances in science that have revealed so much about our spatial intelligence and the ways in which we create our shared mental space through the building of our own individual histories in space. So it is often possible to catch them out as they unwittingly transfer assumptions from their own mental space into other situations. None of them has a manifesto explicitly claiming the territory, but in significant ways they act as if they were aware of the boundaries of their own mental space, as if conscious of the individuality of their own histories in space. This becomes most apparent when their individual positions are examined outside the encyclopaedic tradition, seen not as independent chronological strands, but as braided into the discourses of their times, which I suggest here are best understood as contributing to intellectual change when engaged with worthy adversaries in the field.

We cannot reverse what has happened; we cannot retreat to a pre-encyclopaedic situation in which architectural reality existed as a unified system of mental space, place and form. We have to attempt to move on, using the best currently available knowledge – and in this context that includes, as I have argued, the latest understandings of the workings of our spatial intelligence. Gadamer has proposed that we advance by enveloping existing descriptions with new and better ones, but that these latest descriptions depend on their adjacency to the previous best descriptions for their potency.² Fisher has a lovely description of this through a study of the rainbow and how it has been described through the ages in his marvellously titled book *Wonder, the Rainbow, and the Aesthetics of Rare Experiences*, a title that sets up a dialogue between emotion engendered by experience, accurate description of the experience itself, and reflective practice around both.³

Pioneers in the conscious use of personally inflected mental space: Peter Zumthor, Sean Godsell, Herzog & de Meuron, Zaha Hadid, Kathryn Findlay

So in this chapter I look at individuals who I believe can be regarded as pioneers of looking at architecture not simply as 'guild' activity – dependent on secret knowledge passed down generation by generation through the educational processes of the architectural profession or guild (see final chapter) usually in the form of a recognised canon of precedents admired by the guild – but as the workings of a human capability, shared by us all, differentiated by individual experience, aggregated by what we hold in common with our communities but relegated to the humdrum by the pressures of daily life, and held in conscious care for society at large by those of us who are trained to exercise and extend spatial thinking on behalf of us all. When we succeed in this custodian role, we design and build works that reawaken individual eidetic memories in those who encounter our designs; memories that have the startling freshness of our early experiences of the world through our senses of taste, smell, touch, hearing and seeing.⁴

Peter Zumthor in east Switzerland

The architect who possibly above all others today – perhaps anachronistically as some internationalists would argue, given the globalisation of culture that we experience in the Anglophone world – operates within a single unified mental space is the Swiss architect Peter Zumthor (1943–), although many would assert that the Portuguese architect Álvaro Siza (1933–), who is renowned for the sensitivity of his insertions into landscapes (such as the Santo Domingo de Bonaval Park, Santiago de Compostela (1993–4)) is just as eminent in this way. Zumthor however has accepted (so far) that his architecture, characterised by an obsessive invention of a process unique to the physical realisation of each work and thus also driven to an essentialism in the conception of each work, as if working through the elements of earth, air, water and fire, makes sense only within the ambit of his community's mental space; while Siza,[5] whose most admired works subtly enhance and amplify existing site conditions,[6] has ventured outside his community – with results, as in his housing at The Hague (1983–93),[7] where he reaches out rather forlornly it seems to Venturi, Scott Brown in the attempt to connect, putting into question the possibility of translating such architecture from one spatial community to another. Peter Zumthor, who came to architecture through carpentry, has such an acute appreciation of site and social situation that his buildings have an uncanny sense of inevitability about them. It is as if they did not exist, they would have had to be spontaneously invented. The little Sogn Benedetg Chapel at Sumvitg (1989)[8] perhaps encapsulates the immense power of the limitations that he imposes on himself as an architect. The chapel replaces one that was swept away by an avalanche, and is sited on the ridge of a spur above the hamlet it serves, where its predecessor was tucked – seemingly sheltered – into a fold between spurs that became in the particular circumstances of an exceptional winter, a funnel of destruction. Such chapels in this region were dimly neoclassical in form, contrasting with the alpine hut vernacular of the farmhouses that often combine stabling on a lower floor with living space above, reached by external stairs and a balcony sheltered by the oversailing pitched roof.

The first problem facing the architect of the new chapel therefore was how to find a form that could ride on the ridge and yet seem to belong to this place. His answer was to trace an ellipse symmetrically across the spur with its long axis aligned with the ridge. From this he then pulled a tower form upwards, and this tower deforms from the base: as if made from a leg of panty hose, it has been stretched upwards from that ellipse to a slighter smaller ring of vertically articulated clerestory windows that terminate the tower at high level. Over this is set the roof, its overhang reaching out to the width of the ellipse at the base. The tower is clad in shingles, and the drip line from the eaves causes a differential weathering where the shingles flare out at the base, lipped over a concrete base that seems to be a natural stub from the spur. From the slopes below there seems to be no possible entrance to this tower, and the ancient fairy tale of Rapunzel locked away in her inaccessible tower comes irresistibly to mind. No need for a guess at names, however: a track inclined easily against the inside flank of the spur leads up from the last hutments of the hamlet to the temporary level of a hairpin bend just above the uppermost point of the ellipse of the tower, and here a simple, detached step affords entry into the chapel. The magic is not over yet, for the simple elliptical space within is lit evenly but brightly from the clerestory window ring above, and this has the effect of dissolving away the ceiling; and the space is defined by a palisade of closely spaced vertical timber ribs that reveal the structural simplicity of the tower in a startling contrast to the scaleless shingled outer skin that has one imagining what one now realises were implausible immensities.

Peter Zumthor, Sogn Benedetg Chapel, Sumvitg, Switzerland, 1989. The chapel replaces one that was swept away by an avalanche, and is sited on the ridge of a spur above the hamlet it serves.

Peter Zumthor, Sogn Benedetg Chapel, Sumvitg, Switzerland, 1989. The space is defined by a palisade of closely positioned vertical timber ribs and the floor is, it seems, a floating platform.

And further to this the floor, struck at a level just off the point at which the track reaches the spine, is a seemingly floating platform, held in place inside the ring of the ribs with no visible supports. The pews are made of a lighter timber and formed of horizontal planes that – in their turn – float above the timber floor.

This tiny chapel has immense architectonic subtlety, all of which can be traced back to precedents identified by the theorists discussed in Chapter Four, but – as in Cao Xueqin's 18th-century critique of poetry also discussed in that chapter – the qualities are differently arranged, and add a new layer to our canonical conception of the temple. The poetic is subtle too. Nothing here is mimicry; the design reads the site with mathematical

Peter Zumthor, Thermal Baths, Vals, Switzerland, 1994–6 – a cool rationalist conception in layered slate with cave-like interiors lit mysteriously from hidden apertures.

accuracy, defining the ellipse as if a natural topological derivative of the spine, striking the level of the platform a weather-excluding step or two above the hairpin bend of the track and thus making a walk from the hamlet a ready and natural possibility; and the whole seems to be part of this place, despite its avoidance of any symbolic representation of what was there before. To this it adds a narrative flourish that arises from the softness of its form, which seems to have grown here like a magic mushroom, and induces reveries of ancient tales. Architects recognise the unity of place, time and culture, and know intuitively that they cannot replicate this elsewhere, and no one has even tried to do so.

They can, however, be inspired by Zumthor's approach, because Zumthor is not a rural fantasist. While the Thermal Baths at Vals, Switzerland[9] (1994–6), a cool rationalist conception in layered slate with cave-like interiors lit mysteriously from hidden apertures, and the Bruder Klaus Field Chapel at

Mechernich, Germany (2007)[10] – result of an almost alchemical notion that a space could be created by burning away the complex spiral of formwork around which a shell was cast – also convey the sense that they have grown out of site, cultural circumstance and construction logic, and are also in remote situations and can be argued to be privileged by that fact, this architect is very conscious of what he is doing, and can do it in an urban situation too, as with the Kunsthaus at Bregenz, Austria (1997).[11] This gallery is in some ways the chapel writ large: a structure (a massive concrete box)

Peter Zumthor, Kunsthaus, Bregenz, Austria, 1997 (exterior) – a massive concrete box clad in shingles of large rectangular sheets of obscured glass.

Leon van Schaik   147   Chapter 5 Pioneers of mental space – tracing the use of spatial intelligence

Peter Zumthor, Kunsthaus, Bregenz, Austria, 1997 (interior) – the wall-ness of the walls, floors and the overcast sky of the glazed ceiling.

is clad in shingles (of large rectangular sheets of obscured glass), and once inside there is only the wall-ness of the walls, the floors and the ceilings in the lower gallery (all in the same material, and with works fixed only by drilling into their mass, and a store of absolutely matching sand and cement mix for repair after each show), and the overcast sky of the glazed ceiling on the upper gallery. The building asserts its position on the edge of Lake Constance in the same authoritative manner. At night, neon tube lighting in the space between the outer glass wall and the box asserts a very urban role for a building that is also intimately immense.

Sean Godsell in Melbourne

An architect who has grasped the unity of Zumthor's architecture, and who has been spurred by this into developing his own uncompromisingly unified approach, is Sean Godsell, an award-winning Australian architect[12] who was predisposed to this by his admiration for traditional Japanese architectural values, such as those Platonic ideals associated with the regular reconstruction of temples at Kyoto, complying with an 'ideal' first realised in the 17th century. Such admiration is not generally a promising generator of an architecture that has an independent manifestation and that illuminates the particular spatiality of the culture in which it is attempted. Usually the transfer fails because there is a literal replication of the admired architecture as an object – a process that severs the veins and arteries of the architectonic, poetic and narrative specificities of the original from the body of its architectural reality, and delivers nothing more than a dry, academically correct husk. Or some spirit of the Japanese is conjured up in a concocted symbol. We can see this latter writ large in Bruce Goff and Bart Prince's 'bizarre Pavilion of Japanese Art of 1978–1988, a zoomorphic folly'[13] at the Los Angeles County Museum of Art (LACMA), and the former in any number of Tatami rooms or gift gardens that, while faithfully copied from a Japanese original, woefully fail to evoke its specific qualities.

Godsell does not replicate. Having completed several internationally publicised houses[14] and a science wing for a school, he is currently designing his first major inner-city building, located on Melbourne's civic spine: RMIT's Design Research Institute (2007–10). This project owes something to the

Bruce Goff and Bart Prince, Pavilion of Japanese Art, Los Angeles Museum of Contemporary Art (LACMA), USA, 1978–88 – 'a zoomorphic folly'.

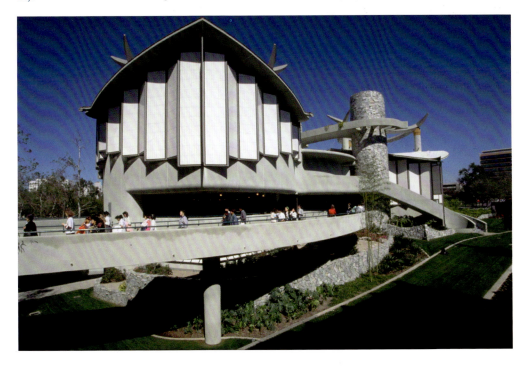

Leon van Schaik   Chapter 5 Pioneers of mental space – tracing the use of spatial intelligence

Sean Godsell Architects, Peninsula House, Victoria, Australia, 2002. The design demonstrates the architect's unerring ability to strike a level.

research his practice conducted for their project (ranked second, 2005) for the Australian National Portrait Gallery in Canberra, particularly in the development of its adjustable external screening, but in its double-banked circulation it resonates with the Peninsula House on the Mornington Peninsula south of Melbourne (2002). This design demonstrates why Godsell can be mentioned alongside Zumthor without condescension to either architect. The house is reached up a track that tunnels through the coastal scrub behind the dunes in an area that has been subdivided on a simple grid. The house is set down a steep slope to the north of the track, and all that can be seen from the approach is a car port – a space for two vehicles within the open end of the double skin cladding – an upside-down 'U' formed by an oxidised steel portal (30 x 7.2 metres), that runs away at right angles to the road. This skin has an outer screen of timber laths that are deliberately allowed to settle into their own profiles, the slight irregularities animating the grillage, and an inner skin of double glazing. There are two possible entrances to the house, one each side of a storeroom that sits across the back of the car port. One of these is somewhat concealed, intended for use by the owner, and leads through a courtyard past the bedroom and down a stairway to the kitchen. The other along the other side of the box, having announced itself with a lip of paving as the way in, leads down a stairway between the building's external skin and a blind wall enclosing the courtyard bathroom and bedroom to which the other entry gives direct access. You sink down this slot of space, which becomes double height as you descend, arriving at the kitchen and living level, and here the external skin can be pivoted upwards in several leaves to open the house to a terrace that stretches east, tucked into the dune with a low concrete retaining wall topped with a broad seat. The north end of the outer box is open towards the sun, and a full-width glass wall can be hinged up to open out to the median level of the site. Fully opened out, this entire rectangle of space incorporates the terrace, the kitchen and the living area into a free-flowing reception area. Cut into the dune behind the kitchen is the cave-like library – the only room that has a window to the west. There is a fireplace in the retaining wall on which the house is anchored, a wall that also stabilises the dune. And in the double wall to the west of the kitchen there is a concealed doorway to the stairway that leads up to the bedroom; and to the west of the double-height living room this wall contains another fireplace.

Like Zumthor, Godsell has an unerring ability to strike the levels for the design that seem so 'natural' to the local spatiality as to seem inevitable or 'natural'. This finding and establishing of levels is the key to the poetic power of the designs of both. Both then capture the levels with a structure that seems to be independent of them, appearing to frame them spatially rather than to hold them in place. This creates an architectonic hierarchy of parts – outer double-skinned box, inner untrammelled spaces, separate circulation zones – that gives the impression that the architecture is severely rational. We are also invited to inspect the making of the buildings – every attachment appears to be shown, and we have the feeling that given the right tools and the time, we could take the building apart, and then reassemble it. In this it appeals to the 'toy' instinct that resides within us, as we saw in Chapter Four. While seemingly very abstract in form, the buildings are very theatrical, because they are visualised around the rituals and behaviours that they will induce: we choreograph ourselves into the weekend barbecues on the opened-out entertainment level, and imagine

Fellini-esque parties in full swing here, on the fringe of the metropolis. We anticipate being invited into the library as the winter draws in, sitting near the fire, and opening monographs on the wide ledge in the fading western light. And we can envy the owners their retreat up that secret stairway to their oversize bedroom cantilevered over and compressing the space of the kitchen, and imagine bathing in the large bathroom looking into that enclosed raked gravel courtyard as clouds race across during a change in the weather from the southwest. A transferable narrative has woven this architecture into being, but it is so nuanced by its place that we marvel at the spatial intelligence through which it has been wrought.

Herzog & de Meuron exporting from west Switzerland

Zumthor has not attempted to export his understanding of his region's architectural reality. Mostly such export fails, but architects who emerge from a single mental space and who put the 'delight' afforded by their own mental space to the fore have perhaps the greatest success in translating their work from one context to another. I would put the Swiss partnership Herzog & de Meuron at the head of this category, and their Laban Contemporary Dance Centre in Deptford (2002) as their best work outside their home base – because not all of their exports have worked as well as this one. The Laban Centre is indisputably the product of their core spatial intelligence. It has the stretched-skin, structure-obscuring surface that they have made their hallmark, and that is said to be derived from their early experience in designing graphics and fabrics – in which they pioneered the growing connections between fashion design and architecture. The building consists of a series of dance studios, workshops, rehearsal rooms and a theatre, a library and a café, and administration for an organisation that promotes dance. The building is entered through a slowly arcing double-skin glass facade that glows faintly from the differently coloured panels of the inner skin in daylight – more brightly at night when light from the inside streams through. The entrance is two-thirds along the face to the south, and once through the screen you are presented with a view of a ramp that rises upwards through ticket control gates towards the studios and the theatre on the left, the library on the right. Another ramp – open access – leads down under the library past a café towards a bookable seminar room, workshops and a car park at the rear. This abuts onto the embanked tributary of the Thames, Deptford Creek. If you take the upper ramp you rise in a fairly informal route – wide at first because here this is the foyer to the black-box theatre around which the ramp snakes, narrower and increasingly close

Herzog & de Meuron, Laban Contemporary Dance Centre, London, UK, 2002. The steeple of a church to the west is the generating point for the radius of the slow arc of the facade.

to the roof plane as it becomes a corridor between studios and rehearsal rooms. Coiling around the theatre, the rehearsal rooms and studios all have an external wall that is double-skin glass, most have mirrored walls with bars, and the doors to the corridor are glazed – affording a vicarious view of classes and rehearsals to those passing (or so it was intended; there are reports of these doors being papered over – perhaps we are not so community minded when we learn, after all!).

Why does this transplant work? The site was an abandoned industrial site once served by lighters up the tidal inlet to the east at its rear. The outer skin of the rear wall of the building is a translucent industrial cladding system, pierced by the workshop roller doors – cost effective and resonating with the prevailing aesthetic of the site's working history. Not much context remained away from the inlet, except the white stone steeple of a church to the west. The architects have taken the steeple as the generating point

for the radius of their slow arc facade; each of the facade's facets reflects the steeple, and as you walk along the pavement you see a cascading series of images of this remnant of the London that once was. The jumping image links dance and civil in what was for a long time 'terrain vague', which as we saw in Chapter Four is a form of spatial ruination that is readily appropriated by people. The Laban Centre design is an affectionate and acute act of appropriation, and it succeeds not only because of the ease of its architectonic arrangements, which have a pedigree that stretches back to the ramps that penetrate Le Corbusier's Mill Owners' Association in Ahmedabad (1954) and the same architect's Carpenter Center for the Visual Arts at Harvard (1965). The success in Deptford lies in the swallowing of the architectonic drama by internalising the ramp, and then deploying screens that talk to their surroundings empathetically. The Laban Dance Centre takes an architectonic tradition and adds to it, it plays with its surroundings in a manner both poetic and narrative, and it speaks very much of its origins and its membership of a body of work originating in the culture of Francophone Switzerland – much less of the earth and the elements, much more of the eye than Zumthor's east Swiss sensibility. Few native London works have dared to be so laconic, and few English works since Tudor times have essayed such informality. The much lesser success of Herzog & de Meuron's Tate Modern, which in the abstract solves a similar problem – an insertion of a new programme into a formerly industrial site – demonstrates, despite the success of the Laban Centre, just how delicate is the business of translating from one mental space to another.

Zaha Hadid's layered mental space

Le Corbusier, Mill Owners' Association, Ahmedabad, India, 1954. The ramp that coils through the building is a canonical precursor for the Laban Centre ramp. Here it culminates in a view across a river.

Le Corbusier, Carpenter Center for the Visual Arts, Harvard University, Cambridge, Massachusetts, USA, 1965. Originally intended as a pedestrian thoroughfare, the ramp here continues through the building as at the Laban Centre and is used for circulation within the building.

Working in thin or tight circumstances suits architects – even though they seldom think so! Prime amongst architects who pursue architecture through a multi-spatial heritage is undoubtedly Zaha Hadid. Kenneth Frampton's early article on her work was entitled 'A Kufic Suprematist: the world culture of Zaha Hadid',[15] but perhaps her ability to operate so convincingly in a variety of spatial milieus arises from her Hobsbawmian enchainment of mental spaces from Baghdad to London via the international lounge that the Architectural Association School (the AA) had become during its heyday under Alvin Boyarsky, rather than from a specific Middle Eastern tradition. Certainly it was at the AA that she discovered that she could find the kernel of a powerful architectural response to a site and a programme within the folds of a spatial imaginary far larger than the site in question itself. Her seminal work, the

The Peak- Confetti; Suprematist Snowstorm by Zaha Hadid Architects, winning competition entry. The project coopted the entire mountain into Hadid-defined tessellated surface.

competition-winning Hong Kong Peak project (1982), coopted the entire mountain into a Hadid-defined tessellated surface into which the programme was slid on small rectangular shelves, as if a bookcase of Barcelona Pavilions had exploded into a compost heap. Her earliest built project, the Vitra Fire Station (1993), which is a breathtaking reconciliation of heap and pavilion, arises from a similar cooption of the wider terrain, and the edit from that of the part to be constructed. What this approach does is very different to what the Barcelona Pavilion does. Certainly Mies's breakthrough is into a flowing space, but that is constrained within actual or implied rectangles of the plan and the curtilage of its surroundings. Hadid's design approach transforms our reading of a terrain far bigger than the project purlieu. In this, as Frampton notes, she shares an expansiveness with Libeskind, but her cooption is spatial rather than notational, a reading-from rather than a reading-into. It is easy to be overwhelmed by the technical virtuosity that her office brings to the realisation of her designs, funded by clients willing to pay for the results, but with the Maggie Centre at Kirkcaldy in Scotland (2006) the exigencies of a very tight budget ensure that Hadid's ideas are to the fore as the concept wraps the tarmac of the existing hospital car park into a folded ribbon on the edge of the cavity of a wooded former quarry, and sets this knot against the

Zaha Hadid, Vitra Fire Station, Weil am Rhein, Germany, 1993. The design arises out of a cooption of the wider terrain, and the edit from that of the part to be constructed.

flank of the hospital's slab of rooms, so as to make the pavilion resonate with Le Corbusier's canonical parti at the Cité de Refuge in Paris (1929–33), with which the slabs are dimly resonant.

The fold has become almost a cliché in design today, but in Hadid's hands it makes compelling sense. Imagine a strip of a material that is black and tarmac-like on the outside, and white and plastered on the inside. Imagine unrolling this from one side of a large tarmac car park, black side down. You keep rolling along the edge of a steep declivity into that abandoned quarry until the programme of a Maggie's Centre – a kitchen for making coffee and snacks, a large table adjacent for round-table discussions, a service area for the kitchen, a library, a quiet zone for spiritual contemplation, a sunny outlook – is accommodated. First you allow space for arrival, signalled by the angle of a ramp from the car park, then you allow for an island in the space held by a concave wall that brackets the kitchen units and cups the big table. You float a library cupboard pivoted on a hinge to act as a valve to regulate the degree to which people can pass behind the island, and you

Zaha Hadid, Maggie's Centre, Kirkcaldy, Fife, UK, 2006. The concept wraps the tarmac of the existing hospital car park into a folded ribbon on the edge of the cavity of a wooded former quarry, and sets this knot against the flank of the hospital's slab of rooms.

pull the shelves of the library around the front of the island, enclosing in its centre the services and offices. Then you allow the ribbon some slack and it falls away from the far side of the island and opens out headroom for a space for solitary reflection. Then you twist and fold the ribbon back on itself, so that it returns to the car-park edge, and you nudge it forward from its base so that in profile it juts forward like a ship's prow. Then glaze both ends of the resulting tube, running the glass inwards from the far end on the south overlooking the quarry to create a long, thin, triangular covered terrace that complements in the plan rectangle the long triangle of space divided by that central island that sits inside the glass wall. You puncture the ribbon with triangular openings that reinforce the triangulated sense of the spaces, and you pull a triangular strip of the ribbon past the rear window wall to mask the service yard at the rear. From the hospital at the rear, the pavilion has the profile of an ark, prows to both ends. From the grounds you discover that the ribbon has been so folded that its angle aligns with the steep flank of the quarry. The inside is white, and suffused with daylight. The outside is dark and gritty. From the grounds it is a jewel that shines in front of the mute slab behind, which it retrospectively activates into grace.

Zaha Hadid, Maggie's Centre, Kirkcaldy, Fife, UK, 2006. The ribbon returns to form a sheltered arrival platform.

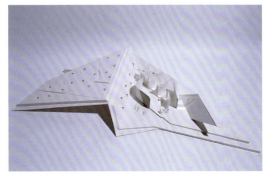

Zaha Hadid, Maggie's Centre, Kirkcaldy, Fife, UK, 2006. A ribbon is folded away from the car park along the side of an old quarry.

This is as simple as one of those pavilions blasted into the compost heap in the Hong Kong Peak project, but here – effected with complex wit – it affords no easy, single-blow-to-the-eye reading. It has become a contemplative object, a puzzle that you seek to hold in your hand, and turn slowly as you unravel its secrets. This wrapping and folding of a material – the substance of which, and the making of which are not disclosed – is a very different approach to the carefully exposed architectonics of Zumthor and Godsell. Hadid's idea is simple enough to dominate our experience, the dexterity of the realisation is wondrous, and the poetic of place is as convincing. Here – as with Herzog & de Meuron's Laban Centre – a 'terrain vague' setting has been ennobled by the creation of a narrative that resonates with the architectural canon, and a place with a powerful poetic has been created by the act of coiling the ribbon along the northern edge of the now-verdant quarry. This is spatial intelligence at work.

Kathryn Findlay's search for resistant mental space

Yet to be invited to do a Maggie's Centre is Scottish architect Kathryn Findlay (1953–), whose Ushida Findlay partnership[16] with Eisaku Ushida (1954–) forged an architectural approach out of two very different mental spaces, uniting a classical Japanese sensibility with its concern for the raw and the undressed with a Scottish narrative imagination in the pursuit of some wonderfully delightful fantasies. Chief amongst these, for its revelation of a Japanese client's mental space, I would put the 'Soft and Hairy' House at Baraki (1992–3) – the title came from the client with the brief – though their most influential joint work is probably Truss Wall House in Tokyo (1990–3), a project which showed that designs as organic as those of Frederick Kiesler (1890–1965), the neo-plastic architect whose 'Endless House' (1950) is emblematic of the approach,[17] could be realised. Ushida Findlay's technical inventiveness also showed that the 'organic' which Hugo Häring (1882–1958), architect of the Cow House at Garkau Estate near Lübeck (1923),[18] nurtured as an alternative to the standardising drive of those concerned to capture

Ushida Findlay, 'Soft and Hairy' House, Baraki, Japan, 1992–3. The name defined the client's brief.

Ushida Findlay, Truss Wall House, Tokyo, Japan, 1990–3. Swimming pool construction techniques are used to create a shell-like house protected from the noise of the high-speed trains across the road.

the traditional industrial means of production, was a possible way to provide customised space for middle-class clients – something that had eluded all those interested in complex spatiality. The innovation in the Truss Wall House is both structural (the architects persuaded a swimming pool manufacturer to adapt his processes to realising the flowing forms of the design in concrete hosed into a structural net) and representational. The drawings for the house use a pointillist method to show only the skin of the internal spaces of the house. Dot by dot, the outer limit of the space of the house is charted and indicated as a transparent veil, enabling you to see the interior as if by x-ray. These hand-drawn studies are a significant moment in architectural representation, focusing as they do on that which the design most concerns – its spatiality. Photographs convey the object, rightfully, on the cover of their monograph: it is exquisite, and appropriately shell-like in its internal arrangements, given that the house is situated adjacent to a railway line along which high-speed trains pass. The drawings however reveal so much more as they convey the space that is occupied within, and show every fissure and blind limb of the spatial design, which is wondrously indeterminate and reverie-inducing. This work heralded the re-emergence of a 'Non-Standard' architectural movement – even though the exhibition of that title at the

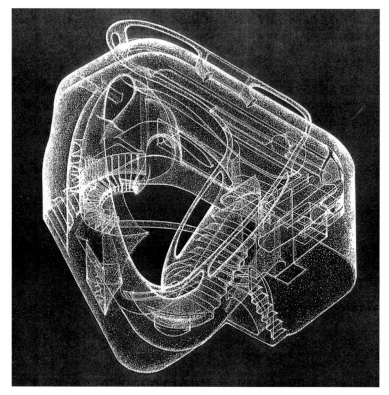

Ushida Findlay, Truss Wall House, Tokyo, Japan, 1990–3. The drawings for the house use a pointillist method to show only the skin of the internal spaces of the building.

Centre Pompidou (2003)[19] bypassed Ushida Findlay's contribution to an understanding that such architecture was now realisable – perhaps because they did it manually rather than digitally. This is unfortunate, because today software that enables you to generate such images is generally in use, but what it fails to provide is the spatial thinking time that building up a drawing dot by dot affords. I doubt there could have been such a fruitful marriage between the two mental spaces brought together in this partnership without this laborious, but mutually engaging drawing process, resisting as it does, at every dot, an easy resolution of where to dot next.

What my pioneers share is an awareness of their mental space, even if only because they manifestly ricochet against its edges. The way in which these architects are manifestly subject to their own mental space – do not discard it but build upon it, and use its energy to drive their architectonic and narrating skills in the forging of poetics that amplify in their projects the best qualities of particular places – has been the theme of this chapter. I conclude by paraphrasing Bachelard's formula: 'each one of us' then should speak of' our spatial intelligence and of our mental space. We should interrogate the role of this capability in the works of those we admire, describing 'the drawings that we have lived'. Thus we will use our mental space consciously, rendering the deep structure of our intuition accessible to ourselves and potentially to all.

References

1 Romaldo Giurgola, from an interview with C Hamann, *Transition*, No 26, 1988, pp 51–6.
2 Richard Rorty, 'Being that can be understood is language' (review of a paper delivered in Heidelberg by Hans-Georg Gadamer on the occasion of his 100th birthday on 11 February 2000), *London Review of Books*, Vol 22, No 6, 16 March 2000, pp 23–5.
3 Philip Fisher, *Wonder, the Rainbow, and the Aesthetics of Rare Experiences*, Harvard University Press (Cambridge), 1988.
4 We should note that – as Ted Krueger, PhD candidate at RMIT has discovered – those working on the neurology of the senses now routinely describe more than 30 different sensate states, and some scientists define more states than this.
5 Álvaro Siza, *Architecture Writings*, Skira (Milan), 1997.
6 Álvaro Siza, *Three Projects: Assemblage 2*, MIT Press (Cambridge, Massachusetts), 1983.
7 Álvaro Siza, *Inside the City*, Whitney Library of Design (New York), 1998, p 60: housing project.
8 Leon van Schaik, *Mastering Architecture*, Wiley-Academy (Chichester), 2005, p 29.
9 David Chipperfield, 'Thermal Baths at Vals by Peter Zumthor', in Mary Walls (ed), *AA Files*, No 32, Architectural Association (London), 1996, pp 72–6.
10 Joe Rollo, 'Klaus Field Chapel, Mechernich, Germany, by Peter Zumthor', *Cement Concrete & Aggregates Australia* (Melbourne), No 07, November 2007, pp 12–29.
11 'Peter Zumthor, Kunsthaus Bregenz', in Christine Spiegel (ed), *Archiv Kunst Architektur Werkdokumente*, Hatje Cantz Verlag (Stuttgart), 1997.
12 Leon van Schaik, *Sean Godsell: Works and Projects*, Electa (Milan), 2004. First published in English in 2005.
13 Martin Filler, 'Broad-minded museum' (review of *The Broad Contemporary Art Museum at the Los Angeles County Museum of Art, 2008*, Los Angeles Museum of Art (Los Angeles), 2008; Renzo Piano, *Renzo Piano Museums* (with an essay by Victoria Newhouse), Monacelli Press (New York), 2008; and 'Collecting Collections: Highlights from the Permanent Collection of the Museum of Contemporary Art, Los Angeles', exhibition at the Museum of Contemporary Art, Los Angeles, 9 February– 19 May 2008), *New York Review of Books*, Vol LV, No 4, 20 March 2008, pp 15–18: states that the museum evokes a fossilised mammoth.
14 His Glenburn House (2007) has been published in *Monument* (Australia), December 2007, *Casabella* (Italy), February 2008 and *Architectural Record* (USA), April 2008. Other projects have been published in *Domus* (Kew House, December 1999).
15 Kenneth Frampton, 'A Kufic Suprematist: the world culture of Zaha Hadid', in Mary Wall (ed), *AA Files*, No 6, London, May 1984, pp 101–5. Ironically Frampton predicts that: 'Libeskind's work is ultimately a speculation about the impossibility of architecture … where for Hadid the modern project is not only incomplete, it has hardly even begun.'
16 'Introduction' in Leon van Schaik (ed), *Ushida Findlay Works*, *2G International Architecture*, No 6, Gustavo Gili (Barcelona), 1998.
17 Yehuda Safran (ed), *Frederick Kiesler, 1890–1965*, *AA Files* (London), No 20, 1990.
18 The design seems to prefigure much that Temple Grandin argues for in Oliver Sacks, *An Anthropologist on Mars*, Pan Macmillan (Sydney) and Picador (London), 1995, pp 241–62.
19 Frédéric Migayrou, 'Orders of the non-standard', and Zeynep Mennan 'Of non-standard forms: a "Gestalt switch"', both in *Non-Standard Architectures*, exh cat, Editions du Centre Pompidou (Paris), December 2003.

6

New futures for architects: new roles for practitioners

> Some have wondered why we should bother to analyse Personal Development in the context of the network society. The reason is that this … can throw some … light on the central issue of the logic of economic networks that [Manuel] Castells raises in *The Information Age*. He asks what the 'ethical foundation of the network enterprise', this 'spirit of informationalism' is and goes on to specify: 'What glues together these networks? Are they purely instrumental, accidental alliances? It may be so for particular networks, but the networking form of organization must have a cultural dimension of its own.'
>
> Pekka Himanen[1]

Peter Lyssiotis, *New futures for architecture (real and virtual) opened up …*, photomontage for *Spatial Intelligence*, 1998 – completed as part of an Australia Council New Media Arts Fellowship at RMIT, Melbourne, Australia.

As we have seen, Henri Lefebvre, our lonely observer, locked away in his study, thinking, found things to tell us about how our spatial experience of the world has been changed by the screens – be they car windscreens, TV screens or computer terminals – through which we look at it. He was working before the age of 'informationalism' that was ushered in by the

World Wide Web around the time of his death. What would he have made of this new world? A world in which letter writing has become a very rare event, in which search engines make finding information something that is more readily done from your desk than through a visit to a library, in which people seek each other out in the virtual space of online 'chatrooms' more readily than they do by going out into the public spaces of their cities, a world in which new democratic engines that gather what we think almost instantaneously are emerging? He might well conclude that our spatial sense is becoming even more compressed.

Architectural reality now: the real environment

We architects must ask ourselves what becomes of architectural reality now? Already, as we have seen, architecture has been so critically undermined by the analytic procedures of the scientific revolution, with its dissections and taxonomic classifications of architecture into bits and parts, that too many of us have come to regard it as a transferable consumable. Time and again the results of such thinking are very disappointing. I examined the case of Rafael Moneo (1937–) in *Mastering Architecture*,[2] somewhat to the chagrin of some of his supporters, but here is what Martin Filler – the architecture critic I currently most admire – has to say, while pondering the effects of the globalisation of architectural practice: 'Some who execute exemplary buildings at home seem unable to excel abroad. The Spanish master Rafael Moneo – architect of the admirable new addition to the Prado and the brilliant Museum of Roman Art of 1980–86 at Mérida in southwest Spain – has had considerably less luck with his lacklustre American museum commissions.'[3] My argument differs from Filler's in that I think that the problem lies in Moneo's failure to acknowledge that his work arises from a specific mental space, and he acts as if he is a master of all mental space, which is in a sense to argue that his mental space trumps the mental space of those outside his home ground. Outside his home ground he therefore lacks the 'resistance' that his internalised mental space affords in the places where his spatial history was forged, and his design intelligence spins where at home it would have traction. Of course nobody's mental space is static, because our brains form a million new connections for every second of our lives.[4] But being unconscious of our spatial history makes it easy to dismiss the new in favour of the old and the entrenched, and thus avoid resistance. Resistance is the term used by artists to describe the qualities of a medium in which they work: a good medium offers resistance to their immediate impulses and, in so doing, causes a dialogue between artist and medium that the best amongst them welcome. We have Vasari's account of Michelangelo's relationship with each block of marble he worked, and anecdotes of how Paul Klee (1879–1940) used broken pens to impede the too-easy fluidity of his natural line. All really great works arise when there is 'resistance'; this is why, for example, Zaha Hadid's Maggie's Centre is so much more evidence of her genius than other better-funded works. In my argument Moneo, when abroad, usually brooks no resistance from local mental space, and a too-easy transplanting of his ideas, so much influenced by the light and air of the Spanish Alto Plano – that high plateau on which Madrid is situated – takes place.

Architectural reality now: the virtual environment

If this is so in the case of traditional architecture, how much more is it the case for architecture that is designed within the virtual environments that computer-aided design provides, with its built-in assumptions about the qualities of light, shade, tone, hue and form? This is what the leading exponents of what used to be called 'digital design' have been confronting as they surf the frontiers of what is becoming possible in architecture in the age of informationalism, and this chapter begins with a view of that experimental situation. The chapter continues by posing a different question. We know that over 80 per cent of the communication between us is passed on through nonverbal clues. Some of these are to do with body language. There is now evidence, for example, that if we like the look of someone our eyebrows flick upwards for a sixteenth of a second – a barely perceptible signal, but one that is invariably read.[5] What is less studied is the information that we pass on by the ways in which we relate to and occupy space. These less than consciously enacted behaviours influence the ways in which we work with each other in real environments in which we fondly believe that we are communicating with words. If we are not even consciously aware of this when we are in the same room together, how much more are we at risk when in environments where we cannot 'see' each other – or the rooms that we are in – as we communicate? There are new roles for architects in learning from this, both for traditional design and in order to become designers of the spatiality of virtual environments.

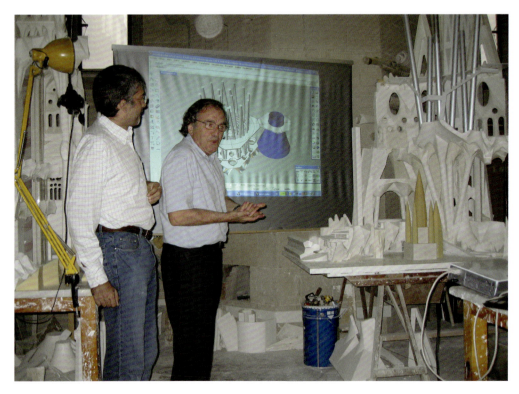

Architectural reality now: the real and virtual environments combine

Mark Burry is one of the acknowledged masters of digital design.[6] Paradoxically perhaps, the engine for this lies in his lifelong fascination with La Sagrada Familia, Gaudí's uncompleted masterpiece in Barcelona (1884–ongoing). Burry, a New Zealander studying at Cambridge and touring in Catalonia, encountered the cathedral as a young man and, asking what he could do to assist in its completion, was given the problem of translating what remained accessible of Gaudí's intentions (the crypt was desecrated in 1936 and his archives and models were destroyed)[7] into instructions that would make them buildable. Driven by this great passion, he pioneered 'parametric' design – not, as one might have thought in the 1970s, a process of designing in NASA systems engineering listings of parameters that must be met by a design, but a joined-up system of notation such that when any one point in the description of a three-dimensional object is moved, the

Design conversation in the Sagrada Família modelmakers' workshop, Barcelona, Spain. In the photograph, engineer Carles Buxadé contributes to early-stage design discussions with the architects, modelmakers and fabricators. The project has always demanded models as the primary vehicle for design decision-making, involving all parties to the design process in a conversation from day one. Today handmade models, rapid prototypes and projected digital 3D models are combined without difficulty or priority.

impact of its movement on all other points is automatically generated. While, as he wryly acknowledges, some still regard the progress as glacially slow, his procedures have enabled construction of this handcrafted building to proceed. The difference between my first sight of it in the early 1990s, when progress was slight enough for many to argue that the building should be abandoned in its 'ruin-in-reverse'[8] state, and the current situation in which there is a wide eagerness to discover what the completed space will be, is vast, and is a tribute to Burry's genius.

Burry was not content to apply his system to this great work from the past, but sought out opportunities to apply it to contemporary works, such as those emerging from Frank Gehry's (1929–) office, as well as to experimental works prefiguring a new future architecture. In the late 1990s Burry and his students convened an early digital design conference ('Morph', 1997), and it was here, listening to Greg Lynn (1964–) – perhaps the doyen of experimenters[9] – that I discovered for myself what has since become known as 'the stopping problem'. This problem is perhaps the most important single piece of evidence for the existence of and the importance of mental space, constructed from our individual histories in space, through the use of our spatial intelligence (linked of course to our other intelligences, be they linguistic, logical mathematical, musical, bodily kinaesthetic, inter and intra personal or naturalist)[10] and the inherited capability that it is based upon. So I will dwell on this problem here.

Mental space revealed in algorithmic design

Lynn described setting up algorithms related to the conditions surrounding a site – passing traffic flows, noise levels, light interference and so on – and then setting the algorithmic model free to run its course within the constraints of the site dimensions and the numerically identifiable aspects of the programme (including an anticipated compromise between functional areas and available budget).[11] Once running, these algorithms could roll on indefinitely, responding to new information as it arrived, the internal and external data at war with each other like two cats in a bag. The problem for the architect was determining when, in the interests of documenting something that could be built, the process should be stopped. Given that there were no glaringly obvious omissions from the model, and that the model had broad acceptance from the stakeholders in the project, it became saliently evident that the architect would choose to stop it when it 'looked good'. What was the basis for that decision if not the innate aesthetic preference of that architect? And, we would ask, what 'mental space' was the architect acting out through that aesthetic? Far from the mathematical process having given rise to an objective design process, digital design took the designers deep into the territory of their unexamined spatial history, a journey for which little in their education had prepared them.

We now encounter a generation of architects who struggle with this problem, a struggle captured in one frame in the *Non-Standard Architectures* exhibition at the Centre Pompidou, Paris in 2003-04.[12] Here Bernard Cache (1958–) grappled with the scalelessness of algorithmic products, slithering in a newly seamless way between landscape, inhabited form, furniture and worn form.[13] Here Kas Oosterhuis (1951–) struggled with new modularities in a search for ways to construct the new forms – Greg Lynn's Korean Church (1999)[14] had demonstrated conclusively that mainstream construction processes could not satisfactorily match design intent, and Tom Kovac's pioneering constructions[15] were huge, handcrafted simulacra of what the current generation of 3D printers now routinely create at small scale, and what product manufacturer Alessi is also pioneering in small-scale industrial processing.[16] On display was all the extraordinary energy that one intuits to have been present at the Crystal Palace during the Great Exhibition of 1851, when – as we have seen – manufacturers went over the top to demonstrate how they could now imitate materials and spatiality at will. Yet it was always possible to detect what had been 'stopped' by KOL/MAC, what by NOX[17] and so on – except when the audience was invited into a virtually realised space, when, almost without exception, we were in a turning 'torus' of space that flowed past uniformly, differentiated only by the specific information the architects chose to project onto the walls, a new design field they called 'hypersurface'; but this essentially graphic design approach eluded spatial definition as much as does Times Square. The battle for this new architecture continues, assiduously documented by *Architectural Design* through the efforts of Neil Spiller and Michael Hensel[18] in particular, but I suspect that it will simply revolve on the spot until its proponents find a way to work overtly with their tacit mental space.

Starting again, conscious of mental space

These 'Blob architecture' conundrums arise from the desire to create architectures that are responsive to their sites and to their users, and they confirm unwittingly the vital importance of mental space. This poses my second – rather more significant, I feel – question, which is the 'starting' problem. We would encounter this problem in the heyday of modernism in architecture, when the three poles of motivation that distinguished Le Corbusier's politics (statist), Walter Gropius (1883–1969), Hannes Meyer (1889–1954) and Ernst May's (1886–1970) strategies (means of production) and Frank Lloyd Wright's inspiration (libertarian democracy) were the alternative starting points for architecture. All these architects, even when it was largely a post-rationalisation (as we may conclude it was in Le Corbusier's case because he suppressed evidence about the particularity of his designs), felt the imperative of working to or from a 'starting' position about society. Indeed architecture is sometimes described as 'the social art' – by those who seek to define what distinguishes it from public art, for instance.

In the 1990s Ernest L Boyer conducted a major investigation into architectural education in the USA, attracted by the learning-by-doing model used in architectural education, and concluded that the social mission of architecture needed refreshing.[19] If we conceive of architecture as the exercise of spatial intelligence as a body of knowledge held in custody and nurtured for society by architects, it has to be more than the production of branded consumable form. It is part of our deep history, capable of benign and malevolent influence on our lives – depending on whether our society is one that uses culture (in particular theatre and sport) to control us through heightened stress and violence against individuals, as seems to be the evidence from the earliest known towns in Catalhöyük in Turkey,[20] or whether it uses culture (in particular music) to promote social cohesion through shared joy, as is the evidence of the earliest discovered towns of South America – possibly the oldest in the world – where there are no defensive walls, the largest structure is an auditorium, burials all show lives lived to their natural term, and the entire site is littered with clay flutes. Can Architecture become whole once again as it was long ago before the scientific revolution, when it had not been cut up into stylistic components or separated from the mental space that it served? Perhaps it can. Just as 'standard' architecture can emphatically engage us in specific places when it is conducted in a dialogue between the mental space of the architect(s) and that of the clients, users and citizens of a place, non-standard architecture offers pathways towards much more specifically tailored space design, promising – if we understand the process – a new customisation to the cultures of specific places. It also offers ways of designing a spatialised virtual environment in which our Internet lives can be much more richly lived out: a new realm for architecture.

Philosopher of science W Zimmerli argues that members of a profession around the world have – due to their acculturation to a common body of knowledge – more in common with each other than with members of their own families who are in different professions.²¹ This is a trap for us, whatever profession we inhabit, but it is particularly devastating for architects whose business is – I argue – our spatial intelligence, and our professional focus on 'master-building' has led architects to believe that our mental space is uninflected by our experience and by the places where we live.²² The room (be it cave, tent or hutment, temple or cathedral, library or office) has played a very substantial role in our proceedings, colouring them. The room is an instrument, used unconsciously, just as King's College Cambridge has become an instrument for a choir of boys' voices, tuned by them, tuning them in turn; integrating the verbal and the nonverbal spatial might advance the quest in ways that have yet to be explored. Be this as it may, Internet-accessible environments currently exclude this major area of communication – one that Australian novelist Frank Moorhouse (1938–) makes a major player in his novels about the League of Nations, in which his lead character demonstrates an acute knowledge of how the layout of a room for a meeting determines in large part the outcome of the meeting.²³ What is 'the room' in the virtual environments that occupy so much of our time today? Is the virtual information environment tuning us? Or are we tuning it? Fortunes turn on this question, as different players seek to provide the 'rooms' in which we engage with each other in virtual space.

Designing with spatial intelligence in virtual space

Asymptote's Virtual New York Stock Exchange (2000) pioneered the use of architectural thinking in virtual space by building a virtual replica of the Stock Exchange that could run in real-time parallel to the actual Stock Exchange, but allowing greater overview, and that could be run in 'action replay' mode when specific trading events merited closer examination. In this it began to design interactive virtual information environments that more and more determine how we live. That exchanges should be early adopters of the technologies that enable informationalism is not perhaps surprising. What Pekka Himanen points to, however, is a background story to the Internet that argues that it is returning us to the possibility of organically multidisciplinary learning communities last seen in the small university towns of Europe in the 17th century before the Humboldt reforms that created the modern specialised and hierarchical institutions with which we are so familiar. This return is only possible, argues Himanen, in open-source environments where people put their inventions out free of charge in the expectation that others will join them in taking the ideas as far as they can be taken in the spirit of what Stanford intellectual property lawyer Lawrence Lessig describes as a 'creative commons' – a concept for which he has drafted contracts that facilitate sharing and define monetary benefits where arising from such cooperation.[24] An example of the possibilities is Wikipedia, which invites different levels of participation, from browsing, to editing, to boundary riding in defence of the knowledge captured in this unprecedented process of pooling ephemerally vast amounts of private scholarship.[25]

What is ironic about Himanen's enthusiastic account of the ways in which we can return to organic learning and escape the artificial hierarchies of curricula, the straitjackets of credit point systems and all of the panoply of central control that have normalised learning into an unwieldy bureaucratic process, is that it evokes the small university town without considering how the physical character of these towns – their architecture – contributed to the quality of the propinquity that fuelled the collegiality of the learning. Pioneer ethicist Immanuel Kant (1724–1804) attended a university with 300 members in all – around the number of people empirical evidence suggests is at the upper limit of the contacts that we can keep active through time. Forgetting that universities in that heyday had a physical aspect is a bit like forgetting that banking – or at least its British manifestation – began in encounters between traders and lenders in coffee houses, which amnesia would make a puzzle of the way that finance still clusters into tightly defined physical locations. The omission raises the question of what is missing in the new learning networks if they are operating without architecture, and whether architects can provide that quality of the real in some way in the virtual environment.

Kovac's LAB 3000 Digital Design Biennale (2003)[26] was a physical manifestation of an architecturally organised virtual environment, showcasing the Virtual Concourse that he has been developing as an online learning environment, configured to accept a range of visits from casual browsing to progressively more committed forms of membership supported with increasing levels of service, and is imbued with spatial qualities that can be read architecturally. The same architect's design for a Virtual Australian Pavilion at the Venice Biennale (2004),[27] realised with the assistance of John Gollings, pioneered this thinking in architecture (it housed a virtual exhibition of 'Design City Melbourne' in 2006) and had the potential to be built. What drives Kovac is the potential for people to create spatial environments

Tom Kovac, Virtual Australian Pavilion, Venice Biennale, Italy, 2004. The pavilion housed a virtual exhibition of the 'Design City Melbourne' for 2006.

through their actions in garnering and evaluating information in the virtual realm. He and his colleagues – some five generations of students, Sean Kelly, Alvin Low and I – have explored the ways in which 'blobs' can be derived algorithmically from the interactions between people in a learning environment, and how a connoisseurship of the 'blobs' can help people in those interactions, assisting them in identifying positive learning behaviours and avoiding those that lead to dead ends.

Much of Kovac's motivation lies in capturing in a virtual architecture the full excitement of those moments of intensity in interactions in real situations – like gallery openings and conference intermissions – and replicating them in their full emotional and sensate form in a virtual space. One device used in this pursuit is the recording of people's tagging of information – a well-established process in visual fields which utilises clouds of keywords that swell and shrink depending on the number of 'hits' they get from habitués of the field. Kovac is intent on a virtual world in which the boundaries that a group construct for themselves in the pursuit of friendship and learning – both information-intensive activities – are defined in a similar tagging action. In a new sense this is architecture defined by users within ground rules laid out by the architect. This is architecture working with the mathematics of networking,[28] a by-product of informationalism, a science driven by the ways in which we are 'connected as never before' through websites that specialise in our interests whatever they may be;[29] shaped by the new ways in which we seek out shortcuts to people and ideas through a new mathematical understanding of how massive, swarming networks operate;[30] influenced as we better understand the number of people we can realistically expect to relate to (critical understandings for those aiming to design learning environments);[31] and organised through new understandings of networking that are changing even our understandings of how to organise airports, shifting from 'hub and spoke' systems to 'point to point' systems[32] as our knowledge about the power of redundancy in non-hierarchical networks grows.[33]

Kovac dreams of designing as Chris Anderson, editor of the IT journal *Wired*, wrote his book *The Long Tail*, posting every chapter on the web (starting in 2004) and seeking feedback from all comers, getting it certainly from his peers but also from his many thousands of readers, and producing a book that was in a sense 'co-authored' around an intellectual framework created

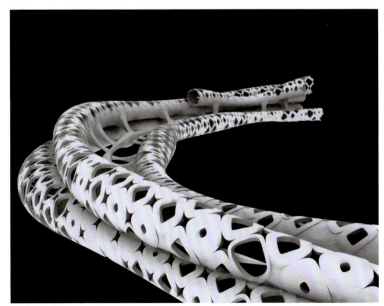

Tom Kovac and students, RMIT Melbourne. The latest iteration Visualising the Virtual Concourse, a research studio led by Tom Kovac based on an operating system devised by Sean Kelly as exhibited at the Seville Architecture Biennale (2008). Each strand documents the learning experience of an individual, the cells on the wall of the stands thicken when the operating system indicates concentrated activity. Synapses between the strands are formed where the operating system indicates a conversation has taken place.

by Anderson as lead-author.[34] Kovac has designed as lead designer in a collective with like-minded students for many years, and appreciates the power that comes from such collaborations, even though they are always project specific, and contingent on the collaborators' own career trajectories. Everyone gives everyone else a hand up, so to speak. What Kovac now dreams of is evolving architectures in real and virtual environments, using the kinds of refining conversations that Anderson used so effectively in his book – which arrived on the shelves in 2006 already reviewed.

Designing with shared mental space: real and virtual environments

What is becoming clearer in this pursuit is that such environments cluster according to the degree to which the mental space of users is shared. The phenomenon in Internet dating in which people meet someone with whom they have been in long discussion and find them off-puttingly unlike what has been imagined is not – as Paul Theroux so tellingly reveals in his story about a woman (staying in the hotel he was managing) who was distraught from meeting a man she described as fat and gross, and who Theroux later discovered to be handsome and athletic – simply about deception: it is about the way each of us constructs our mental space.[35] We do not see things 'as they are' – they are as we see them. These misunderstandings arise because in emails we are using 20 per cent of our communication ability, relying on words alone, when whole environments are what we have evolved to appreciate. When we are deprived of the clues that architectural reality gives, our spatial intelligence is in free fall, and we are, when we re-engage (as was the protagonist in Theroux's story) subject to such spatial stress that only our surface mind can engage. Consider now the kinds of space that we are invited to inhabit through the Internet. Mostly we confront a world of click-through pages that animate space at best like a flicker book. Usually when we are invited into a three-dimensional experience, we are afloat in an endless torus of sameness punctuated with cascading imagery, sound and information factual and numerical. Even in the most sophisticated of 'game-engine' space we float without resistance. No wonder our decision-making is often so impoverished when we leave the well-understood rituals of the auction and the search, and enter realms requiring our emotional intelligence.

Following his daughters growing up in Tokyo, Akira Suzuki documented a generation that negotiated their way through their electronically enabled city, building networks by text messaging and swarming to where the action was in ways incomprehensible to their elders.[36] Suzuki sees <u>an interaction between the real and the virtual in which the real is animated by what the virtual allows.</u> This is a potent partnership, and it can be experienced in many degrees in widely different situations. Visiting Venice (a city that has this at least in common with Tokyo – no easy way of finding a location relative to a street map) and planning to meet collaborators from elsewhere used to require much static planning and watch synchronisation, with injunctions to meet at a well-known landmark at a given time. Today friends swarm towards each other, using text messaging, with no prior planning needed. At RMIT, one annual graduation ceremony is held in a large stadium. Several thousand students graduate simultaneously from a dozen stations around the rim of the playing field, observed from the raked seats by three or four friends and relatives each. This is in an architectural sense an immense event, with pipe bands, oversize video screens around the stadium, and an individual screen at each graduation station. It may seem, at first glance, impersonal. But if you observe what is happening, the entire event is cross-laced with text messaging, including the transmission of photographs, video-clips and voice mail. There is an intimacy in the immensity created by the mobile phone network.

There are real spaces – and we all know this – that support us, buoy us up in our endeavours, but we forget to demand them! I have in mind a room in a turret of the Victoria Railways Administration Building in Melbourne, a domed space with views down Flinders Lane for the full length of the central grid of the city. In the mountains of my youth there was a deep room in the centre of our cottage that opened without windows or doors onto a raised green lawn. We children would fight to sleep outside here; once I awoke to find a small snowdrift on my outer blanket. Rising early we would go out onto the lawn to catch the first rays of the morning sun. Breakfast was out on the lawn. Trips up the river valley would follow, and late lunch was served in the deep shade of the room when we returned seeking refuge from the high midday sun that shone into every crevice of the valley. After lunch the readers amongst us would retreat to the beds that lined its sides, edging slowly towards chairs at the openings, the folds of the mountains always distantly visible, and emerge onto the lawn as the shadows crept across the mountain flank and the grass fell into shade. After dark we would go deep inside the cottage to a room with a large fireplace and very small windows. Reading and reverie followed this same pattern. Even today, for me, reading a book seems to flow through the same diurnal pattern. This is a room that entices thought upwards and outwards. In Stockholm there is a lecture theatre at the

College of Surgeons that has all it takes to create fluid and open dialogue. The room is square in plan, with one end holding the stage in what could be a stasis-inducing, full-frontal broadside between presenters and audience. But the room is made dynamic by two vaulted wings that run off beyond the sides of the square, creating a spatial ambiguity and tension well able to stand for what is not, perforce, said.

All of this is so obvious when we are led to confront it, and yet we do not expect it or have it as one of our primary aims when we design space for our societies. It is difficult enough to surface this in the architecture of the physical world; how then do we achieve this in the space of the Internet? We cannot go back to that time when there was a unity of space, place and culture, even if the most intense of architects, like Zumthor, can in small specific moments achieve an alchemy that seems to unite them again. This is not the general condition because we are, as our lonely observer noted, evolving. As USA psychologist Clare W Graves (1914–86) noted in a seminal statement: 'Briefly what I am proposing is that the psychology of the mature human being is an unfolding, emergent, oscillating, spiraling process marked by progressive subordination of older, lower-order behaviour systems to newer, higher-order systems as man's existential problems change.'[37] We are designed to learn and to grow in awareness, even if genetically predisposed to be polarised between those who prefer order to experiment, who are introverted rather than extroverted, who are conscientious rather than adventurous.[38] Graves's insight has given rise to new ways of integrating the different kinds of awarenesses that have evolved and that are contained within us in layers, like Gadamer's onion.

Architecture's move into the digital and the virtual has set it on a path with the potential to create a new understanding of how all the possible states of architecture nest,[39] potentially integrating the 'primitive' as in survival shelters (still engaging the imaginations of architects like Sean Godsell), through the evocation of magic and myth (evident in the architecture of pavilions and gardens), the service to power and sexual domination (as in the designs for Prada stores), the instrument of order (as in airports and, sadly, most hospitals) and (as in Gottfried Semper's neoclassical building for ETH Zurich)[40] mimicking taxonomic knowledge structures, through to ecological awareness (as in the latest works of Morphosis in Los Angeles and San Francisco) and through to the service of the creative commons (as in the emerging architectures of the virtual world).

In that virtual realm, still a 'thin' environment, tendencies are starkly visible to us when we don the spectacles of Graves and Gadamer. In the experiments of this world some things are now clear. The 'stopping' problem reveals that we are, as Iannis Xenakis (1922–2001) so wonderfully put it in an interview in his later years, 'prisoners of ourselves'.[41] To be so without being conscious of the fact is to put architecture in double jeopardy, trapped in its own global guild history and unaware of our own histories in space. The 'starting' problem is a crucial issue for every designer. It separates the stylists and brand imitators from those who seek to help society in its varied quests for betterment. In the networks of the information society the architectural dimension of their newly emerging culture – that necessary glue that Castells identified – is only just beginning to be considered and invented. Here lies an enormous opportunity for the exercise of spatial intelligence, by a freshly constituted profession that has our spatial capability and the mental space we construct with it as its core body of knowledge. In the next chapter I consider what this means for the profession of architecture.

References

1 Pekka Himanen, *The Hacker Ethic and the Spirit of the Information Age*, Secker & Warburg (London), 2001, p 122. Manuel Castells, born in Spain in 1942, is Professor of Sociology and Planning, and Chair of the Center for Western European Studies at the University of California, Berkeley. His book *The Informational City* was published by Blackwell (Oxford) in 1989. He was appointed in 1995–6 to the European Commission's High Level Expert Group on the Information Society.
2 Leon van Schaik, *Mastering Architecture: Becoming a Creative Innovator in Practice*, Wiley-Academy (Chichester), 2005, pp 178–81: 'Failing to elevate innovations into a metropolitan discourse'.
3 Martin Filler, 'Miracle on the Bowery' (article on SANAA's (Sejima and Nishizawa and Associates) New Museum of Contemporary Art, Manhattan Lower East Side), *New York Review of Books*, Vol LV, No 1, 17 January 2008, pp 20–2.
4 Helen Phillips, 'How life shapes brainscape' (report on research by neuroscientist Colin Blakemore, University of Oxford and Chief Executive of the UK Medical Research Council and others), *New Scientist*, Vol 188, No 2527, 26 November 2005, pp 12–13: 'from meditation to diet, life experiences profoundly change the structure and connectivity of the brain'.
5 Rowan Hooper, 'A little flirting goes a long way', *New Scientist*, Vol 195, No 2622, 22 September 2007, p 10.
6 Professor Mark Burry holds an Innovation Chair at RMIT, where he was founding director of the Spatial Information Architecture Laboratory (SIAL) and is director of the Design Research Institute. He holds an Australian Research Council Federation Fellowship in design, the only one awarded in that field to date.
7 Gijs van Hensbergen, *Gaudi*, HarperCollins, St Ives, 2001
8 Robert Smithson, 'A tour of the monuments of Passaic, New Jersey', in Nancy Holt (ed), *The Writings of Robert Smithson*, New York University Press (New York), 1979, p 54; first published as 'The monuments of Passaic', *Artforum*, December 1967. Smithson coined this wonderful description of the construction process.
9 Greg Lynn, *Folds, Bodies and Blobs: Collected Essays* (edited

by Michele Lachowsky and Joel Benzakin), La Lettre Volée (Brussels), 1998.
10 Howard Gardner, *Intelligence Reframed. Multiple Intelligences for the 21st Century*, Basic Books (New York), 1999.
11 Lynn, *Folds, Bodies and Blobs*, op cit.
12 Frédéric Migayrou, 'Orders of the non-standard', and Zeynep Mennan 'Of non-standard forms: a "Gestalt switch"', both in *Non-Standard Architectures*, exh cat, Editions du Centre Pompidou (Paris), December 2003.
13 Bernard Cache, *The Earth Moves: The Furnishing of Territories* (edited by Michael Speaks, translated by Anne Boyman), MIT Press (Cambridge, Massachusetts), 1995.
14 'Korean Presbyterian Church of New York, Queens, New York City: Douglas Garofalo, Greg Lynn, Michael McInturf', in Michael K Hays (ed), *Assemblage*, No 38, MIT Press (Cambridge, Massachusetts), April 1999, pp 6–21.
15 Leon van Schaik (ed), 'Introduction', in *Tom Kovac*, Architectural Monographs No 50, Academy Editions (London), 1998, pp 6–13; pp24–8, 'Neither Carved nor Moulded: An Architecture of the Third Term'.
16 Alessandro Mendini (ed), *Tea and Coffee Towers* (featuring Tom Kovac and others), Electa (Milan), 2003, pp 110–17.
17 Lars Spuybroek, *NOX: Machining Architecture*, Thames and Hudson (London), 2004.
18 Michael Hensel, Michael Weinstock and Achim Menges (eds), *Techniques and Technologies in Morphogenetic Design*, Architectural Design, Wiley-Academy (Chichester), May 2006.
19 Ernest L Boyer and Lee D Mitgang, *Building Community: A New Future for Architecture Education and Practice*, Special Report, The Carnegie Foundation for the Advancement of Teaching (Princeton, New Jersey), June 1996.
20 Steven Mithen, 'When we were nicer' (review of Daniel Lord Smail, *On Deep History and the Brain*, University of California (Berkeley), 2007), *London Review of Books*, Vol 30, No 2, 24 January 2008, pp 24–5.
21 W Zimmerli, *The Principles of a Non-Principle Orientated Ethics*, paper delivered at RMIT University (Melbourne), 1989.
22 Leon van Schaik, 'Problems of … individual emergence', 'Problems of … the room', conference proceedings, in Prof Dr G de Zeeuw, Martha Vahl and Ed Mennuti (eds), 'Problems of Emergence', Systemica, Lincoln Research Centre (Lincoln) 2007 pp 439–46.
23 Frank Moorhouse, *Grand Days*, Picador (Sydney), 1993 and Frank Moorhouse, *Dark Palace*, Random House (Sydney), 2000.
24 Lawrence Lessig is Professor of Law at Stanford Law School, and founder of the School's Center for Internet and Society. He is CEO of the Creative Commons project. http://lessig.org/info/
25 Nicholson Baker, 'The charms of Wikipedia', (review of John Broughton, *Wikipedia: The Missing Manual*, Pogue Press (Farnham), 2008), *New York Review of Books*, Vol LV, No 4, 20 March 2008, pp 6–10.
26 Leon van Schaik, *Mastering Architecture*, op cit, pp 228–9.
27 Ibid, p 213.
28 NETWORK ANALYSIS: It is a commonplace that in the knowledge economy connections between people add value to information, that clusters of people create critical mass for activity and that the quality of an organisation is measured by the quality of its network.
What is emerging in the literature is a domain of network analysis that tests the quality of connections, clusters and networks.
'Five years ago … Albert-Lazlo Barabasi, a professor of physics at the University of Notre Dame in Indiana … sent a software robot crawling around the web to analyse the links between websites. [He] expected the robot to reveal that websites are connected to each other at random. According to a branch of mathematics called graph theory, most websites would have roughly the same number of links. So [he] was shocked to find that lots of sites connect to just a few others, but a very small number of websites have huge numbers of links.' (*New Scientist*, No 2408, 16 August 2003 pp 32–3).
Studying a wide array of networks has shown that 'a few highly connected "nodes" in the network, be it of people, viruses or other biological organisms – are crucial to its operation. Without these hubs, the structure of the network falls apart.'
This has been validated in history by a study of the Inquisition, by Andrew Roach, a medieval historian at the university of Glasgow; and Paul Ormerod, an economist at Volterra Consulting in London, is working on the science of networks, such as the Internet and groups of friends. It was not until the Inquisition focused on a few hubs that they were able to suppress heresticum. Conversely, to grow a network, you may well need to build hubs.
'David Kempe and his colleagues at Cornell University have found a way to identify who you should talk to if you want your ideas to spread to as many people as possible' (*New Scientist*, No 2421, 15 November 2003, p 14). Studying a community of 10,750 article physicists, they found that 'only certain people are able to influence a large proportion of the network'.

The study used an algorithm, applied thousands of times. A physicist with 20 links might only influence 20 people, while another with two links might influence thousands because of the quality of those links. The work was commended by sociologist at Columbia University, Duncan Watts, author of *Six Degrees: The Science of a Connected Age* (2003).

Knowing your position in such networks is a crucial part of self-curation. 'People tend to build sub-groups of around 150 people … studies have shown that most people can identify a group of about three to seven very close friends to whom they turn in times of distress, a group of about 15 who provide sympathy and support, and a wider community of about 35 who represent their personal community' (*New Scientist*, No 2479/80, 20/27 December 2004, p 61).

Using this network effectively is more complex than it might seem. Using random links can be much quicker than going to the obvious sources of connectivity, because they are often obvious to many people, and become jammed. Random links can reduce the number of steps needed to cross a network governed by 'nearest neighbour' steps by a factor of 100,000 (*New Scientist*, No 2430, 17 January 2004, pp 32–5).

Airlines are evaluating the substitution of hub and spoke networks with point-to-point networks, which it seems are more efficient for just the same reason (*New Scientist*, No 2425, 13 December 2003, p 32).

The implications for the protocols governing access to a network and behaviour in a network are enormous. In evaluating an existing network and its performance, or working out how to make best use of networks, or build an effective network, certain principles seem to apply:
- Know your network of contacts, and constantly refresh it.
- Understand where the nodes of highest connectivity are, BUT
- Be aware that some relatively unconnected nodes can have enormous influence. SO
- Distinguish between influence and connectivity AND
- Systematically engage in random connections within your network, BUT
- Not at random across networks – that is SPAM.
- Work with those who are establishing algorithms to understand your domain.

29 'Connected like never before', *New Scientist*, Vol 191, No 2569, 16 September 2006, pp 44–56.
30 Mark Buchanan, 'Know thy neighbour', *New Scientist*, Vol 181, No 2430, 17 January 2004, pp 32–5: 'whether you are an actor seeking Hollywood contacts, or an email whizzing across the internet, short cuts are hard to find. But the theory that brought you six degrees of separation is at last helping to locate those mystery links'.
31 Meredith F Small, 'The magic number: The circle of friends on your Christmas card list speaks volumes about our hunter-gatherer past', *New Scientist*, Vol 180, No 2426/7/8 (combined issues), 20 December 2003/27 December 2003/3 January 2004, pp 60–1. Meredith F Small is a writer and professor of anthropology at Cornell University, Ithaca, New York.
32 Paul Marks, 'The shape of wings to come', *New Scientist*, Vol 180, No 2425, 13 December 2003, p 32.
33 Michael Brooks, 'Dangerous liaisons', *New Scientist*, Vol 180, No 2408, 16 August 2003, pp 32–3: 'It is all about the network connections, not the nodes.'
34 Chris Anderson, *The Long Tail: The New Economics of Culture and Commerce – How Endless Choice is Creating Unlimited Demand*, Random House (London), 2006, pp 75–6: 'each year 200,000 books are published in English. Fewer than 20,000 will make it into the average book superstore. In 2004 950,000 books out of the 1.2 million tracked by Nielsen Bookscan sold fewer than ninety-nine copies. Another 200,000 sold fewer than 1,000 copies. Only 25,000 sold more than 5,000 copies. The average book in America (USA) sells about 500 copies. In other words 98% of books are non commercial' – but, he argues, still valuable over time, thanks to the arrival of the search engine!
35 Paul Theroux, *Hotel Honolulu*, Hamish Hamilton (London), 2001, pp 255–60 (www.aloha.net).
36 Akira Suzuki, *Do Android Crows Fly Over the Skies of an Electronic Tokyo?*, Architectural Association (London), 2001.
37 Don Edward Beck and Christopher C Cowan, *Spiral Dynamics: Mastering Values, Leadership, and Change – Exploring the New Science of Memetics*, Blackwell Business (Cambridge), 1996, p 28.
38 Jim Giles, 'Born that way: your political leanings are imprinted in your genes', *New Scientist*, Vol 197, No. 2641, 2 February 2008, pp 28–31.
39 Leon van Schaik, 'Movimento moderno de segundo orden en arquitectura', Ignasi de Solà-Morales, Xavier Costa, Suzanne Strum (eds), Metropolis, Gustavo Gili (Barcelona), 2005, pp 64–78.
40 Harry Francis Mallgrave, *Gottfried Semper: Architect of the Nineteenth Century*, Yale University Press (New Haven, Connecticut and London), 1996.
41 Bálint András Varga, *Conversations with Iannis Xenakis*, Faber & Faber (London), 1996, p 71.

7

New professionalism – new practice manifesto

Where is this rebel avant-garde today, if indeed it exists anywhere, in a liberal Western context marked by a progressive falling off of strong ideological positions in architectural practice? Is it possible for an activity that intrinsically involves a degree of complicity with financial and political powers to have a critical attitude that amounts to more than showy rhetoric?

We can distinguish three attitudes: … those who have thrown themselves into a pragmatic maelstrom strong in official professional institutions … promoting business administration that responds to … pressures formal and bureaucratic … ; fundamentalists of a series of transcendental values and immutable essences that have never existed … (running) schools of architecture … as museums where mistakes are forbidden … ; and practices that venture to construct working and research contexts … on their particular interests … .

Peter Lyssiotis, *The dawn of a new professionalism*, photomontage for *Spatial Intelligence*, 1998 – completed as part of an Australia Council New Media Arts Fellowship at RMIT, Melbourne, Australia.

Quaderns Manifesto[1]

Professions are the products of social contracts between specialists and society.[2] In this chapter I consider the implications for architects of establishing a contract that is based on spatial intelligence being the body of knowledge that architecture arises from and nurtures. These contracts provide professionals with sufficient autonomy for them to offer advice that may not be what their clients want to hear; like judges, they also need to be removed from the temptation to offer advice that is in their own financial interest. Professionals, we believe, should not be compelled by financial considerations to provide what a client wants; they should have the autonomy to be able to advise their clients on what is good for them. We feel uneasy, for example, when doctors prescribe on the basis of too close a relationship to a drug company. Architect Cedric Price (1934–2003) was supremely professional, calculating (for example – there were many such instances in his practice) that a client wanting to build care centres for the elderly would be better off paying to send the aged they had to care for on ocean cruises every winter.[3] Much that we need to think through in this chapter lies in the nature of the contract that sets up a profession, because currently that contract between architects and society is a ligament that has been stretched almost to breaking point by policies stemming from the ideology of the market promoted by the Chicago school of economics and embraced wholeheartedly in the Anglophone world by President Ronald Reagan and Prime Minister Margaret Thatcher. The latter espoused the doctrine so enthusiastically that she argued that there was no such thing as 'society', and as she legislated policy without 'society' in mind, one party to the professional contract was progressively removed. Deregulation was introduced (legislation drafted by lawyers – the only profession to escape its rigours!) and the effects of this were (or so it seemed at the time) to remove the last vestiges of autonomy from the practice of architecture, and to fatally diminish the role of the architect in society. In fact, despite widespread feelings that the game was lost, there are more architects per head of population than ever before – at least in the USA, even though they tend in the main to be 'embedded' (as the current jargon has it) in the corporations that deliver housing, manufacturing and commercial facilities, and work without having an outward face as architects at all.[4] The problem is thus not about the disappearance of the species, but about the quality of the advice that can be given, since – lacking 'autonomy' and working as employees in non-architectural companies – these architects do not operate as 'professionals'. Let us see why this is the case.

Rebuilding architecture as a profession

The ability to establish at least a degree of autonomy underpins the ability to give professional advice. Architecture has sought to maintain that autonomy unsuccessfully because it has failed to articulate spatial intelligence as the area of human capability that it holds in custody for society at large. That professional autonomy – a condition which we need to understand, because there are powerful arguments[5] to suggest that without it there can be no such thing as a profession – persisted in other countries, and was still in evidence in Catalonia in the 1980s and 1990s during the emergence of Barcelona as a 'Design City'. Here the contract was well crafted, balancing carefully the privileges and the duties. We will examine this a little later. There has been general dismay in the profession at the waning of the autonomy that architects enjoyed in the post-Second World War reconstruction efforts in Europe (thanks, it must be said, to Le Corbusier's statist push at the Congrès International d'Architecture Moderne (CIAM)[6] and in the re-tooling of the military industrial complex to domestic ends in the USA (an outcome foreshadowed by the Bauhaus's representation in CIAM by Ernst May and Hannes Meyer) and, consequent on that waning, the ebbing of the influence of the professions (though, as we shall see, there is a possible return in the spirit of Frank Lloyd Wright's Usonian democratic vision). Some thinkers herald a final collapse of the regulatory powers of the 'guilds' that gave rise to the professions almost 1,000 years ago as a terminal disaster for professional practice.[7] Others, as we shall see, disagree,[8] arguing that practices run through their own informal competitive behaviours (much is made of the fact that Switzerland has no professional association of architects and yet has a very high general standard of service to the community); and, as I have indicated in the previous chapter through the work of philosopher of technology Pekka Himanen in 2001,[9] some argue that the age of informationalism – as Castells wryly insists on naming it, forcing us to understand that we embrace the information age from the position of assuming that information per se is good for us – gives rise to the conditions which allow for a reconstituting of professionalism in new, much more democratic and inclusive ways, without in any way compromising, but rather enhancing, the contribution that a gifted specialist can make. And indeed our societies have always relied on the contributions of such gifts. What will emerge in this chapter is that there are new opportunities for crafting autonomy, and they arise from the new appreciation of the spatial intelligence and the mental space knowledge base of architecture that this book calls for; from an embracing of the ethics that support increasingly open practice; and from the new information environment that is enabling us to communicate more interactively and inclusively as never before.

Lets us begin with the notion of what it is to be a professional. A former Governor of Victoria, Davis McCaughey, argues[10] that a professional contract with society depends on having custody (on behalf of society) of a body of knowledge that it is that profession's duty firstly to maintain and advance, and stemming from this a profession has the duty to act upon that knowledge with the intention of helping society. This is a 'Knowing, Doing, Helping' triad. A group of scholars is not a profession if it confines its activity to scholarship; and a group of practitioners is only a profession if the practitioners have sufficient autonomy from financial need to provide dispassionate and independent advice. In the past, regulation has been the mechanism whereby autonomy was assured for architects, ensuring such autonomy widely (as in Belgium) by requiring that all building projects were controlled by architects; more usually in the Anglophone world regulation defined only who might use the title 'architect' (still very common) or (now rare) governed fees to ensure that competition was based on the quality of service offered rather than on price. With deregulation that autonomy was undeniably diminished, to the point that in Britain in 1999 the Government instituted the Commission for Architecture and the Built Environment (CABE) to redress the collapse in quality that had flowed from deregulation. CABE has with considerable success rebuilt structures of professional autonomy, such as exercising its power to call significant projects in for peer review. In the Catalonian system, fee regulation brought specific advantages to clients – who were in a sense captive to the system as all buildings had to be designed by architects. But as well as ensuring the autonomy of the architects and thus the independence of their advice, the system delivered a guaranteed level of service to every client. Fees at a fixed scale were paid up front by the client into a trust account held by a bank run by the College of Architects; the fees were disbursed to the architect on the completion of the stages of the works, on certification by the College, and all the stages of work were subject to peer review, thus ensuring high standards of service. This persisted until recently, perhaps because it was so much part of the 'mental space' of a largely homogenous region. This is a kind of contract that became unthinkable in the Anglophone world, subject as it was to an extreme form of market ideology, but that is not the only problem for architects as a profession.

The unique knowledge base of architecture

As I have argued in previous chapters, architecture was – in fits of engineer envy – professionalised not around our spatial intelligence but around the wrong body of knowledge: one unrelated specifically to any of the basic human intelligences, but rather related to a broad amalgam of capabilities that can be seen to underpin aspects of construction engineering, building and technical drafting. The crucial key to being a profession – custody of a body of knowledge – was thus never secured for architecture. The way is now open to redress this inherent error by embracing the knowledge that flows from our spatial intelligence, one of the seven basic inherited capabilities of humans, as the domain over which architects – thanks to their ability to think spatially – have a unique hold, and for architects to reawaken society to the benefits that are to be had from an environment customised to its various mental spaces. Some canny architects have appreciated this and benefited from it solo. In the 1960s I encountered Johannesburg-based architect George Rhodes-Harrison, who had a practice that specialised in milling installations. Part of his vision was traditional – he was always looking for new forms for silos, for example. His milling equipment tender analyses, however, were extraordinary, because he insisted on constructing a three-dimensional model of what each tenderer listed as being supplied. In this way duplications and omissions became evident, and on at least one occasion a cartel was exposed. This experience had a profound impact on me, but Rhodes-Harrison as far as I am aware kept this approach to himself – like a trade secret. It certainly gave him an edge in that market.

New opportunity for inclusivity in professionalism

The case for medicine being a profession based on a specific body of knowledge is readily made even in Anglophone countries; we live – and have lived for many centuries – in some awe of the mechanisms of our health and rely on the specialists to advise us, medicate us, heal us. We place our confidence in the profession even though there is much evidence to show that the 80/20 rule applies here – in that, as one London practice found by analysing its records, 20 per cent of patients are definitely helped, 20 per cent may well have been hindered, and 60 per cent benefited at best from a placebo effect. Complementary medicine has become increasingly prominent, as have traditions from other than Western cultures – China in particular. Medicine has become steadily more inclusive thanks to the interplay between epidemiology and practice-based research. In recent years that inclusivity has taken off, thanks to the self-regulatory effects of web-based search engines, examples of which are constructions of communities of interest around particular symptoms; and those practitioners open to interactivity with their patients have benefited from a vastly more informed clientele. Each of us has a story to tell in this regard. My mother turned 80 only to succumb to a form of osteoporosis in which the nibs of the spinal column were under attack. She was allergic to all the medications prescribed, and all seemed bleak until her niece did a web search and came up with a treatment that had not been suggested by the specialist. When my mother advanced this to him, he was unthreatened enough to go onto the Internet himself, and agree to a trial – which worked. This is an example of an informationalist relationship between professional and client. Are such relationships possible in architecture?

Through the work of Tom Kovac and others (see previous chapter), we have had a glimpse at how architecture might be practised in an inclusively interactive information environment. This is a moment at which the 'high unit cost, low turnover' economy of architecture seems set to add a 'low unit cost, high turnover' string to its bow. (General practitioners in medicine operate on a 15-minute billing period; architects are run on billing periods that stretch in stages across a number of years on a single, modest project.) Kovac, for example, is working on pavilions customised to client and site needs through a design process that is hosted in an online discussion that economically captures stakeholder desires, and in parallel he is developing with timber companies and technology institutes planar structures capable of being laser cut directly from an agreed prototype through CAD/CAM. Even if this does not happen soon – and micro-charging for texts and text fragments has as yet eluded even publishing, which is already a 'low unit cost, high turnover' business – the quality of interaction with client stakeholders is set to become so much more effective than heretofore that benefits must flow. Lyons Architects in Melbourne, specialists in designing for complex user clients like universities and health providers, have (for example) developed a single information environment in which stakeholder inputs and consultant propositions and solutions are managed and disseminated in real time. In this process there is a continuous flow of design realisation feedback that replaces the lumpy design proposal and critical response loops that we are familiar with. Client satisfaction has grown exponentially, so much so that Professor Franklin

Becker at Cornell University is now studying their approach with the intention of making the system generally available.[11]

Spatial intelligence and ethics of practice

Enhanced interactivity such as this changes the traditional ethics of practice. This is difficult for us because ours is a tradition with centuries behind it, as Hopkins' account of Baldassare Longhena's winning competition entry for Santa Maria della Salute in Venice (commissioned in 1631) demonstrates.[12] From the moment that the Venetian Parliament set out to select an architect, to the moment that it appointed Longhena following an 'international competition', the entire process – including legal challenges from a shortlisted but losing architect – is eerily familiar. The arguments have been rehearsed over and again. In the main they concern avoiding conflicts of interest that could arise at all stages of a project, when advice or specifications of materials could – without an ethical position – enrich those providing the advice at the expense of those they are advising. Now, in the new information economy, which puts such a premium on the potentials of the information that every stakeholder could bring to a project, we have to rework our ethical arguments from scratch, including what we now know about our spatial intelligence and how mental space works for us and on us. To do this, we have to reacquaint ourselves with the principles of ethical argument – principles that have grown in layers, once again, like Gadamer's onion,[13] each layer an advance on the previous layers, but still dependent for its shape and position upon their continued existence. So it is that ethical argument begins with the principle of 'universality' – the concept (first articulated by Kant) that anything argued for must be generalisable to all people. We cannot ethically demand special treatment for ourselves. This has been extended in time to the principle of 'humanity', an argument that all life must be held in regard; and the more apparent the fragility of our biosphere becomes, the wider the interpretation of that regard. These interpretations are supporting the work now being done on reintegrating our deep history into our understanding of ourselves,[14] and in this parallels with the deep histories of other species teem. We can expect more exhibitions such as the wildly successful blockbuster in Norway (2007) concerning what is 'natural' – or deep – in sexuality.[15] The evidence mounted here publicly for the first time by zoologists and biologists revealed that every conceivable practice and preference was exercised amongst mammals, challenging the notion that there is a norm in nature. Perhaps an inspired curator will one day show how spatial intelligence plays out in the lives of all species, and how each benefits from its mental spaces (if the evidence for other traits is anything to go by, there will be a wide spread of mental spaces within each genus, depending on where its spatial capability has unfolded – something that an alert watching of natural history films already sporadically reveals).

Out of the foundation principles of modern ethical argument discussed above arises the principle of 'informed consent' – the concept that we may not do anything to others, even if we believe it to be for their own good, without their informed consent. I am writing this on the 13th of February 2008 in Australia, a day on which the Australian Prime Minister, his Government and the Parliament have apologised to the Aboriginal community of Australia for past parliaments having subjected them to social engineering on which they had no opportunity to be informed, and no opportunity to consent. No matter that past parliaments enacted statutes with good intention, the basic principle of informed consent was not even available at all until the 1967 referendum recognised Aboriginals as citizens of Australia. 'Well may they say'[16] that the road to hell is paved with good intentions.

The next principle of ethical argument is the principle of 'content'. This counters the tendency to believe that ethical argument is advanced by general codes like the Declaration of Human Rights. Such codes (more moral codes than ethical arguments) are open to legalistic interpretation – as recent events in the USA have shown. 'Water-boarding' is torture in the Geneva Convention, but for a time it became legitimated force – thanks to the sophistry of an Attorney General claiming 'the greater good'. Scientists concerned at the way in which their 'pure' research has given rise to weapons of mass destruction have added this new layer of principle, arguing that all ethical argument must have 'content'; it is not ethical to put forward general principles, you must apply these to the specifics of your research and its likely outcomes. Such ethical arguments are as 'falsifiable' as are the propositions of the research itself – and this is just as essential a quality of ethical argument as it is of scientific process. The latest layer to this ethical onion (we can be sure it will not be the last) is the principle of 'generosity' propounded by the great cybernetician, early proponent of biological computing (and therefore one of the pioneers in understanding the systems of the information age) Heinz von Foerster, who argued that in analysing ethical arguments, the better argument was the one that opened up 'generously' most options for future action, the worse that which foreclosed future action in favour of a proscribed solution.[17]

So, if we can construct a profession on the 'Knowing, Doing, Helping' triad that is based on our inherent capability of spatial intelligence and on our understanding of the processes by which we construct and then sublimate our mental space – now newly (as I have shown in the opening chapters) available to us thanks to the scientific advances of the last 20 years – how might that map onto these layers of ethical argument? The argument for this has universalisability at its core. Everyone has the capability, and everyone constructs a spatial memory and builds a mental space, which we all internalise in the same way. What is being argued here is that the architectural profession takes care of this area of knowledge and develops practices based on it – as the precursors, intuitives, pioneers and new practitioners discussed in previous chapters have done. The position is also extendable to include all life that has a spatial intelligence – in Chapter Two we encountered the amazing spatial capabilities of homing pigeons – even if this journey into our 'deep history' is relatively new for us. Then the ways in which the new practitioners in the previous chapter are exploring the potentials of our new knowledge is within the relatively new technologies of the information age. These technologies and the software they support – blogs, wikis, and so on – make possible design interactivity between architects and stakeholders in real time, that is online and at the same time as we design. The potential for 'informed consent' has grown exponentially since the establishment of the World Wide Web. At least in the developed world – over 90 per cent of Australian households have broadband connectivity, but the costs are not great and developing countries are not far behind, except perhaps in Africa.

The principle of 'content' has to be argued case by case, as I am doing here, and, as with informed consent above, and following the example of how *The Long Tail* was written,[18] peer review around specific arguments is more readily effected than ever before. And on 'generosity', while there are arguments which suggest that being online can become a substitute for real political action (we can feel that we have achieved something because we have joined an online petition when in fact actual politicians are able to ignore these protests because – unlike a march or demonstration – they have no physicality)[19], nevertheless we do seem to be witnessing the emergence of new democratic forms thanks to the web, and democracy's main advantage over other forms of government is that it opens up options, rather than

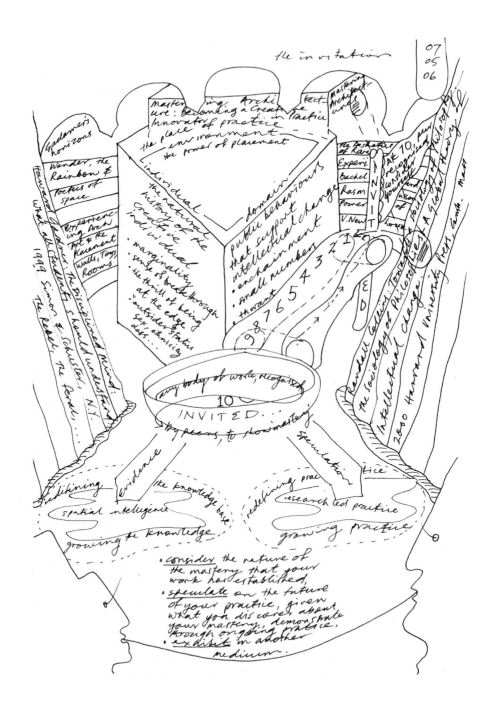

closing them down. Certainly at micro-scale the opportunity to argue for options has probably not been as great since the city state of Athens, and today the slaves are electronic.[20]

The case for a wider, more collectively motivated profession based on spatial intelligence

So we seem to have a good case. At the least, thanks to the serendipitous arrival of neuroscience, network theory and information technology, ethical arguments can be constructed that seem to support an argument for a profession based on spatial intelligence. Where does that take us? It takes us to a consideration of how we architects – who are not neuroscientists, network sociologists or information technologists – care for the body of knowledge that we now claim as the unique basis of our practice. The ethical arguments sketch in ways in which our traditional skills can become more interactively accessible to our clients. Those skills are all still relevant, especially those to do with three- and four-dimensional thinking, but we need to see them now through lenses constructed from our embrace of mental space. Every age has had to do a re-looking – this new evidence provides our opportunity. It is now incumbent on schools of architecture to find ways of enabling student architects to become aware of their spatial intelligence, their spatial histories, their mental space and the mental space they share with others. Some of this is to do with making sure that they are abreast of the latest research about the way their mental space is created. As we have seen, some of the more taxonomic approaches to this have inherent problems in architecture, and my recommendation is that the design studios embrace a tri-polar approach: some exploring canons of good architecture, some the emergence in information culture of new rule-based, algorithmic approaches, and some exploring mental space, individual and communal. Mini-conferences could then service these studio streams, opening up awareness about the impact of mental space on architectures past, present and future. A structured review of past works along the lines of the programme that I have pioneered[21] for architects who have been in practice for some years has proved to be enormously effective in opening up to the practitioners the hidden structures of their intuition, much of which is – in architects – spatial.

We should also encourage practices based on spatial intelligence as a continuum across the professions that act upon our environment. Such

Leon van Schaik, *Ideogram*, 2006. Practitioners observe a cube reconciling the natural history of the creative individual and the role of groups in supporting intellectual change.

continuums are evident in new collaborative practices such as that of two allied collectives at RMIT, one calling itself Urban Interiors, the other Spatial Information Architecture. These have since 2007 built a gradient of shared interest from 'worn form' (Fashion Design), through the 'aesthetics of air' – a designing of the air movement in spaces (Industrial Design), to 'aural form' – the designing of soundscapes (Music Composing), to 'furnished form' (Interior Design/Architecture), through 'composite form' using large-scale three-dimensional weaving (Architecture, Textiles and Aeronautics), through to 'urban time form' (Landscape Architecture), 'inhabited form' and 'bio-form' (Architecture), on into 'information form' (Spatial Information Architecture) which loops back through the virtual environments to a new concept of 'worn form'. These practices all have different takes on the dimensions of space and time. For too long this has divided them. Emerging now is a continuum within design, but more importantly, a continuum with human experience that has eluded design ever since architecture embarked on its exclusionary politic of monopoly statism, that Faustian bargain that Le Corbusier fought so hard to make – to the exclusion of other designer modes, as Beatriz Colomina has so excruciatingly demonstrated with her discovery of how Le Corbusier literally 'painted' industrial designer Eileen Gray out of play and out of the house she designed and built for herself on the shores of the Mediterranean.[22]

Early in this book I discussed the spatial and bodily kinaesthetic intelligence of those who excel in sports – there is an easy acceptance of the continuum between the experience of everyone who has ever thrown a ball and these masters. That is the kind of connectivity – familiar enough to be unremarked in pre-industrial society and sought after by the Bauhaus – that beckons to us in design today, thanks to these new collectives. But let us not get carried away here into a new internationalism. The new collectives such as those I describe above that are emerging in design – fluid in membership, and often enigmatic in their naming (like muf in England,[23] the north European OCEAN NORTH,[24] or the antipodean Antarctica)[25] – are effective precisely because they design scenarios for specific situations and relate to the actual mental space that washes over these situations. This new mode of practice has yet to encounter the excesses of the financial rewards that draw designers into the mass production of a 'brand' – though that trap lies in wait for anyone. My precursors, intuitives, pioneers and new practitioners are so consumed by curiosity and in the latter case by the ethics of mental space that they avoid this trap. So to understand ourselves as new professionals we need to become systematically conscious of the mental spaces that we inhabit. Earlier we saw how this can be achieved through the uninflected documentation of visual evidence – I cited the books *Barcelona Lab* (2003)[26] and *Households* (2006)[27] as exemplars, the latter being especially interesting here because it documents three different sites in which mental space has been constructed by (in part) people from the same social context. Rather as in the heyday of psychoanalysis psychiatrists had to undergo analysis themselves before they could become analysands, we need to ensure that designers have consciously and exhaustively documented their mental space before they can practise on us. This needs to be as much part of the 'putting them in the position of being architects' as is the study of the canons of great works – however defined. Each individual's internalised 'canon' must be exposed and contextualised with its communal environments.

Thus we would be always uncomfortable with the formulation 'Dutch Architecture', or 'Australian Architecture', or 'English Architecture', and always insist on discussing 'Architecture in the Netherlands', 'in Australia', 'in England' without imagining that mental space extends as far as national boundaries. You just have to listen to a Lancastrian in England seething about a signpost on the fringe of London that carries the sweepingly singular legend 'The North' to appreciate the violence that is done to perceived reality by such sloppy formulations. Thus we should fight for a finer grain in our histories, appreciate that the Design City Graz[28] phenomenon arose – as Colin Fournier, coauthor of the Kunsthalle there, avers – out of a challenge posed by the prior emergence of a Graz school in literature, a successful manifestation of regional mental space that critics observed had eluded architecture. Architectural critic Dietmar Steiner describes[29] how the phenomenon of the Graz School emerged as an informal collective of architects concerned to address the 'atmosphere' of their region, developing an angular expressionist approach epitomised in Günther Domenig's (1934–) Stein Haus (1984). So singular was the approach, with its rejection of historical conformity and postmodern eclecticism, that its efforts were noticed and an exhibition toured Europe and the USA in 1985.

As to the phenomenon of Design City Barcelona, thanks to its extraordinary trajectory onto the world stage after General Franco died in 1975, the Catalan story is well known but still capable of being misunderstood locally – as by the politicians who observed that if local architects could build such a reputation, how much more could be built by importing stars from the international stage? My book, *Design City Melbourne* (2006), attempts to capture some of the curatorial dynamics that have underpinned that city's flourishing design

Günther Domenig, Stein Haus, Steindorf, Germany, 1984. The Graz school in literature begat the Graz school in architecture, whose approach is epitomised by this building.

culture. These histories are allied to the personal investigations that our new practitioners need to engage in so as to relegate the 'stopping problem' to the humdrum and focus on the 'starting problem' – to which new modes of practice are so rapidly emerging. (See previous chapter.)

New architectures of the real and the virtual combined

Isn't this new environment rather thin? Can it really sustain viable practices? Like Himanen, architect Kovac argues that a new economy of practice awaits those who understand the re-energised communities of collaborative research and learning that 'open-source' development processes rely upon. Slowly even the music industry is abandoning copyright protection in favour of providing enhanced services around the music that they once saw as their creative capital and their financial base. Firms like DEGW were founded by pioneers who understood this, but their practice is rather interactive in the old sieve process, reliant on workshops that distil stakeholder information into formulaic form, wringing out its 'resistance' and producing printed documents that sit on desks rather than being a real-time part of a design process. There are opportunities – as Lyons Architects (above) have discovered – to go way beyond this if you enter into the designing of virtual environments that hold such information spatially. Kovac's Virtual Concourse pioneered such an integrated spatial model in the early 2000s. Further opportunities arise in the economics of the 'long tail'[30] – a new economy based on the remote but accessible storing of seemingly redundant stock until its time dimension balances out and renders even the shortest production run profitable financially and intellectually. Norbert Wiener (1894–1964) famously remarked that his seminal book *The Human Use of Human Beings* (1950)[31] – probably the book that launched the information age by arguing that an organism is a message – was cited once or twice in the year of its publication, then not at all for a decade, then in exponentially growing numbers as its time came. Perhaps we will discover an architectural position that can take advantage of the newly available depth of and accessibility of information.

Inevitably as we probe into our spatial histories, we assess what lies there emotionally. We cannot be purely analytical, dissecting what we find abstractly. Can we look at Le Corbusier's paintings in the same way, once we know that he painted that mural of nude women onto Eileen Gray's walls, working in the nude, angry at her refusal to succumb to his charms (when she had already made her preference very clear to him)? We also have to access ways of understanding how our emotional intelligence inflects what we discover – and how we use it. A question that is exercising neuroscientists today is the way in which we play out our 'message': how our emotional intelligence is also – like our other capabilities – in part inherited in our genes, in part formed by the way our predispositions play out in our interaction with the places in which we grow up and live. Researchers are now validating the Jungian psychology-based Myers-Briggs personality assessment tool (in modified form) by the slow pinpointing of those parts of our cranial intelligence that 'light up' around our extroversion, agreeableness, openness, conscientiousness and neuroticism.[32] Psychologist Daniel Nettle argues that 'each trait is advantageous under some circumstances'. As biologist Richard Lewontin also argues in his praise for Stephen Jay Gould, a species will most probably display a full range of combinations of these basic characteristics, and different times will favour different combinations.[33]

As we discover more about ourselves, our inherited capabilities and the ways in which they unfold in the world, there is a shift in the assumptions underpinning many of our professions. Even the field of economics is beginning to grapple with the deep engines of our happiness, finding in worldwide surveys much that is confirmatory to those who are studying evolution at the level of our genetics and positing an 'unselfish gene' as central to our make-up. Economists like London School of Economics Professor Richard Layard (1934–)[34] are rethinking economics on the basis of what actually makes us happy, challenging the dualistic and materialistic approach of the statisticians who have created the ideology of the unbridled market that has governed policy making in the Anglophone world for half a century. Layard's central finding is that we are happiest when we are not separated from others by wide gulfs of difference. We are unhappy, however, to achieve this egalitarian state by evening down; we desire an evening-up process.

There is much to be hoped for as this is followed through, because any equalising must include greater access for all to a satisfying and supportive environment, and that requires architecture forged in the mental space of our communities. Even more important for us as architects who aspire to design spaces that inspire wonder is the understanding, arising from neuroscience today, that our brains grow new cells all through our lives, that new cells make us feel happy, and that the growth is stimulated by powerful eidetic experience, and diminishes almost to stasis when we are in boring environments.[35] No wonder the bland sameness of international architecture has given us such a bad name!

The good news is that our potential new professionalism combines the real and the virtual in an architecturally facilitated coupling of information spheres that enriches both environments by asserting the power of the 80 per cent of communication that is nonverbal. What would our lonely observer make of this? The new practice of architecture so enriches the virtual that we are no longer viewing the world through the screen. We are becoming less and less aware of its presence. Is this compressing space even more? Or are we now passing through the looking glass into a landscape of differential time/space zones?

References

1 Editorial from 'Manifesto to radical vitality', *Quaderns*, Vol 4.0, No 244, Collegi d'Arquitectes de Catalunya (Barcelona), December 2004, pp 12–13.
2 Davis McCaughey, *Piecing Together a Shared Vision*, 1987 Boyer Lectures, ABC Enterprises (Crows Nest, New South Wales), 1988. In these lecture McCaughey argued the case for the social contract in terms that I will use here.
3 Cedric Price, *Works II: Cedric Price 1934–2003*, Architectural Association (London), 1984. See also Kester Rattenbury and Samantha Hardingham (eds), *SuperCrit #1: Cedric Price – Potteries Thinkbelt*, Routledge (New York), December 2007.
4 Robert Gutman, *Architectural Practice: A Critical Review*, Princeton Architectural Press (Princeton, New Jersey), 1988. Gutman argues this case with the statistics then available.
5 Elliott A Krause, *Death of the Guilds: Professions, States, and the Advance of Capitalism, 1930 to the Present*, Yale University Press (New Haven and London), 1997.
6 The CIAM was the body in which architects argued out the mission of Modern Architecture, usually with the intention of forging a single ideological position, and thus papering over the fundamental differences between those who pursued poetic and libertarian ends, those who saw the way forward through capturing the means of production, and those, like Le Corbusier, who aimed at capturing the patronage of the state.
7 Ibid.
8 Thomas Haskell, 'The new aristocracy' (review of Elliott A Krause, *Death of the Guilds: Professions, States, and the Advance of Capitalism, 1930 to the Present*, Yale University Press (New York), 1997), *New York Review of Books*, Vol LV, No 19, 4 December 1997, pp 47–52. Haskell argues counter to the collapse proposition (p 50): 'monopoly power … is only an incidental feature of the modern professions. … the pecuniary benefits of suppressing competition from outsiders are trivial by comparison with the increase in professional authority that is achieved by fostering competition among insiders. The occupations that rank as authentic professions today are those that most fully embrace competition … .' Page 51: 'What preoccupies today's professionals is competition amongst insiders in non-pecuniary kinds of achievement, such as recognition, reputation, and the technical quality of the work performed. Instead of fleeing competition, professions intensify it as a means of encouraging individual practitioners to live up to whatever standards of conduct and technical performance may be thought important within a particular community of practitioners.' Thomas Haskell is the McCann Professor of History at Rice University, author of *Objectivity is Not Neutrality: Explanatory Schemes in History* (1998).
9 Pekka Himanen, *The Hacker Ethic and the Spirit of the Information Age*, Secker & Warburg (London), 2001.
10 McCaughey, *Piecing Together a Shared Vision*, op cit.
11 Professor Becker is Director of the International Workplace Studies Program. Two major research themes are Workscape 21 and Healthscape 21. Workscape 21 focuses on offices and the workplaces of professionals and service workers. Healthscape 21 focuses on the design of systems and facility systems to improve health and wellbeing.
12 Andrew Hopkins, *Santa Maria della Salute: Architecture and Ceremony in Baroque Venice*, Cambridge University Press (Cambridge), 2000.
13 Richard Rorty, 'Being that can be understood is language' (review of a paper delivered in Heidelberg by Hans-Georg Gadamer on the occasion of his 100th birthday on 11 February 2000), *London Review of Books*, Vol 22, No 6, 16 March 2000, pp 23–5.
14 Daniel Lord Smail, *On Deep History and the Brain*, University of California Press (Berkeley), 2008.
15 8th International Narrative Therapy & Community Work Conference, Kristiansand, Norway, June 2007.
16 This is one of the most famous phrases in Australian contemporary history, uttered by Prime Minister Gough Whitlam as he responded to his sacking by the Governor General John Kerr on 11 November 1975.
17 Heinz von Foerster and Bernhard Poerksen, *Understanding Systems: Conversations on Epistemology and Ethics*, Kluwer Academic/Plenum Publishers (New York, Boston, Dordrecht, London and Moscow), 2002.
18 Chris Anderson, *The Long Tail: The New Economics of Culture and Commerce – How Endless Choice is Creating Unlimited Demand*, Random

House (London), 2006.
19 Jodi Dean, 'Communicative capitalism: circulation and the foreclosure of politics', John Armitage, Ryan Bishop and Douglas Kellner (eds), *Cultural Politics* (Biggleswade), Vol 1, No 1, March 2005, pp 51–73 (www.bergpublishers.com) argues that the Internet allows people to feel they have done their bit if they sign a petition on the Internet, but politicians feel no compulsion to regard this as anything other than a climate to be acknowledged and then ignored. Politics requires actual face to face effort.
20 Chantal Mouffe (ed), *Dimensions of Radical Democracy*, Verso (London and New York), 1992.
21 This is covered extensively in Leon van Schaik, *Mastering Architecture: Becoming a Creative Innovator in Practice*, Wiley-Academy (London), 2005 and was the topic of the Second RIBA Research Symposium in September 2007; see http://www.architecture.com/TheRIBA/WhatTheRIBADoes/ResearchAndDevelopment/ResearchSymposium/RIBAResearchSymposium2007/RIBAResearchSymposium2007.aspx
22 Beatriz Colomina, *Privacy and Publicity: Modern Architecture as Mass Media*, MIT Press (Cambridge, Massachusetts and London), pp 87–8.
23 muf: http://www.muf.co.uk/
24 OCEAN NORTH: http://www.ocean-north.net/content/section/8/85/
25 Antarctica: http://antarc.com.au/ – a collective of architects and designers from Australia and New Zealand, with whom Melanie Dodd of muf collaborates from time to time.
26 Ramon Prat, Anna Tetas and Carles Poy (eds), *Barcelona Lab*, Actar (Barcelona), 2003.
27 Mark Robbins, *Households*, The Monacelli Press (New York), 2006. See also my review 'Home Body', in *Architectural Design*, No 189: *Rationalist Traces*, Wiley-Academy (London), September–October 2007, pp 146–8.
28 G Domenig, H Eisenköck, K Frey, V Giencke and E Giselbrecht, Dietmar Steiner (ed), *Architektur-Investitionen: Grazer 'Schule', 13 Standpunkte*, ADEVA (Graz), 1986.
29 Ibid.
30 Chris Anderson, *The Long Tail*, op cit.
31 Norbert Wiener, *The Human Use of Human Beings*, Sphere Books (London), 1950. See p 85, in which the organism is seen as message. 'Organism is opposed to chaos, to disintegration, to death, as message is to noise. To describe an organism, we do not try to specify every molecule in it, and catalogue it bit by bit, but rather to answer certain questions about it which reveal its pattern: a pattern which is more significant and less probable as the organism becomes, so to speak, more fully an organism. We have already seen that certain organisms, such as man, tend for a time to maintain and often increase the level of their organisation, as a local enclave in the general stream of growing entropy, of increasing chaos and de-differentiation. Life is an island here and now in a dying world. The process by which we living beings resist the general stream of corruption and decay is known as homeostasis.'
32 Daniel Nettle, 'It takes all sorts: what gives you your unique personality?', *New Scientist*, Vol 197, No 2642, 9 February 2008, pp 34–7. Daniel Nettle is a psychologist.
33 Richard Lewontin, 'The triumph of Stephen Jay Gould' (review of Stephen Jay Gould, (edited by Steven Rose and Paul McGarr), *The Richness of Life: The Essential Stephen Jay Gould*, Jonathan Cape (London), 2006 and Stephen Jay Gould, *Punctuated Equilibrium*, Belknap Press/Harvard University (Cambridge, Massachusetts and London), 2007), *New York Review of Books*, Vol LV, No 2, 14 February 2008, pp 39–41. Richard Lewontin is Alexander Agassiz Research Professor at Harvard University. He is author of *The Triple Helix* (2000), *It Ain't Necessarily So: The Dream of the Human Genome and Other Illusions* (2000), and most recently, with Richard Levins, *Biology under the Influence* (2007).
34 Richard Layard, *Happiness: Lessons from a New Science*, Allen Lane (London), 2005.
35 Jonah Lehrer, *Proust was a Neuroscientist*, Houghton Mifflin Company (New York), 2007. 'The power of holidays can be understood through the emergence of neurogenesis as a factor governing how our brains work. We generate new brain cells throughout our life, especially when stimulated by the new' (p 93). 'A drab looking cage creates a drab looking brain' (p 42). 'For some reason, new born brain cells make us happy ... since we start every day with a slightly new brain, neurogenesis ensures that we are never done with our changes ... in the irrepressible plasticity of our brains – we find our freedom' (p 43). 'Newness is necessary [to break] positive feedback loops ... [that make us] increasingly narrow' (p 142). Works like *The Rite of Spring* jolt us out of complacency. They keep us literally open minded' (p 143).

Index

Figures in italics indicate captions.

A

1066 and All That (Sellar and Yeatman) 133
Aalto, Alvar 17-18, *18*
Aboriginal art 26
Aboriginals 15, 111, 190
Ackoff, Russell L. 38
Adès, Thomas: *Powder Her Face* 133
Africa 112, *112*, 191
Agrest & Gandelsonas 76-7
Ahmedabad, India: Mill Owners' Association 155, *155*
Aldrich, Henry 16
Alessi 170
Alexander, Christopher 71, 84, 124
algorithmic design 169-70
Alnwick, Northumberland 59, 65
Altamura, Italy 138*n*47
Alto Plano, Spain 167
Alzheimer's disease 41, 42
Anderson, Chris: *The Long Tail* 175-6, 191, 197
Andreu, Paul 94
Anglo-New Zealanders 107
Antonioni, Michelangelo 49, *49*
ANY (Architecture/New York) conferences (1990s) 85
Arcadia 69, 126
Archigram 53, 62
Archimedes 26
Architectural Association 85
  International Institute for Design summer school (1970) 74
  School of Architecture 49, 155
Architectural Design 170
Architectural Review 71
architecture
  how it might extend its influence 43-5
  marginalised 46-8
  narrative in 88-9
  reclaiming architectural reality 48-53
  reintegrating it into our mental space 62-7
  relationship with the city 59-60
architecture parlante ('speaking architecture') 88
Architecture without Architects (Rudolfsky) 90-1
Argyll, Duke and Duchess of 133
ARM (Ashton Raggatt McDougall) 119-20, *120*
artificial intelligence 23-4
Arts and Crafts movement 62
Astor, Nancy, Viscountess 133
Astor family 133
Asymptote 19, 48, 172
Athens: Parthenon 110, 120
'Athens of the North' sensibility 16, *17*
Auckland, New Zealand 107
Augé, Marc 93, 94
Austen, Jane 48
Australia 14-15, 60, 190, 191
autism 24, 40, 41
awareness
  ecological 178
  hierarchies of 32
  miracles of 25-6
  progression of 31
  shared with groups 29

B

Babylon 45
Babylonian architecture 59
Bachelard, Gaston 36, 39, 86, 105, 117, 163
  Poetics of Space 13, 39, 123, 124
'back-to-back' developments 67, 68
Baker, Geoffrey 95-6
Barabasi, Professor Albert-Lazlo 180*n*28
Baraki, Japan: 'Soft and Hairy' House 160, *160*
Barcelona 16, 17, 54, 67, 134
  Barcelona Pavilion 111, *111*, 121, 157
  Cerdà's plan for 48, 63-5, 65, 68
  'Design City' 185, 195
  La Sagrada Familia 168-9, *168*
  Park Guell 137*n*28

Barcelona Lab (Prat, Tetas and Poy, eds.) 134, 195
Baring brothers 126
Barry, Charles 47, 132-3
Bath, University of 53
Bauhaus 62
Beaux Arts city planning 71
Becker, Professor Franklin 188-9, 199*n*11
Beckett, Samuel: *Happy Days* 40, 41
Beckham, David 25, 34*n*10
Bedouins 114, *114*
Beijing
  Forbidden City temples 101-2, *102*
  Tiananmen Square 60
Belgium 186
Benson, EF 127
  Lucia novels 125-6
Bergman, Ingmar 69-70
Berkeley, George 34*n*4
Berlin
  Potsdamer Platz 89
  Tempelhof Airport 93, 94
Betjeman, John 13
Betsky, Aaron: *Violated Perfection: Architecture and the Fragmentation of the Modern* 86
Bexleyheath, Kent: The Red House 62
Birmingham 65, 67

Leon van Schaik   201   Index

Black, Richard and Michelle 121-2, *123*
Blenheim Palace, Oxfordshire 69, 131
blind people: navigational spatial awareness 24
'blind springs' 102
'Blob architecture' 170
Blow-up (film) 49
body language 167
Boeri, Stefano 79
Boyarsky, Alvin 85, 155
Boyer, Ernest L 171
brain
  containing a persistent representation of the outside world 38*n*28
  plasticity 200*n*35
Bramante, Donato *117*, 118
Bregenz, Austria: Kunsthaus 147-8, *147*
Bremner, Craig 51
Brighton Pavilion 60
Bristol University 84
British Empire 60, 67
Britten, WEF 127
Brown, Lancelot 'Capability' 69, 131
Bruegmann, Robert 78
  Sprawl: A Compact History 77
Buckingham, Duke of 132, 133
Bunshaft, Gordon 105, *105*
Burdett, Richard 79, 81*n*34
Burry, Professor Mark 168-9, 179*n*6
Burullus Lagoon, Egypt 20
Buxadé, Carles *168*
Byzantine architecture 59

C
CABE *see* Commission for Architecture and the Built Environment
Cache, Bernard 170
Cambridge
  King's College Chapel 99, 101, *101*, 172
  Trinity College Library 16
Campbell, Colen: *Vitruvius Britannicus* 95
Canberra
  Australian National Portrait Gallery 150
  Great Hall of the National Museum of Australia 119-20, *120*
  lavatory pavilion 121, *123*

Cao Xueqin 84, 87-8, 145
capitalism 43, 65
Caputh, Germany 79
Carson, Anne 42
Carter, Paul 49
Castaneda, Carlos 106
Castells, Manuel 179, 179*n*1, 185
  The Information Age 165
Catalhöyük, Turkey 171
Catalonia, Spain 63, 77, 185, 186
cave paintings 109-10, *110*, 138*n*47
caves 107, 108-10, *109*, *110*, 115
Cerdà i Sunyer, Ildefonso 72, 77, 137*n*28
  General Theory of Urbanisation 57, 68
  plan for Barcelona 48, 63-5, 65, 68
Chamberlain, Joseph 67
Chambers, Sir William 60
Chen Shaoxiong: *Homescape* 125
Chicago, Illinois
  Frederick C Robie House 128-9, *128*
  Marshall Field Store 127-8
Chicago Board of Trade futures trading hall 18-19
Chicago school of economcis 184
child development 31-2
children's games *30*, 31, 118-20, *118*, 151
China Now exhibition (Victoria & Albert Museum, 2008) 125
Chinese architecture 59
Ching, Francis DK 95
Chipperfield, David 133, *134*
churches, painted (Romania) 44, 45
Churchill, Sir Winston 131
CIAM (Congrès International d'Architecture Moderne) 185, 199*n*6
classical architecture 60, 106
Cliveden, Berkshire 113, 131-2, *132*, 133
  Blenheim Pavilion 132
  Octagon Temple 132
Coates, Nigel 79
cognitive mapping 42
collage 72
Colomina, Beatriz 110, 194
colonisation 14
Colonna, Francesco: *Hypnerotomachia Poliphili* 88

Commission for Architecture and the Built Environment (CABE) 11, 186
Como, Italy: Casa del Popolo 69
complementary medicine 187-8
compulsory purchase 65
computer-aided design 167
computers 119-20, 165
Cook, Peter 48, 49, 85
copyright protection 196
Cornell University 72, 189
country houses 125-7, *126*
Croquet Shed, the Pediment 16
Cross, Chris 53
cross-ventilation 67
Cullen, Gordon ('Outrage' columnist, *Architectural Review*) 71
Cumbernauld, New Lanarkshire 53

D
Dalí, Salvador 122
Danes: settlement of Greenland 15
de Chirico, Giorgio *96*, 98
  Piazza d'Italia 97
deconstruction 86
DEGW 196
déjà vu 29
Des Moines, Iowa: 'Vision Plans' 77
Descartes, René 34*n*4
'Design City Melbourne' virtual exhibition (2006) 173
Design City phenomenon 54
'Design Methodology' 84
digital design 167, 168, 169
digital modelling 119
'disegno' 80*n*2
Disney 15
Disney World, Florida 98, 130
distributed intelligence 24, 25, 26, 28, 36
Domenig, Günther 195, *196*
Domus 79
'dot' paintings 26
dreaming 27, 28
Dresden 16
Dryden, John: *Absalom and Achitophel* 132
Dublin: Trinity College Library 103, 105
Dudley, West Midlands: West Country Living Museum 68
Durham cathedral 107, *108*
Duvignaud, Jean: *Change at Shebika* 50

E
economics 197-8
Edmond & Corrigan 13, 74
Edwardian style 125, 127
Egyptian architecture 45, 59
Egyptian art 45
eidetic memories/recall *38*, 39, 44, 142
Einstein, Albert 79
Eisenstein, Sergei 89
Elizabethan era 125
emotional intelligence 27, 32, 197
empathy 31, 32, 36-7
encyclopaedic method 46, 59, 62, 63, 84, 140, 141
'Endless House' 160
Engels, Friedrich 36, 67, 77
engineers 12, 13, 187
epidemiology 46, 63, 79
Erith, Raymond 16
ethical argument 190-91
Evans, Robin 62
Existenzminimum (minimum-existence housing) 62, 80*n*4
exoskeletal frame 105

F
facades 43
falsification 72, 74, 77
fan vaulting 99
Fanny and Alexander (film) 70
Farnsworth House (Plano, Illinois) 111
FAT 13, 74
Ferriss, Hugh 78
Filler, Martin 166
Findlay, Kathryn 160-62, *160*, *161*, *162*
Fisher, Philip 106
  Wonder, the Rainbow, and the Aesthetics of Rare Experiences 142
Fletcher, Sir Banister: *A History of Architecture on the Comparative Method* 59, 118
Fodor, Jerry 32-3
Foerster, Heinz von 190-91
Folly, Gatley Park, Hertfordshire 16
Fournier, Colin 195
Frampton, Kenneth 84, 87, 106, 157, 163*n*15
  'A Kufic Suprematist: the world culture of Zaha Hadid' 155

202

Franco, General 195
Friedman, Yona 79
'frozen music' 89, *89*
Future Shack 121
Future Systems 119
Futurism 53

G
Gadamer, Hans-Georg 47, *47*, 56n24, 106, 142, 179
Gadamer's onion 47, *47*, 178, 189
Galfetti, Aurelio 30
Gandelsonas, Mario 48, 74, 76, 77
  Invisible Walls (in *X-Urbanism: Architecture and the American City*) 74
Garches, France: Villa 73
Garkau Estate, near Lübeck, Germany: Cow House 160
Gates, Bill 130
Gaudí, Antonio 17, 137n28, 168
Gehry, Frank 169
Geneva Convention 190
'Georgian' facades 43
Gérard, François: *Napoleon in Coronation Robes* 48
Germany 15
Giacometti, Alberto 24
Giurgola, Romaldo 140
Glasgow
  European City of Culture 51
  mental space of Glaswegians 51
Glenburn House 163n14
globalisation 17, 91
Godsell, Sean 121, 148-52, *150*, *159*, 178
Goff, Bruce 149, *149*
Gollings, John 173
Gopnik, Alison 31-2
Gothic architecture 45, 59, 60, 106
Gould, Stephen Jay 197
Grand Tour 69
Graves, Clare W 178, 179
Gray, Eileen 194, 197
Graz, Austria
  Design City 54, 195
  Kunsthalle 195
Graz School 195, *196*
Great Exhibition (1851) 60, 170
Great Rift Valley, Africa 109
Greece, ancient
  architecture 59, 69
  children's games 119
  city states 45

classical tradition 53
rediscovery of the knowledge of ancient Greece 60
Greenland 15
Griffiths, Sean 74
Gropius, Walter 62, 171
Grove, Archibald 127
'guilds' 185

H
Hadid, Zaha 48, 133-4, 155, 157-60, *157-9*, 163n15, 167
Hague, The, Netherlands: housing 143
Hamilton, Richard 71, 81n24
  Hers is a Lush Situation 138-9n69
Häring, Hugo 160-61
Harlow New Town, Essex 53
Harvard University, Cambridge, Massachusetts: Carpenter Center for the Visual Arts 155, *155*
Haskell, Thomas 199n8
Haussmann, Baron 65
Hawksmoor, Nicholas 131
Hegel, G.W.F. 34n4
Helsel, Sand 65, *66*, 67, 72
Helsinki 16-17, *17*
  House of Culture 18, *18*
  Main Railway Station 17
Hemmings, David 49
Henley, Oxfordshire: River & Rowing Museum 133, *134*
Hensel, Michael 170
Herzog & de Meuron 152-3, *153*, 155, 159
High Italianate manner 133
Hill, Professor Jonathan 80n2
Himanen, Pekka 172-3, 185
Hobsbawm, Eric 46-7, 155
Hockney, David 93
home and gardens magazines 125
homing pigeons 37, 191
Hong Kong Peak project 155, *157*, *157*, 159
Hopkins, Andrew 189
Humboldt reforms 172
'humpies' 111
huts 107, 108, 110-11, 112, 115
hypersurface 170

I
iconic buildings 98
Iliad (Homer) 39

Independent Group 71
India 60
Industrial Revolution 68
industrialisation 17, 61
informationalism 165-6, 167, 172, 175, 185, 188
informed consent 190
International Institute for Design summer school (Architectural Association, London, 1970) 74
internationalism 85, 194
Internet 18, 70, 172, 178, 188, 200n19
intuition 44, 55-6n7, 139n88
Inuits 15
Isozaki, Arata 54
Ithaca 39
Ito, Toyo 121, *121*

J
Jackson, John Brinckerhoff 91
Jacobs, Jane 65
Jamberoo, New South Wales: Fredericks Farmhouse 111
Japur, Rajasthan, India: Jantar Mantar Observatory 91, *91*
Jekyll, Gertrude 127
Jenkins, Simon 13-14
Jennings, Humphrey, Mary-Lou Jennings and Charles Madge: *Pandaemonium* 10
Jung, Carl Gustav 124, 197

K
Kahn, Andrea 89
Kant, Immanuel 34n4, 173, 189
Kaplicky, Jan 119
Keeler, Christine 133
Kelly, Sean 174, *175*
Kempe, David 180-81n28
Kerr, John 199n16
Kew Gardens, Surrey (Royal Botanic Gardens, Kew): Pagoda 60
Khutsong, South Africa 53-4, 124
Kiesler, Frederick 160
kinaesthetic intelligence 25-6
kinetic intelligence 26, 27
Kirkcaldy, Fife, Scotland: Maggie's Centre 157-9, *158*, *159*, 167
kitsch 61, 62
Klee, Paul 167
Koch, Christoph 34n4
Koetter, Fred 73-4
KOL/MAC 48, 170
Konstantinidis, Nikos 87

Koolhaas, Rem 79
  Delirious New York 78, *78*
Kovac, Tom 19, 48, 121, *122*, 136n9, 138n50, 170, 173-6, *174*, *175*, 188, 196, 197
Kumamoto Artpolis 54
Kyoto temples, Japan 148

L
La Pietra, Ugo 51
LAB 3000 Digital Design Biennale (2003) 173
Las Vegas 74, 77, 88, 98
  Fremont Street *73*
Lascaux caves, France 14, 108, 138n47
Layard, Professor Richard 198
Le Corbusier 73, 95, 155, *155*, 156, 171, 185, 194, 197, 199n6
  La Ville radieuse 73
  Towards a New Architecture 77
learning
  ceaseless 29
  from literature 43
  progressive development through 31
  through doing 30, 171
Lee, Terence 41
Lees-Milne, James 133
Lefebvre, Henri 10, 22, 33n2, 46, 48, 52, 71, 87, 97, 165-6
Lego 119
Leoni, Giacomo 132
Lessig, Professor Lawrence 173, 180n24
Lethaby, William Richard 44, 45, 61-2, *62*, 89, 126-7, 128
  Architecture, Mysticism and Myth 45
Lewontin, Richard 197
Li Shiqiao 16, 133
Libeskind, Daniel 157, 163n15
Lim, William 54, 77
linguistic intelligence 27, 28, 36
London
  Big Ben 118, *118*
  Centre Point 105
  Crystal Palace, Hyde Park 13, 60-61, *61*, 170
  Euston station 93
  Fitzrovia 53
  Forster House, Bedford Park 127
  Houses of Parliament 47, 133
  Jubilee Line 54
  Kensington townhouses 127

Laban Contemporary Dance
  Centre, Deptford 152-3, *153*,
  155, 159
Pitzhanger Manor, Ealing 119
Regent's Park 60
Sainsbury Wing, National
  Gallery 74
St Pancras Station 13, 93-4
St Paul's Cathedral Choir
  School 16
Serpentine Gallery 133-4
  Pavilion 121, *121*
  Southwark 54
Tate Modern 155
Victoria & Albert Museum
  (*China Now* exhibition, 2008)
  125
West Kensington studio 127
London Architecture Biennale
  (2006) 21
Longhena, Baldassare 189
Loos, Adolf 110
Los Angeles, California 178
  Hollywood sign *88*
Los Angeles County Museum of
  Contemporary Art (LACMA):
  Pavilion of Japanese Art
  149, *149*
'lost limb' syndrome 24
Loudon, John Claudius: *An
  Encyclopaedia of Cottage,
  Farm, and Villa Architecture
  and Furniture* 95
Low, Alvin 174
Lutyens, Sir Edwin *126*, 127
Lynch, Kevin 71
Lynn, Greg 169, 170
Lyons Architects 188, 196-7
Lyssiotis, Peter
  Architecture grows in cities 59
  The dawn of a new
  professionalism 183
  Each one of us should speak
  of his roads, his crossroads, his
  roadside benches 37
  I mean an architect is
  wonderful when he is in his
  own house, maybe beyond
  this he is terrible? 141
  New futures for architecture
  (real and virtual) opened
  up… 165
  The spaces that we first use at
  surrogate houses as we form
  our spatial histories and our
  mental space 83
  Though we are unaware of
  this, we are the prisoners of
  our mental space 9
  We comprehend and
  negotiate space using our
  spatial intelligence… 23

M
'Ma' (space-time) 52
McCaughey, Davis 186
McLuhan, Marshall 48-9
Madison Millard, Mrs George 129
Madrid 63, 167
  Museo del Prado 166
Maggie's Centres 157-9, *158*,
  159, 160
Maki, Fumihiko 52
Manson, Fred 54
Marías, Javier 39
Marie Antoinette 20, 126
Massif Central, France: hipped
  churches in 102
master builders 60
May, Ernst 171, 185
Mayhew, Henry 38, 67
  Asylum for the Houseless Poor
  (from *London Labour and the
  London Poor*) 38
Meccano 119
Mechernich, Germany: Bruder
  Klaus Field Chapel 146-7
Melbourne 54
  '38 degrees South' studies
  80n11
  State Library café 138n50
  Victoria Railways
  Administration Building 177
Melnikov, Konstantin 120-21
memory, memories 29, 30,
  34n15, 36, 39, 55n3, 86, 142, 191
Mendrisio, Switzerland: School
  of Architecture 30
mental space
  distributed intelligence
  proposition supports the
  concept 28-31
  encountering 53-4
  interdependence between it
  and architecture 83
  learning from 40-42, *40*
  reclaiming architectural reality
  48-53
  reintegrating architecture
  into 62-7
Mérida, Spain: Museum of
  Roman Art 166
Meyer, Hannes 62, 171, 185
Michelangelo 167

Mies van der Rohe, Ludwig 111,
  111, 121, 157
migration 49
Milan 51
Milton Keynes, Buckinghamshire
  53
mimicry 29-30, 31
mirror neurons 29
Mitford, Nancy: *Love in a Cold
  Climate* 22, 33
'mobile ground' 89
model-making 168
Modern Movement, Modernism
  45, 53, 127
modernism 17, 62, 63, 95, 111, 171
Moneo, Rafael 166, 167
Moorhouse, Frank 172
'Morph' digital design
  conference (1997) 169
Morphosis 178
Morris, William 61, 62
Moscow: Red Square 60
Murcutt, Glenn 111
music industry 196
Muthesius, Hermann 127
Myers-Briggs personality
  assessment tool 197

N
Napoleon Bonaparte 47
NASA 13, 84-5, 168
Nash, John 60
national styles 16, 47
National Theatre 40
National Trust 133
NATO (Narrative Architecture
  Today) 79
Negev Desert, Israel: traditional
  Bedouin tent 114, *114*
neoclassicism 16, 47, *47*, 111, 132,
  132, 133, 143, 178
neogothic 47, *47*
Netherlands 15
Nettle, Daniel 197
networks 175, 177, 180-81n28
Neuhaus, Paul 99
neurogenesis 200n35
neurological mapping 26, 27
neurone mapping 29, 39
New England 91
New Scientist 41
New York 74, 76
  Grand Central Station 93, *93*
  Korean Presbyterian Church of
  New York, Queens 170
  Manhattan 78-9, *78*
  Times Square 89, 170

TWA Terminal, JFK Airport
  94, *94*
New York Stock Exchange
  19, 172
Nolli, Giambattista 72
'Non-Standard' architectural
  movement 161-2
Non-Standard Architectures
  exhibition (Centre Pompidou,
  Paris, 2003-4) 161-2, 170
Norway 189
Norwich, John Julius 13
NOX 170

O
observation process 50, *50*
OCEAN NORTH 194
Odyssey (Homer) 39
Olalquiaga, Celeste 61
OMA 79
Oosterhuis, Kas 170
Opie, Iona and Peter 30, 31, 119
Orcival church, Auvergne, France
  102-3, *103*
organism 197, 200n31
Orkney: Melsetter House 45,
  61-2, *62*, 127, 128
Ormerod, Paul 200n28
ornament in architecture 107
Ota, Kayoko 51
Otto, Frei 114
Ottoman architecture 59
Oxford
  Head of Schools meeting
  (1970s) 85
  Peckwater Quadrangle, Christ
  Church 16

P
Palladian style 73, 95
Palladio, Andrea 60
Pallasmaa, Juhani 119
  The Eyes of the Skin 86
Paoletti, Roland 54
Paolozzi, Eduardo 71
Papastergiadis, Nikos 89
'para-functional space' 89
Paris
  Centre Pompidou 162, 170
  Cité de Refuge 158
  Eiffel Tower 98, 118, *118*
  Friedman's megastructures 79
  Grande Arche de La Défense
  114, *114*
  Haussmann's plan 63
  as Manhattan's alter ego 78-9
  Sainte Chapelle 99, *101*

Terminal 1, Charles de Gaulle Airport 94
Paris 'Exposition Internationale des Arts Décoratifs et Industriels Modernes' (1925) 121
'party walls' 67
Pasadena, California: Mrs George Madison Millard House ('La Miniatura') 129, *129*
pavilions 120-22, *121, 122, 123*
Paxton, Joseph 60-61, *61*
Peak-Confetti-Suprematist Snowstorm *157*
Penang, Malaysia: 'terrain vague' 90
Peninsula House (Mornington Peninsula, Australia) 150-51, *150*
Penrose, Roger 24, 28, 34*n*5
Persian architecture 59
Pevsner, Nikolaus 13
phenomenology 86, 87, 117
Piaget, Jean 31
Picturesque movement 69-70, 71, 135
'poetics' of space 86
pointillisme 161
Pop Art 71
Popper, Karl 69, 72
Port Lligat, Cadaqués, Spain 122-3
Portmeirion, Wales 15
Portsmouth cathedral 132
Potter, Beatrix 30
Prada stores 178
Price, Cedric 184
Price, Uvedale 69
Prince, Bart 149, *149*
professionalism 11-12, 13, 33, 60
  new architectures of the real and virtual combined 196-8
  new opportunity for inclusivity in 187-9
  rebuilding architecture as a profession 185-6
  spatial intelligence and ethics of practice 189-91, 193
  the unique knowledge base of architecture 187
  a wider, more collectively motivated profession based on spatial intelligence 193-6
professions, evolution of 31
Profumo, John 133
Progettare In Più journal 51
projectory 29, 30
Proust, Marcel 38-9, *38*, 65, 97,

137*n*35
In Search of Lost Time, Volume One: Swann's Way 39
'Provençal' facades 43
Prussia Cove, Cornwall 126
Pugin, Augustus Welby Northmore 47, 133

Q
Quaderns Manifesto 183

R
Randstad, Netherlands 54
Rasmussen, Steen Eiler 85, 86, 87, 105, 118
  Experiencing Architecture 33
Rationalism 69, 70-71
Reagan, Ronald 184
recreating past glories 15-16
Rée, Jonathan 47, 56*n*24
Reed & Stern 93
REM sleep 27, 28, 36
Renaissance 106
Renaissance architecture 45, 60
Repton, Humphry 69, *70*
resistence 166-7
Rhodes-Harrison, George 187
RIBA (Royal Institute of British Architecture) 85
Rice-Davis, Mandy 133
Richards, IA 43, 61
Richardson, Henry Hobson 127-8
Rietveld, Gerrit 112-13
RMIT (Royal Melbourne Institute of Technology) 24, 51, 52, 65, 177, 194
  Design Research Institute 149-50
Roach, Andrew 180*n*28
Robbins, Mark 134-5
  Households 125, *125*, 134, 195
Roman architecture 59
Roman Empire 45, 69
Romanesque architecture 45, 59, 97-8, 102-3, 127
Romania: painted churches 44, 45
Rome
  classical tradition 53
  Grand Tour to 69
  Nolli's 1748 plan 72
  Pantheon 45, 117, *117*, 118
  rediscovery of the knowledge of ancient Rome 60
  S Maria Maggiore basilica 85, 118
  Tempietto (S Pietro in

Montorio) *117*, 118
  Temple of Vesta *117*
  Villa Borghese 133
Rose, Steven 32
Rossi, Aldo 53, 68-9
Rowe, Colin 48, 69, 71, 72-4
Rowe, Colin and Fred Koetter: *Collage City* 72
Ruscha, Ed 134
Ruskin, John 83, 106
Russian Imperial architecture 127
Rykwert, Joseph 106

S
Saarinen, Eero 94, *94*
Saarinen, Eliel 17
Sacks, Dr Oliver 41, 86
sacred sites 102
Sagebiel, Ernst *93*
San Diego Zoo, California *98*
San Francisco 178
  Golden Gate Bridge 118, *118*
Santiago de Compostela, Spain: Santo Domingo de Bonaval Park 143
Schinkel, Karl Friedrich 25
Schröder House (Utrecht, Netherlands) 112-13
'scientific' approach 67
scientific revolution 171
Scottish Baronial style 13, 94
Scottsdale, Arizona: Taliesin West 129-30, *130*
Scruton, Roger 53, 87
Sebald, WG *13*, 43
Second World War 133
Seifert, Richard 105
selection
  for empathy 32
  of values 32-3
  working through and on environment 32
Semper, Gottfried 114, *115*, 178
'set backs' 67
Seville Architecture Biennale (2008) *175*
Shack for a Potter (Green Gully, Castlemaine, Victoria, Australia) 122, *123*
Shane, Grahame 74
Shaw, Fiona *40*
Shaw, George Bernard 46
Shebika oasis, Tunisia 50
Si, Dr Kausik 137*n*35
Simic, Charles 42
Sitte, Camillo 71, 72
Situationists 79

Siza, Álvaro 142-3
Skidmore, Owings & Merrill (SOM) 105
sleep research 26-8
Small, Meredith F 161*n*31
Smart, Elizabeth: *By Grand Central Station I Sat Down and Wept* 93
Smithson, Peter and Alison 71, 113, *113*
Smithson, Robert 91
Soane, Sir John 95, 105, 118-19
social Darwinism 27
Solà-Morales, Ignasi de 29, 89
Sonning, Berkshire: Deanery Garden *126*, 127
Soria y Puig, Arturo 57, 80*n*9
Sorkin, Michael 54
South Africa 48
  Drakensberg 109, 110
  Game Pass Cave 109-10, *109, 110*
  Game Pass Valley 109, *109*
South America 171
South Australia 14
'space race' 84
'Spanish' facades 43
spatial intelligence
  how it builds our mental space
    encountering mental space 53-4
    holistic mapping of 37-40
    how architecture might extend its influence 43-5
    how architecture was marginalised 46-8
    learning from literature 43
    learning from our mental space 40-42
    reclaiming architectural reality through new understanding of mental space 48-53
  the mechanics of distributed intelligence proposition supports the concept of mental space 28-31
    kinaesthetic intelligence: its spatiality 25-6, *25*
    a new basis for professionalism in architecture 33
    the problem of consciousness and intelligence 23-5
    space and emotional

intelligence 127-8
spatial intelligence uncovered 26-7
ways of being in the world supported by new research 31-3
spatial politics 48, 63, 77
'spatial schemata' 41
Spiller, Neil 170
spiritual spaces 101-2
sport 25-6, 29, 34*n*10
Spreckelsen, Johann Otto von 114, *114*
stately homes 131-4, *132*
Steindorf, Germany: Stein Haus 195, *196*
Steiner, Dietmar 195
Stirling, James 96
Stockholm 17
  College of Surgeons lecture theatre 177-8
Stourhead, Wiltshire 69
Strathclyde, University of 53
Sumvitg, Switzerland: Sogn Benedetg Chapel 143-6, *144, 145*
Sunset Strip (West Hollywood, California) 134
'super-graphics' 88, *88*
Superstudio 53
surface tectonics 106
Sutherland, Duke and Duchess of 132
Suzuki, Akira 51-2, 54, 176-7
Switzerland 185
Sydney
  Laurie Short House 111
  Sydney Harbour Bridge 13
  Sydney Opera House 98
systems engineering approaches 84

T
Taipei, Japan, Yong Kung community 65, *66*, 67, 72
Taj Mahal, India 98
Taliesin I-III (Spring Green, Wisconsin) 130
'tartan grid' 114, *115*
tattooing 107, *107, 108*
Telescope journal 51, 54
temples 115, 117-18, *117*
tents 107, 108, 114, *114*, 115
Terragni, Giuseppe 69
'terrain vague' 89, *90*, 91, 95, 155, 159
Terroir 121, *123*

text messaging 177
Thatcher, Margaret, Baroness 184
Theroux, Paul 176
Third Man, The (film) 86
Thoreau, Henry 36, 122, 136*n*15
thresholds 112, *112*, 113, 124
Tilden, Philip 125, 126
Tivoli, Italy: Temple of Vesta 115, 117
Tokyo 51-2, 176-7
  Café Bongo 52
  economic boom 51
  Imperial Hotel 128
  Truss Wall House 160, 161-2, *161, 162*
Tolkien, JRR 125
totalitarianism 72, 73
tourism 14, 49, 51
Trani, Italy: cathedral *96*, 97-8
translation 42
treehouses 98, *99*
Troy 39, 59
Tschumi, Bernard
  Manhattan Transcript 1: The Park 89
  'Screenplays' 89
Tudor England 60, 126
Tudor style *126*
Turing, Alan 23, 34*n*5
Turing test 23-4, 34*n*5
'Tuscan' facades 43

U
Underwood, Guy 102
undesigned spaces 89, 90
United States
  architectural education 171
  begins to take a prominent role on the world stage 133
  corporate city skylines 60
  Upper Lawn Pavilion (Fonthill, Wiltshire) 113-14, *113*
'Ur' architecture 53, 115
urban hygiene movement 67
urbanisation 68
urbanism 71, 77
Ushida, Esaku 160
Ushida Findlay 160-62, *160, 161, 162*
Usonian ethos 128, 185

V
Vals, Switzerland: Thermal Baths 146, *146*
van Schaik, Leon
  analytical drawing (1985) *95*

The Consultant Arrives and Sees 50, *50*
Design City Melbourne 195-6
Ideogram, 2006. Practitioners observe a cube reconciling the natural history of the creative individual and the role of groups in supporting intellectual change 193
Ideogram on Spatial Intelligence 13
Mastering Architecture 166
West London project 49-50, 52
Vanbrugh, Sir John 131
Vancouver 54
Vangelis (Evangelos Papathanassiou) 30
Vasari, Giorgio 167
Vaux-le-Vicomte château, Loire 131
Veneto, Italy 60
Venice 98, 177
  Santa Maria della Salute 189
Venice Architecture Biennale (2004): Virtual Australian Pavilion 121, *122*, 173, *174*
Venice Architecture Biennale (2006) 77
vent brick rule 67-8
Venturi, Robert: *Complexity and Contradiction* 19
Venturi, Robert, Denise Scott Brown and Steven Izenour: *Learning from Las Vegas* 71, 73, 74, 77, 88, 134-5
Venturi, Scott Brown & Associates 13, 77, 81*n*24, 143
Versailles 131, 132
Vesely, Dalibor 45, 46, 84
Viollet-le-Duc, Eugène 137*n*38
Virtual Concourse 173, 197
visual intelligence 135
visualisation 30
Visualising the Virtual Concourse research studio 175
Vitruvius 83
Voronet Monastery, Romania: Church of St George 44
Voysey, Charles Francis 127
Vriesendorp, Madelon 78
  Flagrant Délit 78

W
Wachsmann, Konrad 79
Wahl, Jean 36, 39, 42, 136*n*15
walled gardens 113

Ward, Stephen 133
Warren & Wetmore *93*
Warsaw 16
Washington DC 71
water diviners 102
'water-boarding' 190
wattle and daub 112
'weak architecture' 29, 34*n*18
weapons of mass destruction 190
Webb, Philip 62
Weil am Rhein, Germany: Vitra Fire Station 157, *157*
Weimar Republic 121
Wharton, Edith 93
Whitlam, Gough 199*n*16
Wiener, Norbert: *The Human Use of Human Beings* 197
Wiesbaden 72
Wigley, Mark 86
Wikipedia 173
Wilkinson, Jonny 25, *25*
Williams, Raymond 131
Williams-Ellis, Clough 15
Wilson, Peter 24-5
Winde, William 132
Wired journal 175
Woods, Tiger 25
'World Wide Web' 18, 166, 175, 191
World's Fairs 120
Wren, Sir Christopher 16, 131
Wright, Frank Lloyd 124, 128-30, *128*, *129*, *130*, 171, 185

X
Xenakis, Iannis 179

Y
Yale University, Connecticut: Beinecke Rare Book and Manuscript Library 105, *105*
Yirrkala, Australia: house for an Aboriginal client 112
York, University of 53

Z
Zaloom, Caitlin 18-19
Zeisel, John 41
Zimmerli, W 172
Zumthor, Peter 48, 95, 142-8, *144-8*, 150, 151, 152, 155, 159, 178
Zurich, Switzerland: ETH building 114-15, *115*, 178

Photo credits

The author and the publisher gratefully acknowledge the people who gave their permission to reproduce material in the book. While every effort has been made to contact copyright holders for their permission to reprint material the publishers would be grateful to hear from any copyright holder who is not acknowledged here and will undertake to rectify any errors or omissions in future editions.

Front cover image © Peter Lyssiotis (1949-) is a photo media artist, and completed this work as part of an Australia Council New Media Arts Fellowship at RMIT, Melbourne, Australia in 1998.

p 9, 23, 37, 58, 82, 141, 164, 182 © Peter Lyssiotis; pp 12, 17, 18, 50, 75, 76, 90, 91, 93, 95, 96, 102, 103, 104, 109, 110, 111, 112, 114, 115, 128, 129, 132, 144, 145, 146, 148, 154, 158, 192 courtesy of Leon van Schaik; p 25 © Christian Liewig / Corbis; p 30 © Janine Wiedel Photolibrary / Alamy; p 38 © Mary Evans Picture Library / Alamy; p 38 © Castle / photocuisine / Corbis; p 40 © Robbie Jack/Corbis; p 44 © Mark Fiennes / Arcaid / Corbis; p 47 © Foodfolio / Alamy; p 47 © Walter Bibikow/Corbis; p 48 © The Print Collector / Alamy; p 49 © Cinemaphoto / Corbis; p 52 © Nigel Coates 1988; p 61 © Historical Picture Archive/Corbis; p 62 © Doug Houghton/Alamy; p 64 © Tavisa; p 66 Unclog: legal structures © Lim Hui Yuan + Hung Jia Xin, Clog: legal & illegal structures (swollen rice map with add-on buildings) © Lim Hui Yuan + Hung Jia Xin; p 68 © Gregory Davies / Alamy; p 70 © Stapleton Collection / Corbis; p 73 Bettmann / Corbis; p 78 Gift of Philotecton, U.S.A., Inc., Ridgway, Ltd., and Biltmore, J.V., to the American Friends of the CCA on loan to the Collection Centre Canadien d'Architecture / Canadian Centre for Architecture, Montréal; p 88 © Andrew Gombert / epa / Corbis; p 89 © Bernard Tschumi Architects; p 92 © Bettmann / Corbis; p 94 © Mark Fiennes / Arcaid / Corbis; p 97 © Interfoto Pressebildagentur / Alamy; p 98 © Jan Butchofsky-Houser / Corbis; p 99 © Andrea Rugg Photography / Beateworks / Corbis; p 100 © Mervyn Rees / Alamy; p 101 © Historical Picture Archive / Corbis; p 107 © Bruce Coleman Inc. / Alamy; p 108 © Joe Cornish / Arcaid / Corbis; p 113 © Georg Aerni, Zurich; p 114 © Eddie Gerald / Alamy; p 116 © Bob Krist / Corbis; p 117 © The Print Collector / Alamy (t) Adam Eastland / Alamy (b); p 118 © Hemis / Corbis; p 120 © Architects: ARM / Photographer: John Gollings; p 121 Richard Waite / Arcaid / Corbis; p 122, 174 – 175 © Tom Kovac, Gollings & Pidgeon; p 123 © www.geoffcomfort.com (t); p 123 Times Two Architects / Photograph Michelle Black (b); p 125 © Mark Robbin; p 126 © Arcaid / Alamy; p 130 © BristolK / Alamy; p 134 © Edifice/Corbis; p 149 © ART on FILE / Corbis; p 150 © Architects: Sean Godsell / Photographer Earl Carter; p 153 © Benedict Luxmoore / Arcaid / Corbis; p 156 © Zaha Hadid / Blue Slab Painting; p 157 © Richard Bryant / Arcaid / Corbis; p 159 © Kirkaldy Model / Zaha Hadid Architects; p 160-162 Ushida Findlay office / Photographer Katshuhisa Kida; p 168 © Mark Burry; p 196 © Mediacolor's / Alamy.